WHEN A

TO THOSE WHO MOURN THEIR CHILDREN

SILVER BIRCH, an Indian spirit sage, gave this message for bereaved parents: Do not weep because you think you have forever lost the fairest flower in your garden. The truth is that the flower has been transplanted into a far more beauteous garden where it sheds a greater perfume and is lovelier and more beautiful than ever it could be on earth. It has been spared many of earth's sadnesses and sorrows. It has been spared many cruelties and many blights. Your child will never know much that has darkened your own life. Rejoice that freedom has come to a young soul who will never be distressed by the many miseries that afflict your world. Do not grieve for the child; grieve if you will for your own loss, for you will miss the little radiant face, the childish prattle, the diminutive figure. But though your physical eyes cannot see, and your physical ears cannot hear, your child is ever present. If you stop shedding tears that create a mist in front of our eyes, you will see the truth that in God's great kingdom there is no death and all continue to live in far better conditions in a world which is richer and sweeter than anything you have ever dreamed. Do not sorrow for the child. Know that an all-loving God has given angels to protect her or him and the child will, in fullness of time, be reunited with you.

WHEN A CHILD DIES

SYLVIA BARBANELL

Spiritualist Truth Foundation

First published in 1942
Reprinted 1964, 1984, 1987
This edition 2012

The Spiritual Truth Press
15 Broom Hall, Oxshott
Surrey KT22 OJZ

© Spiritual Truth Foundation

This book is copyrighted under the Berne Convention. No portion may be reproduced by any process without the copyright holder's written permission, except for the purposes of reviewing or criticism, as permitted under the Copyright Act of 1956.

ISBN 978 0 85384 116 6

Printed in Great Britain by Booksprint

PROLOGUE

THE great liner, outward bound for the United States, was ready to sail. A general air of bustle and excitement surged through the atmosphere on board. Porters and stewards rushed hither and thither. "All ashore who are going ashore!" lustily shouted the ship's officials with growing urgency. Final handshakes, hasty embraces, hurried last messages were being exchanged between passengers and those who had come to wish them *bon voyage*.

Two parents gave the small boy who was sailing without them a final hug before they reluctantly made their way down the gangway. A little later, they stood together on the quay as the tall, powerful vessel slipped smoothly away from the shore. Waving their handkerchiefs vigorously, they maintained an appearance of hearty cheerfulness until the form of their only child was no longer distinguishable. Then, they turned to comfort each other; the woman's lips trembled. "I can't bear to think of him making this long journey without us," she said, "even though I know that Miss Halsall will take every care of him on the voyage. I'll miss him so much. Oh, whatever shall we do without our boy?" She began to weep quietly.

"Cheer up, darling," said her husband consolingly. "The last sight of Bobbie was very comforting. Didn't you notice how carefully Miss Halsall protected him as he waved goodbye to us? And he has always been so fond of his old school teacher. I am very glad she is making this trip too. Wasn't it decent of her to arrange to go to the States on the same boat?" He went on, "We both agreed that this journey was the very best thing that could have happened to the boy under the present circumstances."

"Oh, I know all that you say is true," said his wife between her tears. "I'm glad for his sake he has gone. And it isn't as though he'll be going to strangers.

"I should think not," said her husband. "He'll be living with your own family over there. Think how excited they are at the prospect of having him. Bobbie is a lucky boy, for Miss Halsall is so fond of him and will look after him until your father meets the boat on the other side of the Atlantic. Atlantic! Pooh, Herring Pond, I mean. It's no distance really – less than ever these days."

He continued, by gentle, encouraging words, to help his wife gain some composure. She made an effort to control her emotion as they walked towards the train which was to take them back to a lonelier home.

"I'll be quite all right again soon," she assured her husband, trying to smile through her tears. "It's just the thought of Bobbie making his first long journey without us. Of course I know it is all for his good, and he'll be happy living in the States. And actually my father will be able to provide all the splendid opportunities that we ourselves have been unable to give him." She dried her eyes.

"That's my brave girl," said her husband. "We'll be able to visualise all the places he'll be seeing. What with the wireless, the cinema, the books we've read, and all we've heard about America I feel I know the country even though we have never been there."

His wife answered, "That's true enough. He'll have a grand time." Then, a little more wistfully, "But I know he won't forget his Mummy and Daddy."

"I should think not indeed," answered the boy's father. "There's a special bond of love between us that nobody could change. Bobbie's last words were that he would write frequently and tell us all that he is doing, so we can now look forward to his letters."

As they entered the railway carriage he said contemplatively, "After all, it isn't as though Bobbie has left us for ever. We'll see him again later on. He may be a little taller and a little more mature by the time we meet again, but he'll still be our boy."

"Yes," agreed his wife, brightening considerably. "As you say it isn't as though we were never going to see him again…"

As the train steamed out of the station and began to gather speed, the man and woman lapsed into silence, both wondering what the New World would mean to their beloved son.

* * * * *

Another little child was leaving for the New World. She, too, was making her first journey unaccompanied by her parents, who stood close by, ready to bid her farewell. Different, too, was the scene of departure from the one previously described. No bustling crowds, no noise and excitement here, in the quiet sick-room. The steady ticking of a clock seemed, if anything, to accentuate the stillness of the atmosphere. Silently, the mother and father stood by the bedside of the dying child. Hand in hand, they waited for the spirit body to become released from the pain-racked physical form which would no longer be required in the spirit world for which the little one was departing.

They could not see with their earthly vision what was happening around the child's bed. But their knowledge and experience of Spiritualism helped them to visualise something of the processes taking place as Joan's earthly life drew towards its close.

They were aware that her diseased and suffering physical body was but a poor counterpart of her healthy and potentially perfect spirit body. The etheric counterpart, the true individual, was separating from the well-loved form of their daughter.

Throughout earthly life, the spirit body is linked to the material form by a fine psychic thread, invisible to the physical eye, yet as real as the air which we breathe but do not see. The Bible refers to this invisible thread as the "silver cord." It is the anchor which keeps the ship moored in earthly waters.

The psychic rope that holds this earthly anchor may be extended during sleep when the spirit travels into another dimension. Some of us remember our experiences whilst temporarily released from our physical bodies during sleep, unconsciousness, or in states of trance. But only at the call of death does the psychic cord become completely severed from the body. Then the spirit, the true self, finds permanent expression in the plane of existence we call the spirit world.

All this was familiar knowledge to these parents.

The silver cord, which held Joan's ravaged body to earth, loosened its hold. Her parents stood by, knowing that, had they possessed clairvoyant vision – the gift of most mediums – they would have seen at their child's bedside those whom the world calls dead. They knew that many of their dearest relatives and friends who had already passed over were around their daughter's bed, waiting to welcome the newcomer to the world they already inhabited. Joan, brought up in the knowledge that life continued in an uninterrupted stream, would not feel strange or frightened when her spiritual eyes opened and she beheld beloved and familiar faces amongst those who had come to meet her.

Conscious of some of the psychic processes, and the activities that were taking place in the quiet room, the parents watched and prayed. And as their little one drew her last earthly breath and started on her first journey without them, they turned to each other for consolation – the husband endeavouring to control his own emotion in order to comfort his wife. Their grief at this hour was natural, the woman's tears a relief for her pent-up feelings and a blessed help towards paving the way for the calm, assured composure which was hers by right of knowledge. As experienced Spiritualists who had received unchallengeable evidence of Survival, they were confident that their little girl still lived and that only her physical body had perished.

Like those other parents who bade a temporary farewell to their child about to leave for the New World across the sea, Joan's parents exchanged similar words of consolation in their hour of loneliness. "Dry your tears, dearest," said the man to his wife. "Take heart; Joan is in good and capable hands, as we both know. A little later on, when we are both calmer, we can look forward to hearing how our darling is progressing in her new life. She'll have so much to tell us."

His wife answered, "It is a wonderful comfort to know that she has gone to those who love her. But she will not want to lose touch with her Mummy and Daddy."

"Be patient, dear," replied her husband. "She has only gone on a little way ahead. In God's time we'll all be together again."

Without a doubt the greatest solace these parents had in the early days of Joan's departure from them was the knowledge that they would be able to remain in touch with her, until they rejoined her in the world she now inhabited. They would be able to talk with her and acquaint themselves with the kind of life she was leading in the Beyond.

The spirit world vibrates round and about us. It is possible to "tune in," as it were, to the right wavelength and thus communicate with those whom the world calls dead. Mediums have the psychic ability to act as channels of communication between this world and the next. These psychics are attuned to unseen vibrations. They act as transmitters and receivers of messages in much the same way as wireless sets, telegraph and telephone services are the channels for the transmission of earthly messages. If we desire to talk with someone living in another continent, we are obliged to use one of the known methods of communication. It does not matter how close the link of affection that binds us to the friends or relatives abroad, we must accept the means provided for the purpose of talking with them. Then, if the communicating link is in good order, the barrier of distance is temporarily surmounted. Neither wide oceans nor vast tracts of land can prevent our reunion.

In the same way, when a medium acts as a transmitter of messages between the material and the spirit world, space is conquered and we can communicate easily and naturally with those who have passed through the veil of death.

During their long experience of Spiritualism, Joan's parents had, on countless occasions, spoken with their "dead" relatives and friends. Through different forms of mediumship their loved ones had manifested their continued survival as individuals who retained the same characteristics they displayed on earth. They had attended many public Spiritualist meetings where the mediums, exercising the gift of clairvoyance, had given descriptions of "dead" friends and relatives to unknown people in the audience.

Proofs of Survival had often been vouchsafed to Joan's parents at private sittings for mental phenomena where mediums had exercised their gifts of clairvoyance or clairaudience – psychic hearing. Often they were strangers to the medium. The private sitting had been arranged on their behalf by a reputable Spiritualist society. It is not usual for such organisations to give the names of the sitters, or any information about them, to the medium. At such séances the medium is often entranced. During that time, her physical body may be "controlled" by her guide, an experienced and evolved spirit, whose task is to help the ones who have passed over to present evidence of their survival to the sitters.

Joan's parents had attended direct-voice séances where the "dead" had reproduced their earthly voices for purposes of recognition. At materialisation séances, they had seen the apparently solid forms of loved ones who had passed on take shape before their eyes. They had sat for psychic photography. When a medium who possesses this gift takes a picture of a living person, using an ordinary camera for the purpose, there often appears on the plate an "extra." A spirit entity has impinged his, or her, image on the same picture as the sitter. Hundreds of "dead" people have manifested in this way.

These parents, who had witnessed most kinds of psychic phenomena, had, in the intimacy of their own home, when no professional medium was present, held sacred converse with their loved ones who had passed over. Up and down this country there are many thousands of such home circles, as they are called. Members of the family, and perhaps one or two friends, meet once or twice a week at regularly appointed times. The most important requirement for successful sittings is harmony between the members of the circle. Most of us possess some degree of psychic power. It is often latent until it is discovered and developed in the home circle. The members of the circle usually sit round an ordinary wooden table, with their hands resting lightly upon its surface. The psychic power enables the "dead" to communicate by a language of raps or tilts of the table. Each rap or tilt corresponds to a letter in the alphabet.

From what they had learned during their Spiritualistic experiences, Joan's parents had the knowledge that their little girl would grow and mature in the spirit world in much the same way as she would have done on earth. They had no doubts in their minds that, when they passed over, they would know their own child and she would know them. Why, indeed, should she not, since she would continue to spend much time in her own home? Her earthly breath had failed, but her spirit had not suddenly become transported to a vague, far-off heaven beyond the clouds and beyond comprehension. Neither had the act of death transformed her into an angelic, winged being, totally unrecognisable to them.

These parents knew that their child's astral, or etheric, body, whilst being a counterpart of her physical form, would not, in her new state of existence, reproduce any defects of the earthly body. The real individual had, at the moment of "death," stepped out of the physical envelope because it had no further utility in a nonphysical world. The mind and the consciousness of their daughter, not being physical qualities, were indestructible. Her own individuality would continue to express itself in her new state of life. The parents knew – that Joan was the same child the moment after her passing as the instant before its occurrence. Death had not changed her character, or the characteristics which identified her as their own beloved daughter. These qualities would, in future, express themselves through her spirit body instead of the material one.

They knew that in the New World to which she had gone she would have a home, not so utterly unlike the earthly one that she would feel entirely lost and strange. She would join relatives and friends who knew and loved her on the Other Side. It may be difficult for one new to the subject of Spiritualism to believe that houses and buildings on the Other Side are as real and tangible as our earthly homes. But think for a moment of what occurs in dreams. Are not our experiences during sleep just as real, whilst they last, as our waking activities? During the time we are dreaming we do not think, "Oh, this building is riot really solid!" The house is solid, and the experience unquestioned, because during the dream we are temporarily outside the limits of physical dimensions. The spirit world is in no sense a dream condition. It is more real and permanent than the earthly world we now inhabit. The dream comparison is merely presented for explanatory convenience.

Their knowledge of life on the Other Side told these parents that in her new environment Joan would lead a life of activity which, though comparable with earthly existence, would present her with richer and fuller opportunities to express her true individuality and consciousness. A wide variety of interests, a life of happiness awaited their child. She would find friends and companions; she would receive education at schools specially equipped to impart the kind of knowledge she needed. Such gifts as she had displayed in her short earthly life would be fostered and encouraged by those in the spirit world most suited to the task of developing her special qualifications. Moreover, the latent qualities and talents that she had been unable to express on earth would also be encouraged. For genius and talent do not cease to find adequate expression in an individual after "death." All the giants of the artistic world who have passed on, all the famous composers, the illustrious writers, the great scientists and philosophers have not ceased to express their gifts. Because of the greatness of their souls some continue to impart their knowledge to others.

In the spirit world are no square pegs in round holes. Often, owing to pecuniary difficulties, many of us are denied the opportunity to express latent gifts during earthly existence. The soul of a Mozart may be hidden in a coal miner who gets neither the opportunity nor the leisure to develop his hidden talent. On the Other Side, where material values do not operate, and where livings do not have to be earned, each one of us has the opportunity to develop innate gifts.

Joan's parents were fortunate in the knowledge they possessed. Confidence in their child's continued individual existence and the assurance that they would not lose touch with her, helped them over their most difficult days. It assuaged their grief, tempered their emotion and gave them courage to face the future.

But you may be a parent who, in similar circumstances, yearns for tangible help and guidance in your hour of bereavement. Your child's body, once so full of life and vitality, lies still. The young bud, so full of promise, has perished, and the hand of death has plucked the slender stem. Whither has flown the living spark that so recently animated the beloved form? A thousand questions torture your mind. Doubts, fears and perplexities trouble your spirit. Before this sorrow came, you may have had no religious beliefs. Alternatively, you may never have questioned the orthodox and conventional belief in a future life. But now you want to know more. The somewhat mythological conception of a far-off heaven, populated by white-robed angels, becomes unconvincing, unreal. The thought of the transformation of your own very human child into a winged cherub in a nebulous realm brings little consolation in your hour of loneliness.

You feel that such a metamorphosis completely divorces you from the child you knew so well and loved so deeply. Your whole soul yearns to know what has happened to the little one whose spiritual, mental and physical care have been your concern from the moment of birth. You ask, "How is my darling faring without me in the strange new life? Am I missed? Am I needed? What is my child doing and in whose care is my darling? Shall I ever see my beloved again? If so, how shall we be able to recognise each other? Can I really communicate with my spirit child, and is it right to do so? Will the constant return to the earth retard my little one's progress in the spirit world?"

If these are the questions that trouble your mind I hope that the answers which appear in the following pages will help you. It is for this purpose the book has been written.

Chapter 1

A LITTLE GIRL'S CHALLENGE

"IT is wrong to call up the dead." How many times I have heard these words of condemnation directed against Spiritualists! Such a reproach is but an acknowledgment of ignorance of the subject. Spiritualists do not disturb the "dead." In fact, the contrary is often the case and it is the "dead" who disturb us! I have attended hundreds of séances. On more than one occasion I have heard a "dead" person ask that mourning relatives or friends be given the information that the one for whom they grieved had survived the grave. Such spirit communicators have provided proofs of their identity. Because the ones whom they wished to comfort were complete strangers to the mediums, and those present, the "dead" have had to furnish names and addresses before the messages could be delivered.

Spiritualists do not "conjure up" the "dead." If the Great Spirit we call God had not intended the veil between the two worlds to be penetrated, neither the efforts of the "dead" nor the endeavours of the living would have been of any avail.

The pages of ancient and modern history are filled with instances of psychic experiences of those who have held communion with the world of spirit. Prophets and sages, philosophers, social reformers and humanitarians have, at times, received direct inspiration from the Beyond and have translated their revelations into terms of service towards their fellows. Religions have been founded on such experiences. The Christian faith is based upon the teachings of the great psychic, Jesus of Nazareth, who was in constant rapport with the world of spirit. His "miracles" were manifestations of his complete mastery of psychic laws. The everlasting truths taught by the Nazarene later became buried under a mass of dogma and creed. The simplicity of his words, the implications and understanding of his deeds were lost in the complexities of ritual. Attempts to resurrect his teachings have been made from time to time by other inspired leaders.

Throughout the ages revelation from the spirit world has been received by saintly men and women. Their clairvoyant eyes have beheld visions; their clairaudient ears have heard voices from

Beyond. In the western hemisphere alone, Joan of Arc, Emanuel Swedenborg and George Fox are but a few of the great personages who were uplifted by their communion with the spirit world. Joan of Arc chose the stake rather than deny the psychic source of her inspiration.

Yet, in so many instances, the interpretations of the spirit communications have been coloured and influenced by the religious upbringing and orthodoxy of the recipients of the messages. The Maid of Orleans, nurtured in the Roman Catholic faith, identified the radiant personalities of her spirit messengers with the saints she had been taught to revere and admire. It was natural, and perhaps even necessary, for the successful fulfilment of her mission that it should be so.

Emanuel Swedenborg, the great Swedish seer, was the son of a bishop. In interpreting the meaning and implications of his remarkable psychic experiences, he could not break away from his own theological training. The human mind, cultivated in orthodox or theological soil, cannot easily destroy all the weeds of religious prejudices. Through the centuries, evolved spirits have endeavoured to unlock the door of misunderstanding and theological bias and prove that spirit communication is not the special privilege of the exalted few, however unblemished their lives. For the same natural laws which operated when the Nazarene appeared before his disciples after his "death" are in operation today. Young men still "dream dreams and see visions" as they did in ancient times. The laws of the universe are unchanging, unalterable, but our knowledge of their application has increased with a fuller understanding of their operation.

The knowledge that communication between this world and the next is available to ordinary people was first discovered in 1848 not by a great seer, but by two children, whose simple minds were untrammelled by adult prejudices. It all began with the playful request of a little girl. Into a new home in the village of Hydesville, New York State, moved a farmer named Fox, with his wife and family. They had not inhabited their wooden homestead very long before they began to hear strange noises in the night. Knocks and rappings resounded all over the house. Efforts to trace the cause of the disturbances completely failed. As the weeks went by, the unwelcome supernormal happenings increased both in violence and frequency of occurrence. Furniture was moved about, unseen hands pulled at bed-covers and footsteps were heard all over the house.

At first, the children were as disturbed as their parents by the unwelcome happenings. But gradually, becoming accustomed to the phenomena, they began to be amused instead of frightened. Lying in bed one night in their parents' room, the strange rappings seemed louder than ever to the children's ears. Perhaps rendered extra bold because her mother and father were there, 12-yearold Katie sat up in bed. To the unseen disturber of their slumbers she said, "Here, Mr. Split-foot, do as I do!" With this, she clapped her hands. Immediately, the sound was followed by the same number of raps. Not to be outshone by her younger sister, Margaret, who was 15, then called out, "Now do as I do – count one, two, three, four." Instantly, four raps were heard. Thrilled with the new game, Katie next made silent motions with her finger and thumb. The invisible intelligence gave a number of raps corresponding to the number of noiseless motions Katie had made. "Only look, Mother," said the astonished child, "it can see as well as hear!"

Further questioning by Mrs. Fox received intelligent replies by the method of raps. "Is it a human being that answers my questions so correctly?" she inquired. There was a silence. "Is it a spirit?" she demanded. "If it is, make two raps." Two raps immediately followed.

Although this method of communication was of necessity long and laborious, it was ascertained that the raps were made by a "dead" man, a pedlar, who said he had been murdered at the age of 31 in that very house and that his body lay buried beneath the cellar. He told them the manner in which he had been murdered and by whom the deed was accomplished. He gave particulars about his wife and family, and referred to events that had happened since his passing. The statements made by the spirit communicator were investigated and found to be accurate.

His remains were discovered in the place he had indicated.

And so, with a child's playful challenge to an unseen intelligence, Modern Spiritualism was born.

Chapter 2

THE VITAL SPARK

THE physical life of every individual begins, after conception, as a single cell in the human body. This germ of living matter so small that it is hardly visible to the naked eye contains the full potentialities of a complete male or female body, with all the hereditary material contributed by the parents. Within this tiny fertilised seed are the elements which will develop into eyes and hair, teeth and finger nails, organs and tissues of an individual who in due course may reproduce his or her own species. The human fertilised germ contains potentially, not only the puling infant, but the aged, wrinkled adult. They are of the same material, a speck of life, within the womb of the mother. The miracle of birth is surely the most amazing of all natural phenomena. It is enacted so often in our midst that we take the process almost for granted. But what is life itself without which the development and growth of an individual could not take place?

The inventive powers of man have performed remarkable feats of ingenuity, skill and imagination. He has devised scientific instruments of great precision with which he is able to control and even conquer many of the elements. He has stemmed rivers, bridged channels and sent tall buildings towering upwards. His machines fly in the air. He has wrested secrets of nature from her bosom. His artistic accomplishments are manifold. Yet even though man can stimulate, transform, transpose and perform all sorts of tricks with living matter, he cannot create even the lowest form of animate life. The chemicals that compose the physical human being may be bought for a shilling or so. Yet no man has even been able to make one of God's lowliest creatures. The brain of man has conceived and put into practice fearful methods of destroying healthy life. In war, we kill each other by various and dreadful means. With all our knowledge and scientific accomplishment, we have not yet learned to respect sufficiently the life we cannot create, the vital spark that we cannot kindle of our own volition. The secret still eludes us.

Our bodies are not animated by physical material. When life is withdrawn, the body dies, even though the physical components are exactly the same the moment after breath has ceased. The heart and lungs are still there, however inadequately they may have functioned before death actually occurred. Death takes place because something has happened to the physical body that prevents the spirit from continuing to express itself through the same earthly vehicle.

As has been demonstrated by the marvels of modern plastic surgery, many different parts of a living body can now be replaced, when necessary, by sections taken from another physical body, either human or animal. Numbers of the disfigured victims of the Great War were obliged to wear masks over their poor, injured faces, or else were kept hidden from the sight of their fellow-men.

Plastic surgery has made rapid strides. Many of the dreadful facial and other disfigurements caused by the disasters of modern warfare are now treated so skilfully that, under the surgeon's expert hands, a patient practically receives a new set of features in place of the disfigured ones. New noses and chins are shaped from bone and cartilage. Destroyed eyelids are replaced by fresh ones fashioned from flaps of flesh removed from different parts of the human body, not necessarily that of the patient. It is unlikely that even the genius of Shakespeare ever anticipated that Shylock's demand for a pound of flesh from a living person would one day be made possible by modern surgery for humane instead of vicious reasons.

Today, sections of cartilage and bone taken from dead bodies can be preserved for long periods until they are needed for plastic operations. It may perhaps strike one as gruesome that victims of a disaster should go through the rest of their lives with new noses, chins and ears shaped from the bone formations of dead bodies. Yet these skilful replacements enable the patients to continue their lives amongst their fellows. The alternative, permanent, ghastly disfigurement and perhaps voluntary banishment from human society, has been avoided. But the "repaired" individuals do not assume – in part or in whole – the personalities of the ones whose physical components have replaced their own by the process of surgery. Patients continue, as hitherto, to express their own personalities. You can patch up or replace physical discrepancies by other physical components. But you cannot repair the individual's spirit body with part of another spirit body.

The earthly form is not the individual. It is merely the temporary habitation of the spirit body which is a perfected reflection of the earthly one and does not reproduce the purely physical discrepancies of its temporary habitation. When the spirit can no longer express itself through matter, the material body is cast aside like a useless cloak. Life being indestructible, the spirit journeys on...

The two Fox sisters, who as children discovered that communication between this world and the next is possible, were the first mediums to give public demonstrations of this stupendous truth. They were the torchbearers of modern Spiritualism. Since their day other mediums have followed the trail they blazed, keeping aloft the flaming brands of inspiration. The volume of evidence of personal survival has accumulated and increased.

Such illustrious scientists as Sir Oliver Lodge, Sir William Crookes, Dr. William Brown and Sir William Barrett – to mention a few – have investigated the claims of Spiritualism and proved to their own satisfaction the stupendous fact of personal survival and spirit communication. These men, trained in scientific observation, have publicly testified to the truths they have ascertained. In common with scores of other respected men and women of the highest integrity and motives, they have announced to the world that the spark of life is not extinguished when the physical body perishes.

There is wealth of evidence now available that after death man retains his individuality, consciousness and memory. In recent years the scientists themselves have destroyed the case for materialism by their own investigations. With the knowledge that the atom was capable of being split went many preconceived notions as to the indestructibility of matter. It is now realised that "solid" matter is something of an illusion. It has been scientifically demonstrated that material substance consists of a collection of electrically charged particles. Our physical bodies, the houses we inhabit, the furniture we use, the food we eat and the books we read, must all be considered in terms of electronic radiations. Matter itself cannot be destroyed. Only its form can be changed and transformed into other substances. A piece of paper consigned to the flames is changed into ashes. In their turn the ashes may be resolved into chemical compounds. The physical body of an individual, apparently so solid, can be disintegrated and transformed into non-material substances.

Since even the discarded matter, a dead physical body, continues after disintegration to exist in a changed form, it is unreasonable to assume that the superior mind which controlled the body's mechanism should become extinct after vacating the earthly vessel. Leaving aside the mass of evidence for Survival, such a belief is illogical and unsound. Complete negation is not the law of the universe planned by the Master Mind. Death takes place when the life-force has withdrawn from the physical body. Then the etheric or spirit body, no longer limited by material conditions, continues to express itself in the non-physical plane to which it belongs.

Individuality, character and memory continue to function through the spirit body because these non-material qualities were: never part of the physical covering through which they formerly expressed themselves. Newcomers to the world of spirit find themselves in a sphere in many respects similar to the one they have left.

The astral or etheric world to which the spirit gravitates can be compared with our own, but it is a mental world, since the material aspect of life is no longer necessary to the etheric body. But absence of physical conditions does not imply that the spirit world is less tangible than the present one. The contrary is true. Life there is infinitely more vivid and vital. It may be said that in the Beyond thought action takes the place of physical action on earth. In a mental world, mental effects are potent and real.

Hundreds of spirit communicators have told, in séance rooms all over the world, of life in the next world. Rarely do they contradict each other on any important point. We learn that we are personally responsible for the lives we have led and the characters we have formed and developed on earth. Life in the next world is conditioned by the character we take with us when we pass over. Nevertheless, retribution can be made for mortal errors and eternal progression is available to us all.

Chapter 3

SOME SHALL BE TAKEN...

THE "death" of a well-loved aged relative or friend is deeply felt by those left behind. But, after the first pangs of grief have abated, some solace is often derived from the reflection that the "dead" person's mortal span of years was well spent, and a full measure of earthly experience was acquired.

Those who pass over at a ripe age have weathered the storms of life's trials and tribulations. The common lot of human experience has been theirs. They have travelled roads both smooth and rough. They have known joys and sorrows, happiness and pain, at different periods of their earthly pilgrimage. Such individuals have, as we say, "lived their lives," and grief for their passing is softened by this reflective consolation. But when a child "dies," we are denied this solace, unless we consider the physical loss from a different angle.

You, whose little one has perhaps only recently passed on, may have experienced a storm of turbulent emotions after the child's transition. As the sense of separation deepened, perchance you cried out in rebellion against the cruelty of fate. You may never before have questioned God's benevolence, but the loss may have shaken for a time your faith in divine justice and wisdom.

In some bitterness, you may have asked yourself why the cup of life should have been dashed so prematurely from the lips of your darling whose future appeared so rosy and for whom you had made such wonderful plans. When the golden opportunities for leading a useful, active and happy life were so apparent, you could not understand why full human experience should have been denied your little one. These, perhaps, were some of the thoughts that troubled your bitter hours.

I do not pretend that I can supply an adequate answer to the question why some are taken and others left. Individuals who accept the reincarnation hypothesis affirm that those who pass over young have, in their short earthly experience, fulfilled a particular phase in the soul's evolution. Whether such affirmations – which bear no relation to the purposes of the present book – appeal to your reason or not, take courage. Stem your tears; raise your head. Prolonged, intemperate grief is a form of self-pity. We weep for our own sense of loss and separation, our own loneliness.

It is true that full human experience, as we understand the term, will not be your child's lot, although, as you will read, "dead" children do return to earth and spend time with their relatives. Your little one will not, however, in the material sense, know worldly pleasures and joys. But neither will he or she ever undergo the pain of parental bereavement such as you have just experienced. Your child will never know the bitterness of disillusionment, disappointment, thwarted ambition and unfulfilled hopes. Your beloved will never know the anguish of unrequited earthly love, or suffer the miseries of ill-health, or experience the horrors and tortures of war.

Your child will lead an active and joyous life in a world of unimaginable beauty and unbounded opportunity. The lesser has been abandoned for the greater happiness. Only your grief separates you from the little one who has not left you, and will never leave you while the ties of love hold you. The door of death which opened, as you thought, so prematurely, might prove to be the greatest blessing that Providence could bestow upon your child's head. The wonderful plans you made for the future may never have reached fruition. Through the death of the physical body, an appalling fate may have been averted. You do not know.

Do you remember Hans Andersen's *Story of a Mother*? Whilst a poor woman sat watching by the cradle of her sick baby, an old man, whose name was Death, entered, and carried off the infant. Frantic with sorrow, the mother left her home and went in search of Death, hoping he would relent and return the babe to her arms. During her long journey in search of her child, she endured untold hardships. She gave her most prized and cherished possessions to those who demanded payment for information concerning the route Death had taken. One took her eyes, another her long black hair.

Eventually, worn and exhausted, the now sightless woman was led by an old crony to Death's great hot-house where flowers and trees grew curiously together.

"Here were delicate hyacinths under bell glasses," writes Hans Andersen, "and there were great strong peonies; here were water plants, some quite fresh, others sickly with water snakes wound round them and little black crayfish pinching their stems. Here were beautiful palm trees, oaks and plane trees; there grew parsley and sweet scented thyme; every tree and every flower had its name. Each one was a human life, living still, one in China, one in

Greenland, scattered round about the world. There were big trees in small pots, growing in a stunted way, ready to burst their pots; and there were also, in other places, little tiresome flowers in rich earth surrounded with moss, and covered and tended. But the sad mother bent over all the tiniest plants and listened for the human heart beating in them. Among a million she knew her child's at once.

The baby's heart beat within a little blue crocus which hung feebly to one side. She stretched her hands over the delicate plant, but she was warned by the old crony not to touch the flower. She told the mother to await the arrival of Death. Then she could threaten him that, if he took the flower which contained her child's beating heart, she would pluck other floral lives. This would frighten him, said the old woman, for he was answerable to God for all the plants, not one of which could be removed without His permission.

All at once, an icy wind sprang up, and the mother knew that Death was standing beside her. "How didst thou find thy way hither?" he asked. "How couldst thou get here before me?"

"I am a mother," she said.

Death stretched his long hand towards the delicate little flower, but the sightless woman sensed his purpose towards her child's life. She clutched his hand, fearful that he should touch one of the sickly leaves. Then Death breathed upon her hands. His breath was colder than the most icy wind, and her hands fell numbly away from his own.

Telling the mother she had no power over him, he assured her that he was only there to do God's will. "I am His gardener!" he said. "I take all His flowers and trees and plant them in the Garden of Paradise."

Despairingly the mother begged him to return her baby. She clutched two beautiful flowers which were growing close at hand. "I will pull up your flowers, for I am in despair," she cried.

"Touch them not!" said Death. "Thou sayst that thou art unhappy, yet wouldst thou make some other mother equally unhappy."

The poor woman removed her hands immediately. "Some other mother," she repeated, letting go the flowers at once.

"Here hast thou thine eyes back again," said Death. "I fished them up out of the lake, they shone so brightly; I did not know they were thine. Take them back again, they are brighter than ever. Look down into the deep well close by. I will name the names of those flowers thou wast about to pluck, and thou shalt see their whole lives, and all that future thou wast about to destroy."

And as she looked down into the well it made her happy to see that one of the lives became a blessing to the world and was surrounded by joy and pleasure. Then she saw the life of the other. It was one of sorrow and need, sin and misery.

"Both lives are according to the will of God," said Death.

"Which of them is the flower of misery and which of blessedness?" she asked.

"That I may not tell thee," said Death; "but I may tell thee that one of the flowers was thy own child's; it was thy child's fate thou sawest, thine own child's future."

Overwhelmed with terror, the mother cried, "Which was my child? Tell me that. Save my child from all the misery... Bear it into God's kingdom."

"I do not understand thee," answered Death. "Wilt thou have thy child back or shall I take it whither thou knowest not?"

The mother fell upon her knees and wrung her hands in grief, praying to God, "Do not listen to me when I pray against Thy will, which is best; do not listen, do not listen." She bent her head in submission.

"Then Death carried her child into the Unknown Land," concludes this beautiful and touching story of a mother's love.

But to Spiritualists, the Beyond is not an "Unknown Land." Time and time again "dead" children have returned to tell their parents of the wonders of the world to which an all-seeing Providence has thought fit to call them.

Chapter 4

THE VEIL IS LIFTED

FOR more than two years I attended voice séances at the home of Estelle Roberts, the famous medium whose high standard of public clairvoyance has convinced thousands of people of life after death.

With very few exceptions, voice and materialisation séances are held either in darkness or in red light. White light has a deleterious effect on certain kinds of Spiritualism's physical phenomena in much the same way as it is destructive to photographic plates, which have to be developed in darkness or in red light. Physical phenomena may, indeed, be compared with the processes of birth. The germination of life takes place in the dark. The growth of the animal and human embryo occurs within the darkness of the body. In the absence of light, seeds begin their growth in the earth. The physical phenomena of the séance room, materialisations in particular, entail a temporary "speeding up" of the forces of life itself. I have attended hundreds of materialisation séances, held in good red light, but, in any case, it is neither the presence nor absence of light at sittings that is of importance. The evidence of Survival that is received is the only test that matters.

The tin, or aluminium cone, used at a voice séance looks like, and is known as, a trumpet. It conserves, directs and amplifies the voice of the spirit communicators, who use it as a megaphone. When the psychic power of the medium functions adequately, the trumpet moves freely about the séance room. At the scores of Estelle Roberts's voice séances I attended, the trumpet never bumped into anything in the dark, or touched a sitter unintentionally as it travelled rapidly about the room under spirit direction. Estelle Roberts's voice séances were held in darkness, but the wide bands of luminous paint applied to the broad end of the trumpet enabled the sitters to follow its every movement with ease.

At the most successful voice circles, the spirit communicators are able to reproduce their earthly voices, so that relatives and friends can often identify characteristics, intonations and mannerisms.

In that Upper Room of sacred reunion between the living and the so-called dead, I have sometimes felt an interloper as I heard touching conversations that have moved me to tears. In contrast, there have been many amusing episodes. Comedy and drama intermingle in the séance room as freely and as naturally as in everyday life. It was at one of these trumpet séances that I received the most strikingly corroborative personal proof I have ever had in my long experience of Spiritualism. But then, I have listened to proof after proof of Survival being received by sitters, many of whom were entirely new to the subject of Spiritualism and quite unknown to the medium.

The dominating spirit influence at these circles was the medium's guide, Red Cloud, whose Indian personality cloaks a highly evolved being of great wisdom, humanity and a profound sense of humour. He is beloved by all who know him. Every well-developed medium has a spirit guide or control whose function is to protect the medium from undesirable influences and to help the "dead" provide their evidence.

There were usually 20 to 25 people present at the voice séances of Estelle Roberts. A few were regular members of the circle; the rest were visitors. I was present one week when Mrs. Madge Donohoe asked Red Cloud if he would permit her to bring "a friend" to the next sitting. She gave no other details. The guide agreed, and subsequently Mrs. Donohoe brought a stranger to the circle. He was not introduced beforehand to the medium or to any of the sitters. Later, we learned he was not a Spiritualist and this was his first séance.

After several spirit voices had addressed relatives and friends, and some excellent evidence had been received, the luminous trumpet moved in the direction of Mrs. Donohoe's companion. We heard the voice of a boy say to him, "Dad, I want you to know I did not commit suicide! The coroner said I did, and the jury said I did. But I did not, Dad. You tried to stop them, but they shut you up." The stranger answered, "Yes, that is true. But how did it happen?"

"You didn't know I had a gun, did you? But Mummy knew."

"Yes," replied the sitter. "I've found that out since, but tell me how it occurred."

Very pathetically, the spirit voice replied, "Well, Dad, I was only a boy like other boys, and I wanted to be a highwayman. I took the gun and went out on the by-pass road. Then I tried to shoot a bird and I stumbled and shot myself. That's how it happened. You believe me, don't you, Dad?"

"Yes, Teddy boy, I believe you," replied his father. It was

obvious that he was having some difficulty in restraining his strong emotion.

"Don't cry, Dad," said his boy, "I'm all right now."

After the sitting, my husband spoke to the father, who was still amazed by the evening's events. "Tell me," he said, "are you sure it was your son?"

"Yes," came the reply, "that was my boy's voice. They said he committed suicide four months ago, but my wife and I found it difficult to believe it of our son."

Wishing to record the story in a book he was then writing, my husband telephoned Mrs. Donohoe a few days later to ask for her friend's name. "I cannot give it to you," she answered. "He has been afraid to tell his wife about the séance. She is a Christian Scientist who is opposed to Spiritualism."

It is not always easy to break down prejudices!

A regular spirit visitor at Red Cloud's séances was a young girl named Louise. She would come and talk to her earthly mother and aunt, two sitters who often came to the circle. Louise, who had been a dancer before she passed over, had a characteristic voice which rose and fell during every sentence. Red Cloud once said, "Her legs have got into her tongue!" One night, after she had spoken to her relatives, she said to us all, "They did not tell me when I was on earth that I was a German, but it makes no difference here." Hannen Swaffer, the famous journalist and dramatic critic, was present that night. The spirit girl's mother said to her, "Look, Mr. Swaffer is over there. You remember how we used to discuss him."

"Yes, I know," Louise replied. "I have been looking at him." Then she added, "You know, Mr. Swaffer, I am afraid of you."

"Why?" he asked.

"Well," she shyly answered, "I am a dancer and you are a critic!"

"That's all right, my dear," he reassured her. "It's dark and I can't see you."

"But I can see you," she said in some surprise. "Why, you must all be dead!"

"It is getting near Christmas," I heard a "dead" boy say to his foster-mother at another voice séance.

"Yes, my darling," replied the sitter. "A week today. What are you going to do?"

"Come with you," was the immediate response, and there followed a long, confidential talk between the child and his fostermother.

Many children brought Christmas greetings to their earthly relatives that night. "Daddy, Daddy," came the excited voice of one little boy. "Daddy, it's Peter... Peterkin." Then, addressing his mother, he went on, "Mummy, I'm so happy. Kiss John and Wendy for me."

"I will kiss them, but what about Mickey?" she asked.

"My brother Mickey," came the reply; "kiss him too."

Peter told his parents that his grandfather had brought him and was helping him to speak. The child mentioned another member of the family who had helped him dress the Christmas tree the previous year, when he was on earth.

"What about my rocking horse in the top room?" was the spirit boy's next question to his father.

"It's still there, darling," his parent replied. "I ride it sometimes."

"Funny Daddy," said Peter, highly amused.

Then the parents told their "dead" child that they were going to put something on the Christmas tree for him at home. Peter was delighted. We heard the sound of kisses coming from the trumpet. "Daddy, I'm not in pain now," he volunteered. "Do not grieve for Peter. I always come with Grandad."

"You come to me when I am sitting quietly at night, don't you?" asked his father. The answer came in a plaintive childish treble, "I always do. Daddy. There is a nice doctor here. He said I died with meningitis. *But I did not die.*"

The spirit child told his parents how he sometimes had games with his earthly sister Wendy, to whom he sent his love. He sent greetings to two other children, Nettie and Johnnie. He said he would be, with them all on Christmas day. "I will make a lot of noise, if I can," he told his parents.

Then he spoke of a new pet in the family circle. "You did not have her when I was there. You have somebody now to take my place."

"Nobody takes your place, Peterkin," answered his father.

"I do not mind," said Peter.

Through the trumpet came another voice, a girl's this time. "I am Daphne," she said. The child began to speak to her mother, but suddenly broke off, apparently embarrassed by the number of visitors present who were strangers to her. Bashfully she said to her parent, "There are such a lot of people here. Tell them not to listen to Daphne." She referred to her earthly brother John. "He has been playing with the barrow," she said. "Daphne plays with the barrow too."

Trying to explain how she spoke at this séance, she stated that all she knew was that a guide said, "Go into the box, Daphne, and you can talk." So Daphne went into the box – no doubt the simple description given to the little girl of the ectoplasmic "voice-box" through which the spirit voices register in the séance room.

About 20 different voices spoke that night, and nearly all of them volunteered the fact that they would be present in their earthly homes on Christmas day.

At another voice séance, we heard a pathetic child's voice say, "Daddy, it is Mickey. It's Mickey speaking." This "dead" child returned that night to comfort his father because, as he said, "Mummy is so ill."

"Have you seen Mummy?" asked his father. "Yes," replied the child. "Granny took me."

The sitter asked how he thought his mother's health was progressing. "She is better now," answered Mickey, "but she is worrying."

"What about?" asked his father. Pathetically, came the reply, "Because I 'died.' One, two, three of us are all here now. Poor Mummy."

It was very touching to hear this little boy say, "Daddy, tell Mummy that Mickey always loves her. I wish she would not be so sad, Daddy."

"When are we going to sit again, dear?" asked his parent, wondering when their home circle would recommence. "Not for a long while," answered the child, "because Mummy must get strong. Mummy had another little Mickey, but he 'died.' Don't be unhappy. We are all together. I love you all the time."

"Blessed are they that mourn, for they shall be comforted," said Jesus of Nazareth. And, in that Upper Room, two thousand years later, a little child was fulfilling the message by bringing solace to a father's heart.

* * *

"Mummy, Mummy, I want Mummy," said a child's voice at a trumpet séance held by Mrs. D. Hadden at the Edinburgh Psychic College. Mrs. Christina Lockhart recognised this voice to be that of her daughter Cathie, who passed over in her sixth year, after an operation for appendicitis. "Cathie was our only child," writes Mrs. Lockhart in a moving letter to me. "She was the sunshine of our lives. Only those who have loved a child as we loved her can understand what her death meant to us. Her passing left a blank that has to be experienced to be understood."

The questioning minds of Cathie's parents had, for many years previously, prevented them from being able to accept the tenets of the orthodox faith in which they were nurtured. Indeed, at the time of their child's "death," they were becoming increasingly agnostic in their attitude to a future life. "In spite of our prayers and our heart-searching, we could not come back to the simple faith of our church membership days," says Mrs. Lockhart. "Many times after Cathie's passing we discussed the pros and cons of an after-life, and, after the coming of wireless into our homes, we began to think more seriously about there being a state of existence outside our ken, in spite of all the materialists might say."

In this attitude of mind, 17 years after Cathie's passing, the parents attended a Spiritualist propaganda meeting. Seated amongst an audience of 2,000 people, they received their first clairvoyant description of their "dead" child. The meeting was held at the Usher Hall, Edinburgh,, where the medium gave them their daughter's first and second christian names. "Your child passed over young," added the clairvoyant, "but she is growing up now." Later, Cathie was able to give further messages to her mother at a private sitting arranged with the same medium.

But it was not until several months later that Mrs. Lockhart had the happiness of hearing her child's actual voice at Mrs. Hadden's trumpet séance. "I knew it was Cathie," she writes. "There was an inflection in the way she used to say 'Mummy' that was peculiarly her own way of addressing me."

In that darkened séance room, the trumpet, which was not near Mrs. Lockhart when her daughter first spoke, moved in the mother's direction and hovered in front of her as the spirit child excitedly said: "Mummy, it's me, it's me, Cathie!" Then time stood still for this parent. "If I should live to be a thousand," she writes, "I can never hope to feel again such a thrill as passed through my being. In that room it seemed there were only Cathie and I – as I said to her, 'Darling, I knew you would come.'"

The trumpet, hovering in the air, touched Mrs. Lockhart with soft, gentle movements before Cathie's voice spoke again. "Mummy, you won't leave me, you won't leave me!" she begged. Mrs. Lockhart writes, "As she said these words, it was as though the years had rolled back and I was again by her side in the hospital ward after her operation. As the surgeon came forward to make his examination, she held my hand and said, in an agitated tone, the same words I now heard through the trumpet." That was the last time Cathie spoke to her mother on earth.

The repetition of her child's dying words seemed to Mrs. Lockhart to rejoin the threads that death had snapped 18 years previously. "I will never leave you again," she assured her newfound daughter. "Daddy did not come," said the child in disappointed tones, before she bade her mother goodbye, promising, however, that she would communicate again.

At the next voice séance Mrs. Lockhart attended, Cathie's voice was stronger and clearer, and she was less emotional. She referred to a little spirit friend named Lucy who had spoken just before her. "Lucy has lovely curls," volunteered Cathie, "but they are not like mine. They are dark." Cathie's hair was fair in her earthly life. Lucy, who was an excellent communicator, told Mrs. Lockhart that Cathie had been teaching her to sing. On earth Cathie had possessed a beautiful voice. Sometimes the little family would sing together, "Drink To Me Only With Thine Eyes," while Cathie rendered the accompaniment on the zither her mother had taught her to play. It was significant that the first time she spoke to her mother immediately followed the playing of that song in the séance room.

As time went on, Cathie became an expert communicator and was able to assist other "dead" relatives and friends to provide evidence of their identity. Once at a sitting with Edith Potts, a well-known North of England medium, the guide spoke of the presence of an infant who had "died" at birth. Mrs. Lockhart did not know the child until Cathie supplied the additional evidence by giving the surname of "Murray." Then the sitter recalled that the wife of her husband's nephew had, some months previously, in South Africa, given birth to a child who had not lived. At this sitting, Cathie said she had brought the baby with her so that her mother could tell the parents, who were taking a holiday in England at that time, about the baby. Cathie said the baby's name was David and he had fair hair. These facts were not then known to Mrs. Lockhart. But when her husband's relatives called on her, she asked them what they had intended to call the child if he had lived. "David," was the reply. "What colour was his hair?" she asked them. "It was fair," they answered.

Since the beginning of her parents' investigation into Spiritualism, which began nine years ago, Cathie has continued to provide proof upon proof of her continued existence. She is able to demonstrate her knowledge of their daily lives by commenting on incidents which occur in their home and business surroundings.

At materialisation séances, the "dead" build a reproduction of their earthly bodies for recognition purposes. They make themselves visible by using the white, vapourish substance, called ectoplasm, which exudes from the medium at the sitting. This substance is partly physical and partly ethereal. It has weight, and has been handled by many scientists.

Contrary to popular belief, these materialisations do not look like the ghostly forms associated with Christmas fiction. They are as "solid" as earthly people. When the materialisation is a complete one, the whole organic system of an earthly body is temporarily duplicated, even to heart and pulse beats, which have been recorded by famous men of science.

At most physical séances, the medium sits behind a curtain, or a piece of material, which is hung across a corner of the room. This "cabinet," as it is called, prevents interference from the psychic vibrations of the other people in the room. When the spirit forms are sufficiently "built up," they usually show themselves outside the cabinet, while the medium remains behind the curtained space. I have, however, often been present when a fully materialised spirit has drawn the curtain aside and the medium – usually in deep trance – has been visible at the same time as the "dead" individual.

In America I was present when the guide of the medium, Ethel Post, came out of the cabinet and, in good red light, walked a distance of some 30 feet into the séance room. This young Indian spirit girl' invited my husband to walk back to the cabinet with her, to satisfy himself that the medium was still there. This he did, whilst the guide remained outside the curtain, visible to us all.

The well-known materialisation medium, Helen Duncan, has been victimised by "psychic researchers" and anti-Spiritualists more consistently, perhaps, than any other psychic of the present time. She has been accused, by her enemies, of swallowing cheesecloth by the yard and then regurgitating it in the form of "dead" people. The fact that these spirit individuals have conversed with, and been recognised by, countless people does not appear to be of import to those who have condemned her.

I have witnessed the most remarkable psychic phenomena at some of Helen Duncan's séances, held in red light, when sitters have embraced and kissed their "dead" relatives, who have given full proofs of their continued survival. I have clasped the hand of the materialised form of my brother who passed over in the Great War. His touch was warm and vital. He gave his name and other information that could not possibly have been known by the medium. He also cleared up a mystery regarding his passing.

Dr. Montagu Rust, supporting Helen Duncan's integrity, has affirmed, "The phenomena that come from that woman are perfectly marvellous and cannot be produced by anyone else in Europe." He described a séance where Helen Duncan was tied in a sack and then placed within the cabinet. At the end of the sitting, she was found outside the sack, the seal of which was still intact. On another occasion, he saw the medium when her body was completely dematerialised from the shoulders downward, and again when there was no physical sign of her body below the hips.

Mrs. Elizabeth Holiday, of Birkenhead, tells in *Psychic News* how her child, a twin who "died" at birth, materialised, 24 years later, at one of Helen Duncan's séances. Although she had never seen this daughter, she recognised the spirit girl by her likeness to herself. She was clad, says the mother, in a "beautiful dazzling robe." Those who have sat with Helen Duncan, when the psychic conditions were good, know how white and radiant are the ectoplasmic robes of the materialised spirits. Mrs. Holliday comments on the extraordinary resemblance between the three members of the family, her "dead" daughter, the twin brother and herself. Since the first manifestation, her daughter has materialised on many occasions. "She always comments on what is happening at home," says this mother.

Some "dead" children manifest at the ages at which they passed on; others at the ages they have since attained in the spirit world.

Three of her four "dead" children have materialised to Mrs. E. M. Reynolds, of South Wales, at Helen Duncan's séances. Two of the children manifested at the ages they reached before their passing. The mother tells me she recognised them easily. Another of her sons, David, who "died" at the age of nine months, materialised five years later as a child of six. He told his mother he had been present in the home a few days previously when, during tea, she said to his father, "I wonder what our little David is doing now." The spirit child reminded her that she had also indicated with her band the height he would have reached had he remained on earth.

Mrs. Reynolds told her little son she remembered the

conversation quite well. "Well, I am 'so high,' Mummy," said the child, repeating the words she had used, and holding his hand the same distance from the ground as she had done when she spoke of him. David also sang a verse and chorus of a song to his mother at the same séance. "It was the sweetest voice you ever heard," says Mrs. Reynolds, "yet it resembled the voices of my other children at that age. When you realise I am the mother of a large family, I have had a reasonably good chance of knowing the timbre of their voices."

This child who passed to the spirit world at such a tender age told his mother how he had been taught on the Other Side to walk and talk. "When I was old enough," he said, "they showed me pictures of you and Daddy, and all my brothers and sisters, so that I might know you all. After a time they brought me to see you." Mrs. Reynolds says that a man who had gone to the séance in a sceptical frame of mind was permitted to pass his hand over the form of the materialised child in order to convince himself of the genuineness of the phenomenon. "He stated definitely that he was satisfied it was the form of a child," she writes. "I know he would vouch for this fact. I vow that what I have written is the solemn truth."

Character is the only assessment of an individual's status after "death." The Other Side is not concerned with earthly rank or power. Evidence of Survival is as available to men and women of simple calling in this world as it is to those of exalted position. I know of royal personages who have been vouchsafed remarkable proofs of Survival. I know of others – well, here is the story of a street sweeper, Mr. F. Spencer, whose daughter returned to him through Helen Duncan's mediumship. This girl, who passed over at the age of 14, materialised, gave her name and supplied her father with accurate details of her last illness.

"Vera came out to me from the cabinet," writes Mr. Spencer. "I held her hand and saw the beauty of her face. It was a night that will live with me for ever." The "dead" girl spoke of her mother and, sending her love to them, named all her sisters.

A little later, Albert, the medium's control, asked Mr. Spencer to encourage the spirit who was about to materialise for him, as she had only left her physical body a few hours previously. Then a form appeared before the sitter and called faintly, "I am Lily." Mr. Spencer asked if she could give her surname. She did so, adding, "I have followed you here. Vera helped me."

Lily was the child of one of his neighbours. She had passed on that morning! The medium's control told Mr. Spencer that the girl was distressed because her parents did not understand that she had not really left them. He asked the sitter to communicate with his neighbours and tell them what had occurred that night. Mr. Spencer said he would do his best, but the girl's parents were fervent Roman Catholics who did not believe in Spiritualism.

The following night, Mr. Spencer called on his neighbours. "Have you come to see Lily?" asked the father. He was somewhat taken aback when Mr. Spencer replied, "I saw her last night," and proceeded to relate his experience at the séance. "I do not believe in such things," answered the girl's father. Just then, his wife entered the room, and Mr. Spencer repeated his story. "Thank God!" replied the mother. "Lily suffered here, and I have been worrying that she would remain in Purgatory, still suffering. Now I know it is not so and I am comforted."

At Mr. Spencer's request, I have not given Lily's surname.

Florence Marryat, the well-known Victorian writer, who stood by the truth of Spiritualism when it was unpopular, describes in her book, *There Is No Death*, a public séance she attended in New York whilst on a professional visit. She was unknown to the medium, M. A. Williams, or to any of the sitters. Her "dead" child Florence materialised and satisfied her mother that she was the same girl who had given her incontestable proof of her identity in England. Florence Marryat, from her seat in the front row, witnessed other reunions between earthly parents and their "dead" children. Not more than a minute or two after the séance began, she heard a spirit voice asking for "Father," whilst three spirit forms appeared through the aperture of the medium's cabinet. An old man left his seat and walked up to these three young spirit girls, who embraced him and talked with him. "I almost forgot where I was," writes the author. "They looked so perfectly human, so joyous and girl-like, somewhere between seventeen and twenty, and they all spoke at once, so like what girls on earth would do… The old man came back to his seat, wiping his eyes. 'Are those you daughters, Sir? asked one of the sitters. 'Yes, my three girls,' he replied. 'I lost them all before ten years old, but you see I've got them back again here.'"

Each spirit form, after the time allotted for communication had expired, dematerialised before the sitters, the forms sinking right down through the carpet as though it were the most ordinary thing to do.

Chapter 5

RUTH ANNE COMES BACK

"BECAUSE of the evidence we have had, my husband and I are convinced that our little one lives and loves and is happy in that life beyond death." This is what Mrs. R. Newton, of Newton-le-Willows, Lancashire, wrote to me when I asked her about her "dead" daughter. Ruth Anne passed over at the age of six and a half, after suffering from meningitis. "It was chiefly through the wonderful trance mediumship of Mrs. Lilian Bailey that the amazing evidence of continued life and love came to us," writes Mrs. Newton.

At private sittings, the psychic will describe the "dead" she clairvoyantly sees or clairaudiently hears. Often at séances for mental phenomena, the guide or control will speak through the lips of the medium whose own consciousness is temporarily laid aside. Only highly evolved spirit beings are elected to act as guides, for such a position is a great responsibility. Some mediums have, in addition, one or more spirit controls, who are selected for their ability to co-operate with the guide, particularly in producing physical phenomena. Controls are not necessarily as highly evolved as guides, but, in many cases, a guide also acts as a control.

The parents' first sitting with Lilian Bailey was arranged by the Spiritualist organisation, the Britten Memorial, in Manchester. "We had never met the medium before and she had not been told our names or our reason for coming," says Mrs. Newton, "yet her spirit guide told us immediately that our little girl was present. He gave her full name, Ruth Anne Newton. He gave her age and birthday, the date of her passing and many details of her illness. All these were correct. There followed accurate descriptions of events that had recently occurred, things we had done together and places we had visited when Ruth Anne was with us. We were told her two grandfathers were with her. My father's name, Josiah, was given, with an excellent description of him and his boyhood home, the names of his brothers and sisters and details of his last illness. The name of Ruth Anne's other grandfather was given, too, with much family history."

Writing of further séances with Lilian Bailey, Mrs. Newton states, "It is impossible to convey the atmosphere of deep love and joy and the reality of these reunions. Poppet, Mrs. Bailey's child guide, who is herself a sheer delight, has spoken to us at each sitting. Apart from the excellent evidence she has given us, she has a charming naive way of expressing herself."

When they neared the anniversary of Ruth Anne's "death," the parents were told by another of Lilian Bailey's splendid guides, W. H. Wooten, an officer who "died" in the Great War, "Today your darling child is here. She is making great progress. I wish you could see her as I do, starry-eyed, full of intelligence and beauty and a happiness beyond your understanding. She is radiating a spiritual glory. She looks at me wondering what I am talking about. I want you to understand she is free; she has no limits. She enters into your life. Often she comes into your home and you entertain an angel unawares. The fact that you know she lives makes her heaven more lovely. Her world would be dulled if you did not know this.

"Have you recently been handling some of her clothes?" he then asked. "Yes," admitted Ruth Anne's parents. "Put her clothes away if you can't bear to part with them, and think of her new life," the guide said. "Do not be sad on this anniversary. Celebrate with her."

Some months after this séance, Captain and Mrs. Newton sat with Hester Dowden, the well-known medium through whose hand automatic writing from the spirit world is received at remarkable speed. The parents had not met the medium before, and she knew nothing about them. Soon after she had taken a pencil in her hand, the following message was written at a very rapid rate: "I'm Ruth. Mother, Daddy, it was hard to wait. I was just longing to shout out, 'I'm here. I'm here.' Daddy. Mother, darling, talk to me." This greeting was followed by pages of writing, the enthusiasm of which, says Mrs. Newton, was most characteristic of her "dead" child's temperament.

At their next sitting with Lilian Bailey, Wootten told them they had recently visited another medium through whom their daughter had given her name as Ruth. He said the child wanted to confirm this fact, and was delighted to have been able to do so. "It means so much to her," he explained, "to be able to convince you she is still alive." He told the parents that Ruth Anne described how, at the beginning of the other sitting, a board, covered with capital letters, had been used. Afterwards, the medium had used a pencil and paper. This was a correct account of the procedure at Hester Dowden's séance.

Wootten then said Ruth Anne was giving the name of the London medium her parents had visited "Mrs. Hester Dowden, whose guide, Johannes, had been very kind." The sitters had not told Lilian Bailey or, in fact, anyone else, of their visit to this medium. Details of two excellent sittings with Rose Livingstone are given by Mrs. Newton. She and her husband were complete strangers to this medium when they met, the sitting having been arranged by the London Spiritualist Alliance on their behalf. "Mrs. Livingstone described our little daughter," writes Mrs. Newton, "giving her age and birthday, and her name, Ruth Anne. She said that our daughter had been with us by a font at about three o'clock that afternoon. We had been in St. Paul's Cathedral at that time. Ruth Anne said her two grandfathers were with her, one she had known and loved on earth, and the other, her Daddy's father, she had met in the spirit world. Many times, family details and events were correctly given, as well as happy, loving conversation, typical of Ruth Anne."

One little incident impressed the parents very much. The medium said that their child wanted to know if they remembered her little tea set. "Yes," they replied, "of course." "But do you remember it when I was ill?" was Ruth Anne's next question. Despite her persistence, they could not connect the tea set with her illness for some time, until it suddenly occurred to Mrs. Newton that she had used the little-teapot as a feeding cup for the dying girl!

A few days after her dog had been "put to sleep," Mrs. Newton had another sitting with Rose Livingstone. Ruth Anne was described almost immediately. "She has a dog in her arms," said the medium, "and she is so excited about it. She says, 'You had him put to sleep, Mother, but he is perfectly all right now. He can't fret for you because we're making such a fuss of him.'"

Because of our common ancestry, animals are vitalised by the same spark of life as human beings. In their long association with man, domestic animals have acquired similar undying attributes and qualities that continue to find expression after physical death. There is a formidable array of evidence to support the case for the survival of our lesser brethren. I deal with this subject in my book, *When Your Animal Dies.*

In her letter to me, Ruth Anne's mother, happy in the knowledge that her child has never really left her, says, "I know you will have realised she was, and is, the joy of our lives, precious and lovely beyond words."

The first time she sat with a medium, Mrs. Winifred E. Clarke, of

Stockport, recognised the voice and mannerisms of her little son, Philip. She and her husband decided to investigate Spiritualism four months after the child's "death." The Britten Memorial arranged a séance for them with Lilian Bailey, of whom the parents had never even heard.

In their critical mood of investigation, they did not wish her to know of their relationship to each other. Their sittings were arranged for the same afternoon but at different times. In accordance with the custom of most reliable Spiritualist organisations, neither their names, nor any other information about them, was given to Lilian Bailey. Contrary to sceptical belief, reputable mediums always prefer these arrangements for preserving the anonymity of new sitters.

Mrs. Clarke's was the first appointment. Lilian Bailey had only been controlled by Wootten for a few minutes when he described a little boy who looked about eight years old. Mrs. Clarke tells me that Philip was nine when he "died," but was small for his age.

The guide immediately followed his description of the child with, "He is your own little son who has recently passed to our world." Then, through the lips of the entranced medium, the voice of Philip Clarke was heard by his overjoyed mother. While the psychic power remained strong enough, the "dead" child's voice sounded exactly the same as it had done on earth. "But," says his mother, "the most striking and evidential part of his manifestation was his characteristic way of speaking, his movements and, in fact, his whole personality. If a mother – critical as I was – recognises her own child's voice and manner beyond any doubt, there can be no mistake about the solidity of the evidence."

At the end of the séance, Mrs. Clarke adjoined to another room. She was aware that her husband would arrive later for his appointment, but she did not encounter him. He told her later that, when Lilian Bailey was entranced, the guide greeted him and remarked, in a rather surprised manner, that the little boy who manifested to the previous sitter was still present. He said that the child appeared to be highly amused and was laughing. Then Wootten paused and said, "Oh, you are his father! He is calling you Daddy." Mr. Clarke admitted this was true. Then, for the second time that afternoon, Philip controlled the medium and spoke to his other parent. Neither Mr. nor Mrs. Clarke gave their names to the medium after their separate sittings.

A few days later, the secretary of the Britten Memorial received a letter from Lilian Bailey, written from her home in Crewe. She wrote that, the previous evening, a little boy, giving his name as Philip Clarke, had spoken to the members of her own voice circle. When they asked him for further information about himself, he could only tell them that he had been able to speak to his parents the previous week. Then his power failed and Poppet took up the story. She said she had brought the little boy because he wanted to send his love to his Mummy and Daddy. Poppet desired this message to be forwarded to the Britten Memorial so that the boy's parents would receive it.

Soon after this voice circle took place, Lilian Bailey sat with some friends at a table séance. Using the alphabetical code of table tilts, Poppet spelled, "I have brought the little boy again. Tell his Mummy and Daddy I am teaching him how to communicate." There was a pause, then, slowly and shakily, the table tilted to the letters "P-H-I-L," followed by this message from Wootten, "This little chap is very anxious to get into touch with his people. Please tell them we are helping him to learn how to use the spirit power in this way."

Lilian Bailey's letter containing Philip's message was shown by the secretary of the Britten Memorial to his parents who, needless to say, were delighted to receive their little son's added and unexpected greetings. Since that time, they have had further sittings with Lilian Bailey, through whose mediumship Philip has manifested again and again. They have also developed their own psychic powers. A simple wooden table, which they use for spirit communication, is the bridge which spans the gulf of death and enables Philip and his parents to spend happy, intimate hours together.

A child who lived on earth but a few hours gave evidence of his survival to his father, Mr. Hugh Stanhope, of Llandudno, a personal friend of mine. Mr. Stanhope waited 15 years to receive a spirit message that he would regard as one hundred per cent. evidential. Although Mr. Stanhope has accepted the Spiritualist case for years, his "suspicious mind," as he terms it, has always demanded "castiron proof" that could not be explained away by any other hypothesis. Lilian Bailey furnished this long awaited proof when she demonstrated clairvoyance at a Spiritualist propaganda meeting at Colwyn Bay.

"I had never met Lilian Bailey in my life," says Mr. Stanhope, "and she certainly could not know by any normal means the names and facts she gave me." He went to the meeting without expecting to receive a spirit message. The medium had been giving trance clairvoyance for a little while before she called the name "Stanhope," following this by perfect descriptions of his "dead" parents and providing their names. She went on to describe a spirit, now a young man, who lived on earth but a few hours. The spirit gave his name, John Stanhope. Many years ago this baby was born to Mrs. Stanhope, but "died" within a few hours in rather sad and distressing circumstances which made a deep impression on the lives of the parents.

Tragedy entered the lives of Mr. and Mrs. Norman C. Sinclair, of Sunderland, when their child Norma, a 13-year-old girl, was struck by a motor lorry and received injuries which proved fatal. Mr. Sinclair owned a small yacht in which the family were in the habit of spending happy week-ends. The fatal accident occurred whilst Norma was on her way to join her parents on the yacht which was moored in the river near Boroughbridge. Grief filled the hearts of the parents.

"Away went our dreams of a happy homely future," writes Mr. Sinclair, "away went joy and laughter and in place – what? Fretting and heartaches, tears and black despair, and my mind filled with ghastly, loathsome, horrible thoughts, too terrible to tell. We were existing in this state of mental darkness, thinking the world a very vile place, and fully convinced in our hearts that it was all rot about there being a loving heavenly Father, when, one day, driving through a Sunderland street, we saw a placard reading, "Psychic News: Life After Death Proved." Mrs. Sinclair went into the shop and bought a copy, which they both hastened home to read. This paper brought them into touch with the Spiritualist movement. In psychic books, too, they read of the proofs of Survival that had been vouchsafed to other people. Thus began their own search for evidence.

When Mr. Sinclair arranged to have a private sitting with the famous medium, Helen Hughes, he was a complete stranger to her – beyond his name, she knew nothing about him. At his first séance, she described a tall girl who was standing by his side. Then, to his astonishment, she went on to say, "Furthermore, the girl has put her arms round your neck, claiming you with love. She tells me you are her Daddy." Mr. Sinclair says that Norma was a tall girl for her age. She had never addressed him as "Father," but always as "Daddy."

When Mrs. Hughes continued, "She has her brother with her," the father's heart sank. Norma was an only child. "That is absolutely impossible," he answered. "I never had a son." But the medium insisted. "My guide tells me," she affirmed, "that it is indeed your own son. He never knew life on earth, as your wife had a miscarriage years ago. In the spirit world, your son has been named John, after your uncle John who has also passed on." He had, until that moment, quite forgotten that, 15 years previously, his wife had a miscarriage. The statement about his uncle was also accurate.

As you will read elsewhere, evidence of Survival has been furnished by many spirit individuals who never breathed on earth at all. Once the spark of life has been ignited, growth continued at whatever stage of earthly life the physical counterpart of the spirit body perished.

This séance was the forerunner of many others with Helen Hughes. But although Mr. Sinclair repeatedly asked the medium's guide to give him Norma's full name, he was always refused. He was informed that his daughter would supply the evidence in good time.

A year passed before he received the eagerly awaited evidence. Then, at one séance, Helen Hughes was entranced by one of her controls, a child, who laughingly said, "Daddy Sinclair, you are going to get a surprise." She asked for a pencil and some paper. Mr. Sinclair handed her a pencil, but, unfortunately, he had only the back of an envelope for her to use. "Oh dear," she said, as she began to write, "this is too little!" Laughing again, she told Mr. Sinclair, "Your Daddy is here and he says I have to write on the wall, as there is plenty of room there."

The séance was held in complete darkness. When, after the sitting, the lights were switched on, Mr. Sinclair examined the back of the envelope. In black letters, the words, "Norma Doreen," were written. And on the wall, he read, "Norma Doreen Couly." His daughter's christian names were Norma Doreen Coulson. He considers the word "Couly" very evidential, for he frequently called his daughter by this nickname, a fact that was unknown to anybody but his own wife. The remarkable part of the writing was that although the words were printed in the dark, not a single block letter overlapped another, either on the envelope or on the wall.

"Spiritualism has given my wife and myself new life," avers Mr. Sinclair. "The black, horrible thoughts have gone and, though we still yearn for our loved one, it is wonderfully comforting to know that there is no death and one day we will all meet again, a little happy family."

Mr. Herbert Hampson, of Barnsley, Yorkshire, tells in *Psychic News* how the cold, perfunctory manner of the service carried out by the minister at her young son's burial started the boy's mother on the psychic quest. Her inquiry into Spiritualism satisfied her that her boy still lived, and provided the consolation that was unobtainable in the orthodox church of her former faith.

The boy, Sydney, one of Mr. Hampson's relatives, was sent by his parents to a Kentish school, where he became suddenly ill and passed on a few days later. A letter from the school authorities telling his mother of his illness was followed by a telegram saying he was "dead." Unfortunately, she received the telegram before the letter. The mother was stunned by the shock. Her son's body was brought home for burial and Mr. Hampson attended the service. As Sydney and his parents were active and loyal members of the village chapel, the minister conducted the funeral service.

"In the light of my Spiritualist knowledge," writes Mr. Hampson, "that graveside service was an insult to ordinary human intelligence. After reading the usual committal words, the minister closed his book, shook hands with the parents and walked leisurely away, leaving the parents in their grief unable to tear themselves away from the graveside." Being the only Spiritualist in the party of mourners, Mr. Hampson told these two mourners of his knowledge of Survival. Not long afterwards, the mother expressed a wish to know more about Spiritualism, for she had received neither help nor comfort from her own church in the time of her greatest need.

Through the Leeds Psychic Research Society, Mr. Hampson arranged a sitting with Helen Hughes. He made the appointment in his own name and gave no information whatever regarding Sydney's mother and grandmother who accompanied them to the séance. It was not long before the medium was controlled by the "dead" boy. He proved his identity by his mannerisms of speech and his knowledge of home affairs. Sydney asked his mother not to grieve for his passing and "not to lift my cap from a peg in the house and cry over it." He informed the sitters of the cause of his fatal illness, one that his parents had already suspected.

"You have some money belonging to me," he went on. "Don't keep it! Buy yourself something with it." The "dead" schoolboy told his mother that the amount of his savings was 2s. 7d. When she reached home, she found there was 2s. 7d. Finally, through the hand of the entranced medium, Sydney wrote his name on a piece of paper.

Though he was an agnostic, Mr. P. H. Holdsworth determined to inquire into Spiritualism when his seven-year-old boy passed. The result was a dramatic reunion. The father has graphically described his search in *Psychic News*.

He began by attending, two months after his bereavement, a séance held by Dorothy Henderson for direct voice and materialisation. He went because, a day or so previously, he seemed to hear his boy calling to him. His frame of mind is explained in his own words, "I was an agnostic, prepared to argue the impossibility of Survival."

He sat there and joined in the singing without the slightest idea of what he might expect to happen. In a way he was rather glad the darkness hid a certain amount of embarrassment he felt at taking part in something that seemed to be very foolish. Presently, after the trumpet had moved about the room in a way for which he was totally unable to account, a luminous slate was lifted up and brought close to him. "I saw clearly the solemn, appealing face of the boy I had lost, he writes. "If I am asked if I recognised him straight away, I will say I did not. I was quite bewildered."

Within the next few days, "sober consideration convinced me that it was indeed my own son that I had seen. Amongst other things, I might mention that his mouth and chin bore a great similarity to mine, and that, catching a glimpse of myself in the mirror the next day, I was startled by the likeness of my own features to those of the materialisation."

Here then, he thought, was food for serious thought. He had made perfectly certain that the medium knew nothing more about him than his name, and that he wished to investigate. On the following week, his wife accompanied him to the circle. The boy again materialised, picking up a bunch of violets from the floor and dropping them in his wife's lap as he brought the luminous slate.

Mr. Holdsworth writes, "My wife at once recognised him and I too – better prepared this time – was able to satisfy myself that there could be no doubt it was he. He still looked very solemn, but we have seen him several times since, and on each occasion he has looked more and more cheerful. Now he smiles happily when he shows himself. At that séance he spoke to us for the first time. He could not manage much, but we had the joy of hearing him call me by a pet name that he had for me when he was living upon this earth. Since then, scarcely a week has gone by without our being in touch with him. Of course, conditions have not been uniformly good, but on some evenings he has spoken up so clearly that everyone in the room has been able to hear exactly what he has said without the least difficulty. His chief concern has been to convince us of his well-being and to comfort his mother."

At one séance, the "dead" boy said, "Mummy, I'm all right. You mustn't cry, because when you do it makes me sad."

On another occasion he asked the parents to take out his toys. Until then his father had kept them in a large box. Mr. Holdsworth went home, opened the box, and displayed the toys. The next week the first thing the boy told them was that he had got his toys, and that he could play with them.

He gave them one remarkable piece of evidence. His father had been trying to do automatic writing. The only result was that his hand shook violently. This, however, was known only to himself, for he had made his attempts in an upstairs room alone, and had told nobody – not even his wife.

Judge, then, his surprise when his little boy said: "Daddy, I've got a message for you. You shake too much." "Do I?" replied his father in astonishment.

"Yes," he went on, "when you write you shake too much."

This led Mr. Holdsworth to make a further experiment, not in automatic writing but in direct writing. His boy had been able to pick up flowers and even a tin soldier from the floor and give it to them. Why should he not be able to write, providing his father gave him the materials? When next Mr. Holdsworth went to the circle he took a writing pad and a pencil sharpened at both ends. These he laid at his feet before the sitting began. At no time during the sitting, however, did he ask that anything should be written, because he felt that if his boy were unable to do what he asked it would make the spirit child unhappy.

"On the third time I carried out my experiment, I was more successful than I had dared to hope," writes the father. "On the lights being turned up there were 11 names written on the pad. Naturally, what delighted me most was to find my boy's name amongst them. Most important of all was that, to the best of my belief, it was actually written in his handwriting.

"Now, in case some people would like to quibble over this

point and say that a boy of seven has no particular individuality as regards handwriting, I would like to point out that I have at home a specimen of his writing of his name made a little while before he passed over. As a bank clerk, I have had some experience at picking out forged signatures from genuine ones, so that my opinion of the matter has some weight behind it."

Soon after this he and his wife had a remarkable experience. To understand this, says the parent, it must be made known that 11 years ago they had a baby who had lived for only one month and who, like the boy they had already got in touch with, was named John.

"Now eleven years is a long time," he writes, "and, though I will not say that I had forgotten this baby, he certainly was very seldom in my thoughts, and consequently to hear from him was the last thing I expected. When, therefore, a materialisation came to us with hands larger than a boy of seven would have, and hair that was curly in place of the hair that I knew was straight, I was very put about to know what to think. Rather grudgingly, I admitted to my wife after the sitting that it might have been our older boy, but I honestly didn't think it the least bit likely."

At the next sitting his mind was set at rest. The younger boy came through and spoke very distinctly. "Mummy," he said. "John's here, and Big Man says we must call him John John so we won't get mixed up." Big Man was the little boy's name for Mrs. Henderson's control.

"After that," says the father, "on materialising, the younger boy put his hand over the luminous slate so that we could see that it was the right size, and he also held the slate against his head in a way that enabled us to see his hair, which was straight and ruffled-up just like it used to be.

"Since then he has mentioned his elder brother several times. They play together and share his toys. John John has not spoken yet, but I am hoping that he will. He materialises, however, almost every week. This he does very strongly. At the last sitting, he put his hand round my wife's neck and drew her to him.

"So far as I am concerned, I have set down the actual happenings at Mrs. Henderson's circle as truthfully as is possible. If some other parent, facing the same kind of loss as my wife and I have had to face, can draw some help from my simple statements, I shall have done all I set out to do. Personally, in Spiritualism, I have found a new belief. Yet, I cannot, if I would, deny the facts that had been presented to me. I have approached the whole subject with, I believe, an open mind. If I have been prejudiced in one way or another, it has been against Spiritualism."

How a young mother's grief, after the passing of her son, was assuaged by spirit messages, was described by Mrs. E. E. Campbell in *Psychic News*. Her story concerns Billie Graff, a 12-year-old soloist at the Episcopal church in South Pasadena, California. Three years previously he "died" in an epidemic of spinal meningitis. All the nurses at the hospital had loved the little fair-headed boy with the beautiful soprano voice. The young mother was crushed with grief.

"After a few weeks," Mrs. Campbell says, "I wrote and asked her if she would read a Spiritualist book which I thought would help her. Later she told me that the book had given her the first ray of hope. I sent her many books and some of my friends loaned her others. Her husband told me he believed the books had saved her reason."

Together with her cousin, Mrs. Campbell attended a séance in Los Angeles with Margaret Bright as medium. Suddenly a child's voice said, "Hello, Auntie Ina." This was what Billie had called her cousin, though she was not his aunt. He told them he wanted to talk to his mother and asked them to bring her. He said he was going to sing to her so that she would know it was really he. They promised, and soon after brought the mother to another sitting. "We were surprised," Mrs. Campbell says, "when the guide, who is Mrs. Bright's daughter, after greeting us, said, 'Hello, Marie.' She likes to call people by their first names and I had purposely not given Mrs. Graff's name. I asked how she knew what name to call her She replied, 'Billie is here and he says, "That's my Mama and her name is Marie."'

"When Billie tried to talk to his mother he began to cry. She was brave and calm and told him not to have any tears. He said, 'I'll be all right in a minute. Let me cry and be done with it.' "

Soon he started one of his songs and when half-way through he said, "Help me, Mama." She joined in and together they finished a song that he was learning before he became ill.

Then they sang "Holy Night," and Mrs. Campbell's "dead" son came and told her that all that day Billie had been singing, getting ready for his mother's visit. After finishing the song Billie asked about his little brother and his father, and said, "I miss my Daddy and I love my Daddy."

Mrs. Campbell describes how they went once again to the medium, taking the father this time. "The guide told us Billie was there," she says, "but was so excited because Daddy was present that they were trying to quieten him before he spoke. Twice other voices were heard talking and Billie's voice called out, 'Hello, Daddy.' When told it was his turn, he said, with much feeling, 'I'm not dead, Daddy, really, I'm not.'"

When Mr. Graff said Billie had told them one day, at the hospital, that the next Thursday he was coming home – instead of coming to their home he had gone to his heavenly home – Billie said, "Daddy, I was just repeating what Grandpa said. He said I was going home then. I guess I was half gone already."

Billie asked what year it was and then calculated which year he was born and how old he would be now. His mother spoke of Christmas, and he told her that last year, when they were all standing around the tree, he heard her say, "If Billie were only with us."

He added, "And I was there. I knocked a big blue glass ball off the tree to show you I was there. I've done that both years and I'll do it again this Christmas."

Mr. and Mrs. Graff assured them that this happened both years. The mother and father went home thrilled, and happy in the knowledge that Billie still lives.

Here, also taken from *Psychic News*, is the story of Mr. E. Beresford, who had lost his faith, became almost an agnostic until Spiritualism proved to him the reality of the spirit world. After attending several Spiritualist church meetings, he decided to have a private sitting with Frank Leah, a psychic artist who, using his clairvoyance, draws the "dead" who usually pose for him.

"I was a complete stranger to him and went anonymously," says Mr. Beresford. "He rapidly described, with uncanny accuracy, the appearances, characteristics, ages and conditions of passing over of several of my family. He told me I was a train driver on the Underground, which I was and am.

"One communicator was my little girl, who passed on 11 years ago at the age of seven years, of whom Mr. Leah drew a very rapid portrait. It has been immediately recognised by everybody who has seen it. This portrait brought conviction and great solace to my wife, who had suffered great grief at her loss since my daughter had passed over."

Here is a case where the evidence for Survival consisted in the giving of facts which were unknown to the medium, but confirmed on inquiry. The incident happened at the home circle of Mr. Fred Rees, a London man.

At the sitting of his home circle, following one at which a woman, a comparative stranger, had spoken to her "dead" son and husband, the control announced that the woman's daughter was present. She appeared to be very disappointed because her mother was not in the circle. This was a great surprise, as the members of the circle were not aware that the woman had a daughter on the Other Side. They explained that her mother was not a member of the circle and that she only attended the previous week by request to receive her brother's message.

The control then said that the girl was apparently all the more disappointed, as she had hoped to bring her mother a gift. The girl was told not to distress herself, but if she would trust them with the gift they would convey it to her mother. This assurance appeared to satisfy her, for in due course a beautiful little rose was brought into the circle with the request that we were to say that it came from Honor, "with love to Mummy." To prevent mistakes, the control carefully spelt the name.

It then occurred to Mr. Rees to ask for a description of the girl. He was told that she showed herself as a little girl of 11 and that her hair was done in two long plaits. The following day, his wife presented herself at the woman's house in Kew and asked whether she had a daughter on the Other Side. "Why, yes," was her reply.

"Was her name Honor?" his wife inquired. "Indeed it was," was the answer. "But however did you know?"

"And did she wear her hair in long plaits?" the mother was asked. "Why, of course she did," she said. Taking the visitor into the drawing-room, the mother showed her a portrait of the little girl in which the long plaits were a prominent feature!

The mother received the gift, with delight, but she is no longer a stranger to this group of Spiritualists, for she is now an enthusiastic member of the circle.

Chapter 6

TELEPATHY IS RULED OUT

BOBBIE NEWLOVE, a child of ten who suddenly "died" from an attack of diphtheria, proved his survival to the Rev. C. Drayton Thomas, a Methodist minister and a Spiritualist, though the clergyman and the boy had never met on earth. The boy's foster-parent, Mr. Herbert Hatch, of Nelson, Lancashire, having read a book on Spiritualism by the minister, wrote to him after Bobbie's passing, saying, "The loss is so dreadful that we feel we must !ask you if we can in any way obtain comfort similar to that recounted in your book... I confess that my education... makes my faith in such matters very halting."

Mr. Drayton Thomas decided to try to get into touch with the "dead" boy, hoping that Bobbie would be able to provide proofs that would convince his relatives of his continued existence. If, at a séance, he gave evidence about himself which was entirely unknown to the sitter, a stranger, this would disprove any suggestion in his foster-father's mind that telepathy could be responsible for the communication. This hypothesis is sometimes expounded by sceptics in order to explain away the evidence received at sittings. For some reason or other, they do not appear to realise that if telepathy is possible between individuals still on earth, mental communication is also possible between discarnate and incarnate minds.

Mr. Hatch refrained in his letter from giving anything but the barest details about the "dead" boy. The clergyman, however, obtained such striking evidence of Bobbie's survival that he recorded his experience in a book, *An Amazing Experiment*. He tells how, first of all, he prayed for guidance, and then asked the aid of his own "dead" relatives in seeking out the boy and bringing him to his forthcoming sitting with Gladys Osborne Leonard. Success crowned his efforts to comfort sorrowing hearts. In a series of sittings with this famous medium, Bobbie returned and provided a wealth of evidential details establishing his identity. The boy recalled some of his favourite walks and rambles. He named streets and vicinities, giving facts which were entirely beyond the knowledge of the medium or the sitter. At one séance Bobbie accurately described an unusual photograph of himself in the fancy dress costume he wore at a gala not long before his passing.

The most convincing evidence was received when he gave details of the way he acquired the infection which led to his "death." He had joined a children's "secret society." The exploits of his "gang" took him to a pool of contaminated water with which he had played over a period of some weeks. This pastime had undermined his health. The whole incident was entirely unknown to Bobbie's family when it was first communicated to them by Mr. Drayton Thomas. The details provided at the sittings had to be unravelled bit by bit and involved correspondence with the Brierfield Medical Officer of Health. All the evidence given by the "dead" boy was confirmed.

The successful results of this one case alone must prove the truths of Survival to any intelligent and unbiased mind. The facts provided were unknown to the clergyman, the medium or the boy's own family.

The hypothesis that telepathy accounts for all spirit communication is destroyed by the story told by Margery Lawrence, the successful novelist and writer. In *Psychic News* she relates how she accompanied a sceptical friend to a sitting with a noted medium. There ensued at this séance a considerable amount of interesting conversation with several entities who told her friend Leila much about herself, her family history and other matters. "But," writes the novelist, "Leila maintained a rather superior smile, as she had previously told me she believed that anything told her would be of necessity 'taken from her own mind' by the medium's ability to read that mind."

When the medium informed Leila that she had a brother on the Other Side who had been born about four years before her, and who had lived only a few months on earth, she could not accept the statement. Margery Lawrence writes, "Startled and offended, Leila declared this could not possibly be true; she was positive that her mother (who had been American – but Leila's father was English) would have told her if she had ever borne another child. But she rang me up a week or so later in a very chastened frame of mind."

The story had so worried her that she had tackled her only surviving relative, a very old American great aunt – and discovered that her mother (who had "died" some time previously) had been twice married, the first time, when extremely young, to an

American adventurer, who, after treating her with great harshness,. ended his life in prison. The shame and distress of this caused the young widow to decide, on her second marriage to an Englishman, to bury even the memory of her first marriage. In this decision she was loyally supported by her family and her second husband; and as she left America for good upon her second marriage, to ignore the past was made comparatively easy. But the most interesting and valuable point of this case is that she had borne a son, who only lived a few months, to her first husband.

Margery Lawrence asks, "Where is your telepathy here? Leila knew nothing whatever about her mother's first marriage – and you can only read in a person's mind that which is already in it."

Another psychic instance which again negatives the theory that telepathy explains away séance communications is told by the same writer. She was present at a sitting where a "dead" girl stated that, eight years previously, she had passed on at the age of 15 from the effects of heart-strain, after playing lacrosse for a well-known girls' school. The spirit communicator was unknown to the sitters.

Margery Lawrence writes, "She gave us her name and the name of the school, also that of the headmistress. As her death was so recent, I took a chance on the same woman being in charge of the school and wrote her a cautious letter, trying to check the girl's statement. But, as I had more or less anticipated, I got a chilly reply informing me that, as I was no relation to the young girl in question, the headmistress had nothing to say to me about her or the manner of her death. But luckily, a little later on, I ran across a friend who had lived there and knew the family, and she checked the story for me and found it quite true.

"Here again, no information could possibly have been 'tapped" from the mind of anybody in the circle. This child, her school and her headmistress were entirely strange to us all."

"I want Norah, I am Nic," said a spirit voice at a direct-voice séance given by Mrs. A. E. Perriman. Mrs. Edith Wynne Mitchell, of Shrewsbury, was present that night with her daughter Norah, who replied that she did not know anyone named "Nic" who had passed on. "Oh, yes, my child, you do!" insisted the voice. "I am Nicol, the brother of your mother, Wynne Jones."

Mrs. Mitchell writes, "Jones was my maiden name and I had then been married over 30 years. I am never called Wynne, but always addressed by my first name, Edith." She had never known Nicol on earth, for he had "died" five years before her own birth. This spirit said he had returned that night to disprove the "subconscious mind hypothesis." Nicol's voice was followed by that of a girl who addressed Mrs. Mitchell, "I am your sister Grace. We are a large family here." Mrs. Mitchell says, "This sister 'died' at the age of two, within a fortnight of my brother Nicol's passing. She was christened Rosa Grace, but was never called Grace, always Rosa."

These two relatives, who "died" before her own birth, had proved, by giving her maiden name and two christian names never used in the family, that telepathy and the "tapping" of the subconscious mind do not account for psychic phenomena. The "dead" are who they say they are – the "dead." It is a much more simple explanation after all.

In Harold Sharp's London séance room are two carved figures of angels. They were given to him by a mother whose sorrowing heart was comforted when she learned, through his mediumship, that her "dead" twin girls still lived. These children succumbed to an epidemic of measles. The, parents were heart-broken and the mother was inconsolable. Some months after the children's passing, their mother read of a London curate who had spoken to his spirit sister at a sitting with Harold Sharp. Thereupon the mother wrote to the medium for an appointment, telling him nothing about her grievous loss. At a subsequent date she sat with Harold Sharp, whose guide, Brother Peter, a "dead" monk, described her twin daughters – one a fair pale child, the other a dark girl with rosy cheeks. The guide spoke of their distress because their mother did not realise their continued presence. To prove that fact, the "dead" children gave details of what occurred at home that very day before she set out for her London appointment. They also recounted events that happened before their passing. Still the mother found it hard to believe the evidence she was receiving. The guide said that, with her children's help, he would give her further proof of their survival.

"When you reach home," he said, "go to your bookcase, the tall one. The end book on the second row is a green-and-gold covered volume. Turn to page 115. Nowhere amongst your many books could you find a page which binds you more closely to your two daughters." At that moment the mother could not visualise the book to which Brother Peter referred. But a few days later she wrote to Harold Sharp, "The more I read page 115 of the book, the more

certain I am that my children inspired your guide to help me." She had found the volume in the position Brother Peter indicated. On page 115 was a poem by Thomas Hood written "To Jane." Jane is the sitter's Christian name. The poem begins:
"Welcome, dear Heart, and a most kind good-morrow:
The day is gloomy, but our looks shall shine...
For love the rose, for faith the lily speaks;
It withers in false hands, but here 'tis bright!"

Rose and Lily are the names of the children she had mourned as dead. Brother Peter finished the sitting with the words, "Their angel faces are around you so very often. You must cheer up and be happy for their dear sakes." And like a wise woman and a loving mother, she has taken his counsel and is comforted.

Bertha Hirst, a medium who has brought much comfort to bereaved parents, gave Mrs. S. Bray, of Thornton Heath, Surrey, striking evidence of her young son's survival. "Your boy is here," said the medium's guide. "He has brought another boy named Jack, about 14 years of age. He lived in the same road as your boy, in a house opposite. Please try and tell his mother that Jack is alive and well. Ask her not to grieve."

Mrs. Bray gave *Psychic News* further details of the séance. "Your boy says he was wheeled about in a chair," she was told by the spirit. "After he had passed over you gave the chair to a hospital. Your son passed over with heart trouble." But now the boy was well. In fact, he wanted his mother to tell his father that if they listened at home they would hear him running up the stairs! The guide went on to interrupt the "dead" boy's message to his mother, saying, "You have a book of his called *The Boy's Book of Adventure*. " Mrs. Bray contradicted this statement. "No," she said, "I gave most of his books away." The guide went on, "Your boy insists that there is a book in the wardrobe, on the second shelf, a big, red book on adventure and ships. When you find it, turn to page 182 and there you will find a message which, in a way, will apply to him."

Much to her surprise, Mrs. Bray found at home a thick, red bound book called *The Boy's Book of Adventure*. It was in the wardrobe, as the spirit had said. When she opened the book at page 182 she read: "For hours he lay senseless, as dead, but towards night the field was searched and he was found alive. He was taken up and carried into a village, his wounds were dressed, and after some time he was able to rejoin his regiment and embark upon still more adventures."

Mrs. Bray says, "I had forgotten that my son had this book and I certainly had not read it. The evidence of the book incident poses of any suggestion of telepathy." Her son had been found "dead" in a field, as the passage in the book described.

Mrs. Margaret A. Tucker, of Cardenden, Fife, sums up her psychic experience in these words: "These experiences have enriched my life beyond expression. I thank God for the privilege of such a wonderful revelation, for it has helped me over many a rough bit of life's pathway." She obtained amazing proofs at a trumpet séance with Margaret McCallum, of Glasgow, which she unexpectedly attended. The sitters had been told that if a spirit voice addressed them they were to answer immediately. Mrs. Tucker replied when a voice twice called "Maggie" without eliciting any response. "I'm sorry," said the spirit. "Don't be hurt, but it is not you who is wanted. There is another Maggie here." Shortly afterwards, a totally different voice called, "Maggie, Maggie." Mrs. Tucker had to restrain an impulse to rise to her feet as she instinctively answered "Yes." Then, remembering, she added, "Oh, but is it I who's wanted?"

"Why, of course it's you, Maggie!" continued the voice. Asked who was speaking, this distinctly resonant voice replied, "Brother." She was about to reply when he forestalled her by giving the name "Archie." Then ensued quite an argument. She said the name Archie was incorrect. The voice maintained it was right. Asked if he could supply the first letter of his name he said "A," and while she was agreeing that was correct, he went on spelling "R-C-H-I-E."

Suddenly her mind flashed back to a photograph of a lovely curly-headed boy she had seen in the family album many years ago. Remembrance brought acute remorse. While she was struggling to apologise he said, "Oh, that's quite all right. You didn't know me, Maggie, but I know you. I hadn't long on your earth, had I?"

"No," she said. "Do you remember what happened, Archie?"

"Yes; I was burned!"

"Do you remember the nature of the burning?" "Yes, boiling water!" He then said that her mother, father and brother Andrew were with him. "That's who you were expecting," he said, as he mentioned the name Andrew.

Asked if there was anyone else belonging to her, he broke in on the question to reply, "Yes, your little Girlie is here." He referred to a still-born baby, whom Mrs. Tucker had not been allowed to see. The medium told her that she saw the little girl clairvoyantly, first as a baby, then as a girl of about 16 or 17. "That was very fine proof in itself as, had she been in earth-life, she would have then been 17 years old," commented Mrs. Tucker. "Since then," she writes, "I have been privileged, through Mrs. Helen Duncan's mediumship, to see her materialised form as a baby and as the young woman she is now – both at one séance."

Chapter 7

MORE PROOFS FROM BEYOND

THE "death" of his two children, both on the same day, was the blow that started Mr. W. E. Harrison, of Balham, SouthWest London, on his quest for the truth about Spiritualism. Before the passing of these children, Mr. Harrison had no real interest in psychic matters. Four of his business associates, unknown to each other, tried to interest him in the subject. But he did not feel inclined to make any real effort to obtain evidence. "Then," writes Mr. Harrison, "as so often happens, tragedy came into my life, which up till then had been uneventful." His daughter, a healthy girl, suddenly became ill and developed pneumonia. Within a few days, her younger brother sickened, too.

In spite of every effort to save them, both passed over on the same day – one in hospital, the other at home! "Little imagination is needed to realise the desolation of our home," writes Mr. Harrison. "All that my wife and I had hoped, planned and lived for was gone in one tragic blow. Somehow we lived through that terrible time…

"Then came the real urge. What had happened to these young lives? Where were they now? I remembered those friends who, a few weeks before, had been urging me to investigate. We got into touch with the Marylebone Spiritualist Association and began the quest which has since brought so much help, happiness and comfort into our lives. I determined to investigate carefully and to keep a record of all that transpired. I have these records by me now."

During that period of critical investigation, Mr. and Mrs. Harrison sat with the majority of well-known mediums and witnessed most phases of psychic phenomena. Within two months of the children's passing, the parents began to receive remarkable evidence of their survival.

From Mr. Harrison's conscientiously kept records of all his sittings extending over some years, he has provided me with details of the proofs he and his wife received which "are those I regard as being the most satisfactory, knowing there could be no possible means of the facts being known to anyone except ourselves and the ones who communicated them from the spirit world." Mr. Harrison was a stranger in the case of every initial sitting with a medium. Much of the evidence was received in group séances, the appointments having been made a day or two earlier with the appropriate Spiritualist organisation. Mediums often take group séances when private sittings are not desired by the sitters, who may number six to a dozen people and are not, necessarily, or generally, known to each other.

"You have two children in the spirit world," Helen Spiers told Mr. Harrison the first time he and his wife sat with her. "One passed with meningitis, the other with pneumonia. They are both here now. The little boy is about three years of age. The girl says she is five." All these statements were correct, with the exception of the boy's age which was over-stated. "They are showing me an old teddy bear," went on the medium, "also a doll. The little girl is playing with something. She is banging it with her hands and saying, 'Toot, toot.' It looks like a motor car, and I think she is playing with the hooter." The children had possessed a dilapidated old teddy bear. Mr. Harrison understood the description of the hooter. When on earth, his little girl often accompanied her parents in their car, and, child-like, she loved to press the motor horn.

The medium, talking of the "dead" girl, went on, "She says her name is Maisie – no – it's Mavis – Mavis Joan." Helen Spiers declared, "She holds a lily in her hands. The child says it is not her name, but a symbol of her name." The "dead" girl's father understood the simile. Lilley is a family surname. Mavis Joan are her two christian names.

Addressing the "dead" children's mother, Helen Spiers said, "The children now come to you. The little girl says you are wearing her beads. She says you are her Mummy." In this group séance, husband and wife sat apart, and there was no reason why they should have been associated with each other by the medium, to whom they were strangers. Mrs. Harrison was, at the time, wearing her little daughter's beads.

Three months later, they attended another group séance, held by the same medium, in which she reiterated some of the evidence already given, but presented it in a different way. "The children passed within a very short time of each other," she told the parents. "It seems they were so necessary to each other they could not be happy apart. The little girl holds a trumpet in her hands. She says she will speak through it one day." The child has kept her promise. On many occasions she has spoken to her parents through the trumpet at subsequent voice séances.

Still maintaining their attitude of critical investigation, Mr. and Mrs. Harrison, under assumed names, sat with Leslie Flint, a direct voice medium. But the medium's spirit control addressed Mr. Harrison by his real name and told him, "You have a daughter in the spirit world. Her photograph is in your pocket. She is six years old now. She is here." The next moment a childish voice called, "Mummy, Daddy," repeating these two words two or three times in her excitement before she went on, "I'm here and I've got my teddy and a kitten, too." She spoke of her blue frock and told her parents she visited them every night. "I like the photographs by your bedside," she continued. "I've got Baby here – little brother – and Auntie's here – Tinny." Every detail mentioned at the voice séance was accurate, says Mr. Harrison.

About six months later, the parents attended a group séance held by the well-known medium Nan Mackenzie. It was not long before she said to Mr. Harrison, "A little fair-haired girl has crept up to your chair. She climbs on your knee and laughs happily. She is a winsome child, unspoiled, but full of mischief. She was about five at the time of her passing. She put her arms around you and tries to climb on your shoulder, a favourite position." Mr. Harrison says this was one of his little daughter's habits.

The medium went on to say that the child was looking for her mother. "She points to you," she told Mrs. Harrison who was sitting apart from her husband. "She has now gone over to you and is kissing you. She says you have a frock and two articles in a drawer which belong to her." The mother acknowledged these statements to be accurate. Then the medium told her the girl was saying, "I like the little vase with the daffodils you put out for me today" – a statement that was evidential.

"Your daughter is often in your surroundings," continued the medium, "and is taking a great interest in all you do. She says her Daddy is going to be a 'preacher man.' " Mr. Harrison comments, "The reference to 'preacher man' has come true. Since those days, I have frequently spoken in Spiritualist churches – something I then thought highly improbable."

Some months later, Mr. Harrison sat with another noted medium, Agnes Abbott, who described Mavis, gave her age and other correct details. "She sends her love to her Auntie Vera," said the medium. "She has a little boy with her, a brother, much younger." The "dead" girl spoke of other relatives and people in her parents' earthly surroundings.

At a later séance with Jack Webber, a materialisation medium, his guide described every detail of Mavis's passing, even to the last drink of water she was given and the effect it had on the dying child. No other medium had ever mentioned these particular details.

In a later section of this book, I refer to the reasons why, at Christmas-time, special séances are held for spirit children for whom a tree is decorated by the sitters. Toys, afterwards given to earthly girls and boys, are provided for the young spirit visitors. These Christmas parties afford great pleasure, linking the "dead" children, at the season they love so well, with their earthly friends and relatives.

Mr. and Mrs. Harrison attended a Christmas séance held by Mrs. A. E. Perriman. Beforehand, they sent gifts for the tree – a rabbit with large ears, a big doll, and a soft woolly toy. No names or messages were put in the parcel containing the toys. At this voice séance, 38 spirit children – two of them were Polish and one Chinese – gave their full christian and surnames. Mr. Harrison writes, "The seventh child to speak said, 'I am Mavis Harrison, with Kenny. My Mummy is here and my Daddy, too.'" The parents greeted their "dead" children and Mavis continued, "I want the dolly you brought me." There was a scrambling noise and, in the darkened room, the sitters heard a few toys fall from the tree. Then Mavis's voice was heard to say, "Where's that dolly? Oh, I've got it! Thank you, thank you, it's lovely!" Next, another childish voice, less powerful, broke in, saying, "I want Bunny with big ears." Mavis again spoke. "He's got it now," she said. "Good night, Mummy, good night, Daddy. Grandma brought us. Good night."

The following July, the parents went to a public Spiritualist meeting where a medium named Harry Dyer gave the mother an excellent description of Mavis and mentioned her age when she left the earth. "I now see a little boy who passed over with meningitis," said the medium. "The girl points to him and says Ben – no – Ken. She says he's her brother."

The medium asked, "Did you go to a Christmas tree séance last year? These children say they were there and spoke to you." He went on to describe a coloured ball belonging to Ken, saying the toy lay in a kitchen drawer in the home. He also told the parents that their daughter was going to try to make herself visible in their own home.

The details given at this public meeting were all acknowledged to be accurate by the parents. Harry Dyer had only recently started giving public clairvoyance, and was quite unknown to them. Their daughter's prophecy was fulfilled a few weeks later when Mrs. Harrison awoke in the early hours of the morning. She distinctly saw Mavis standing by her bed. "This objective vision has never since been repeated," declares her husband.

On the fifth anniversary of her daughter's passing, the mother attended a group séance held by Margaret Bevan, a psychic artist. This medium executed a characteristic portrait of Mavis. Mr. Harrison writes, "The picture was painted in three-and-a-half minutes and is an excellent likeness. Being in profile, it is entirely different from any picture we have. It is certainly the one we treasure most."

Several mediums have conveyed messages from the children to the effect that they are being cared for in the spirit world by their grandmother. In her charge, too, they visit their earthly surroundings. The parents are constantly hearing of the progress their girl and boy are making on the Other Side. Mr. Harrison says, "Mavis has lately told us, through different mediums, that she is now grown up and is helping to 'mother' the children who have passed to her world under war conditions."

In view of the striking evidence he has received, it is not surprising that Mr. W. E. Harrison is an ardent propagandist for Spiritualism. "The proved survival of my children," he affirms, "has given me the urge to proclaim its truth in every possible way for the rest of my life."

When a "dead" child controlled a medium and put round her mother's neck a birthday present, it was the culmination of a series of remarkable spirit messages that had been given through three well-known mediums, Edith Clements, Helen Spiers and Estelle Roberts. This was the story told in *Psychic News*.

Mr. J. Stanford, a City business man, was at a séance with Edith Clements when his "dead" daughter asked him to buy on her behalf a blue bead necklace for her mother's birthday. He said he would. Some time later, he was impressed to draw a design, which he had copied in diamonds and sapphires, the predominant colour being blue, as the daughter intended.

Then Mr. Stanford sat with Helen Spiers and told his "dead" daughter he wanted her to give the present to her mother herself. He would go with his wife to a séance on her birthday and he asked his "dead" daughter to control the medium – whoever it might be – take the present from his pocket and give it to his wife. Nothing else happened until Stanford went to a service at the Æolian Hall, London, where Estelle Roberts demonstrated clairvoyance. The medium gave him spirit messages from his daughter and started to make such pointed references to the present that Mr. Stanford was afraid the secret would be divulged before his wife's birthday!

There were other comments when he and his wife went to another Edith Clements séance, his daughter and the medium's guide, Sunshine, teasing him by making him think they were going to tell all about it and spoil his surprise. "We have got a secret, too," he was told.

The night before the birthday, the husband and wife went to a psychic demonstration by Helen Spiers. Mrs. Stanford was given birthday greetings "for tomorrow" by her two daughters – the one who had sent the previous messages has a little sister, who "died" before she learned to speak. Then the elder daughter told her father about his plans for the morrow, saying he intended to put the present in his left-hand pocket which was true.

Having asked whether she could describe the present she said it was "a metal brooch to go round the neck and it has got diamonds and sapphires." She promised to be present on the next day when the Stanfords had their sitting with Edith Clements. On the important day, Mrs. Stanford's birthday, Sunshine took control of Edith Clements and stood in front of Mr. Stanford and his wife. Then she put her hand in his pocket and drew out the envelope containing the present. "She is going to take it," said the guide.

As they watched, the medium's body straightened and became erect. A different voice addressed them as "Mummy and Daddy" and took two roses from the medium's dress, giving one to each of them. She kissed them both, then took the envelope and tried to open it. "I have forgotten how to undo it," she said, so Mr. Stanford took the necklace from the envelope and gave it to her. He wanted to help her to put it round her mother's neck, but the spirit insisted on doing it herself. Then, with a "God bless you, Mummy and Daddy," she was gone. It was his turn to be surprised when Sunshine again took control of her medium and named the youngest daughter as having helped her.

"Then we realised," he said, "that it was our baby daughter who had done this and had, for the first time in her life and ours, spoken to us directly, as she went over as a baby of ten-and-a-half months of age. It was the greatest shock and moment of our lives when we discovered this. That was the secret they had kept from me – but what a secret!"

"As entire strangers, my sister and I attended a sitting with Mr. Leslie Flint and obtained remarkable evidence of survival." In these words, Mr. S. W. Horne, of North London, put on record in *Psychic News* the results he obtained through the direct voice. First he was addressed by the voice of his "dead" grandfather, whose tones he recognised. Then Mickey, the medium's control, "brought John, my little son."

"Mickey gave me the child's name (slightly incorrectly), age, physical features and cause of passing," said the father. "All this time my hands were placed on my knees, a position familiar to sitters. We had been advised to keep our overcoats on because of the low temperature of the room. Mine was buttoned up securely. I then heard my child's voice quite close to me, and felt my overcoat being unbuttoned. I felt distinctly a hand placed in the pocket of my inner coat and with some difficulty a book was extracted.

"The voice quivering with excitement said, 'This is a cheque book and my photo is inside it. I saw you put it in your pocket before you came.' The book was placed in my hands and I felt fingers close round mine. Then the same hands made for my other pocket, and efforts were made to remove something there, but the power by this time was waning and the attempt was given up. For about five minutes afterwards a most intimate conversation took place with my boy while his hands were resting in mine.

"He gave me his own name, quite correctly this time, his sister's and mother's christian names, and described many intimate details of past incidents, too numerous to mention. He called my sister his 'Auntie Chrissie' and reminded her of his photograph for which she had recently obtained a special frame. He reminded me that I was wearing his mother's wrist watch. I had put this on particularly for the occasion, and it was quite concealed in the sleeve of the heavy overcoat. Every fact mentioned by him was correct in every respect.

"The fact that my cheque book with the enclosed photograph was in my inner coat pocket was known only to me. In my other pocket I had at the last moment before leaving the house hurriedly placed the little cap he used to wear."

This is the story of a "dead" boy who promised through one medium to manifest through another medium – and kept his promise. His parents, Mr. and Mrs. E. J. Farebrother, and his sister

Elsie, of Worcester Park, Surrey, have signed a joint statement attesting the facts.

They called on John Myers, the well-known psychic photographer, and the elder of Mr. and Mrs. Farebrother's two "dead" sons appeared on one plate. I have sat in John Myers's séances on scores of times, and have witnessed many striking demonstrations of his mediumship. These include tests in which the investigators have purchased their plates at shops of their own choosing, signed these plates as they loaded them into the slides, inserted these in the camera themselves, took their pictures and conducted their development in the dark room. All the medium did was to stand in the séance room while the photographs were exposed. And yet recognised extras – as they are called – of the "dead" have been found on the plates.

Soon after the Farebrothers had their experience with John Myers, they had a séance with Estelle Roberts. Jack, the younger spirit son, said he had tried to show his face on the plate on which his brother appeared, but he had not succeeded because the power was not strong enough. He added that if they went to John Myers again, he would manifest. They did – and Jacky kept his promise. He appeared as a spirit extra on one plate. Naturally the parents were overjoyed.

A remarkable communication from an unknown "dead" boy who gave many particulars about himself, all of which were confirmed, was described by a Mrs. Davidson in the *Harbinger of Light*, an Australian Spiritualist journal. The medium was Mrs. Leisk, wife of the Rev. David Leisk, of Brisbane.

One visitor from the spirit world was a child who, speaking clearly, but somewhat falteringly, said, "I want someone to tell my Mummy I am not dead. She is all the time troubling about me, but I cannot be as happy as the other boys because I see her crying, and it makes me sad. Can anyone tell her about it?"

When asked for more particulars about himself, the spirit boy gave his christian names, Stanley Thomas, and his surname, as well as giving the number in Bell Street, Elsternwick, Victoria, where he lived. He said he was nine years old, but had "died" when he was six. Asked whether he had any brothers or sisters, the child replied, "Yes, my big brother Leslie is 15, and Doris is 12. My little sister and brother are Norms and Cliff."

Then one of the sitters asked how he had passed on. "I got a scratch on my forehead, by accident, when I was playing with the boys at school," he said. "But it healed. Then, after that, I had pains in my head and at the back of my neck, and Mummy took me to a doctor, but I did not get better. Then I went to a hospital. The doctor thought I got a germ from the scratch at school. Then I came here, and I do want someone to tell my Mummy not to cry about me."

Mrs. Davidson, who was returning from Brisbane to Melbourne in a few weeks, offered to investigate the boy's story. She found the address in Elsternwick which the child had given, and discovered that the tenant had the name the spirit had said. Having confirmed the other particulars given, Mrs. Davidson asked the boy's mother, "Were his sickness and death caused by an accident at school?"

"At first we did not think so," the mother replied, "as a scratch he got on his forehead healed, but he still complained of pain in his head and at the back of his neck, I got the doctor to examine him thoroughly, and he wished him to go to a hospital in Carlton. Stanley did not get better, and the doctor told us the cause of his death was a germ from the scratch received at school."

The woman could not believe that the information had been given by the "dead" boy himself, for she knew nothing of Spiritualism, and the message bewildered her. Mrs. Davidson, however, left her address and asked her to think it over. If she wanted any further information, she would be glad to hear from her. Two days later, the woman telephoned Mrs. Davidson, asking when it would be convenient for them to call, as her husband was anxious to know more of the message.

"I arranged to go to their quiet little home and help in whatever way I could," wrote Mrs. Davidson. Now, the grief of the parents has been conquered, and the child in the spirit world is happy again.

Chapter 8

SIGNS AND WONDERS

PHYSICAL deformities, whilst they are not reproduced in the spirit body, may be temporarily assumed at a materialisation séance to provide proofs of the "dead" person's identity. The earthly life of Florence Marryat's daughter was restricted to ten days. At the time of the infant's "death," the mother had no experience of Spiritualism. She could not have anticipated that, ten years later, her child would provide striking evidence of her survival by reproducing the peculiar physical deformity with which she was born. How the spirit child persisted until she succeeded in establishing her identity beyond a shadow of doubt is convincingly told by Florence Marryat in her Spiritualistic classic, *There Is No Death*.

Her infant daughter, born during a time of great physical and mental suffering, arrived in this world with a peculiar and rare deformity. On the left side of the upper lip was a mark, as though a semi-circular piece of flesh had been cut out by a bullet-mould, which exposed part of the gum. The swallow also had been submerged into the gullet and, for the short period the child was on earth, she had to be fed by artificial means. The jaw itself was so distorted that, had her earthly life continued, her double teeth, when formed, would have been in the front. This blemish was considered so remarkable that the doctor who attended the mother invited several other medical men to examine the baby. They all agreed that a similar case had never before come to their notice. Florence Marryat points out that this is an important factor in her story. The medical men came to the conclusion that the child's deformity was caused by the trouble the mother experienced prior to the birth. The case was fully reported in the *Lancet*. The little one lived long enough to be baptised Florence, and then passed quietly away. "In this world of misery," records Florence Marryat, "the loss of an infant is soon swallowed up in more active trouble. Still, I never quite forgot my poor baby, perhaps because at that time she was, happily, the 'one dead lamb' of my little flock."

Ten years after the child's birth, Florence Marryat had her first experience of a materialisation séance. She went anonymously to the house of a medium, a Mrs. Holmes, where she received evidence from a "dead" friend. She could not, however, recognise a child who materialised before her with her mouth and chin covered in ectoplasmic substance and who intimated that Florence Marryat was the attraction which drew her to earth. The spirit child was bitterly disappointed when the sitter failed to connect her with anyone she had known. "I was so ignorant of the life beyond the grave at that period," says the author, "that it never struck me that the baby who had left me at ten days old had been growing since our separation until she had reached the age of ten years." The séance, however, made such an impression on her mind that she presented herself at the house of the medium two days later. Again, in the presence of about 30 other sitters, the same spirit girl manifested and failed to obtain recognition from Florence Marryat.

"Have you never lost a relation of her age?" asked the medium, trying to help the spirit child to establish its identity. "Never," answered the sitter with some emphasis. At that declaration, the little spirit sorrowfully retired.

A few weeks later, Florence Marryat was invited to attend a séance given by Florence Cook. Describing the séance room, the author writes, "The double drawing-rooms were divided by velvet curtains, behind which Miss Cook was seated in an armchair, the curtains being pinned together half-way up, leaving a large aperture in the shape of a V."

Being a complete stranger to the medium, Florence Marryat was surprised to hear the spirit control direct her to stand by the curtains and hold the lower parts together lest the pins should give way. From this position, she could naturally hear every word that passed between the psychic and her control. The first face to materialise was that of a man who was unknown to her. Then ensued a frightened exclamation from the medium, "Go away!" she cried. "I don't like you! Don't touch me; you frighten me!" Her guide's voice interposed with, "Don't be silly. Don't be unkind. It won't hurt you."

Immediately the girl's face she had twice seen at Mrs. Holmes's séance rose to view above the aperture of the curtains. The lower part of the features was muffled in ectoplasm as before, but her smiling eyes were directed at Florence Marryat as she stood holding the curtains of the cabinet. Because of the way the spirit girl was always muffled about the lower half of the face, Florence Marryat had named her "my little nun." Describing her emotions at this séance she writes,

"I was surprised at the evident distaste Miss Cook had displayed towards the spirit." When the séance was over and the medium had regained her normal condition, she told her of the "little nun" and demanded the reason for her apparent dread. "I can hardly tell you," said Miss Cook. "I don't know anything about her. She is quite a stranger to me, but her face is not fully developed, I think. There is something wrong about her mouth. She frightens me." This remark, made quite casually, set the author thinking. When she returned home, she wrote to Florence Cook asking if she would inquire of her guides the identity of the little spirit. In her reply, Florence Cook said, "I have asked Katie King" – her famous control with whom Sir William Crookes experimented so successfully – "but she cannot tell me anything further about the spirit that came through me the other evening than that she is a young girl closely associated with you."

Florence Marryat remained, at that period, unconvinced of the young spirit's identity, despite the fact that John Powles, a "dead" friend, constantly assured her that the "little nun" was her daughter Florence. She tried hard to communicate with the child in her own house, but without success. John Powles told her, in one spirit message, "Your child's want of power to communicate with you is not because she is too pure, but because she is too weak. She will speak to you some day. She is not in heaven." Because, at that time, she knew so little about the after-life, this last assertion both puzzled and grieved Florence Marryat. "I could not believe that an innocent infant was not in the Beatific Presence," she records, "yet I could not understand what motive my friend could have in leading me astray. I had yet to learn that... a spirit may have a training to undergo, even though it has never committed a mortal sin. A further proof, however, that my dead child had never died was to reach me from a quarter where I least expected it."

This occurred at the house of Dr. Keningale Cook and his wife – they were not related to the medium bearing the same name – some people she had never before visited. They knew nothing of Florence Marryat's private life. She never spoke of her "dead" infant, even to her intimate friends. The memory of her "death," and the events surrounding that period of her life, was not a happy one. Even her own children were ignorant of their "dead" sister's physical deformity.

During conversation with her host and hostess, the author discovered that Mrs. Keningale Cook was a powerful trance medium. The three decided to have a sitting. After several spirit communicators had spoken to Dr. Cook, the medium suddenly left her seat and fell on her knees beside Florence Marryat, whom she embraced emotionally. "I waited in expectation of hearing who this might be," writes the author, "when the manifestations as suddenly ceased, the medium returned to her seat, and the voice of one of her guides said that the spirit was unable to speak through excess of emotion, but would try again later in the evening. I had almost forgotten the circumstances in listening to other communications, when I was startled by hearing the word 'Mother' sighed rather than spoken. I was about to make some excited reply when the medium raised her hand to enjoin silence." Then came the following words, through the medium's entranced lips, "Mother, I am Florence. I must be very quiet. I want to feel I have a mother still. I am so lonely. Why should I be so? I cannot speak well. I want to be like one of you. I want to feel I have a mother and sisters. I am so far away from you all now." The mother answered, "But I always think of you, my dear dead baby."

"That's just it – your baby," was the spirit reply. "But I'm not a baby now. I shall get nearer. They tell me I shall. I do not know if I can come when you are alone. It's all so dark. I know you are there, but so dimly. I've grown all by myself. I'm not really unhappy, but I want to get nearer you. I know you think of me, but you think of me as a baby. You don't know me as I am."

"Did the trouble I had before your birth affect your spirit, Florence?" asked her mother. "Only as things cause each other," came the rejoinder. "I was with you, Mother, all through that trouble. I should be nearer to you than any child you have if I could only get close to you."

"I can't bear to hear you speak so sadly, dear," replied her mother. "I have always believed that you, at least, were happy in Heaven."

"I am not in Heaven! But there will come a day, Mother – I can laugh when I say it – when we shall go to Heaven together to pick blue flowers. They are so good to me here, but if your eyes cannot bear the daylight you cannot see the buttercups and daisies."

Florence Marryat, who did not learn until afterwards that blue flowers are, in spiritual language, typical of happiness, asked the "dead" child whether she thought she would be able to write through her hand. But her daughter did not think she would be very successful in this form of communication. She told her mother, "I seem composed of two things – a child in ignorance and a woman in years." She went on to say, "Why can't I speak at other places? I have wished and tried. I've come very near, but it seems so easy to speak now. This medium seems so different."

"I wish you could come to me when I am alone, Florence," said her mother. "You shall know me," was the spirit response. "I will come, Mother dear. I shall always be able to come here. I do come to you, but not in the same way."

The child spoke in such a plaintive, melancholy voice that she was asked not to depress her mother. Her reply was very remarkable: "I am as I am. When you come here, if you find that sadness is, you will not be able to alter it by plunging into material pleasures. Our sadness makes the world we live in. It is not deeds that make us wrong. It is the state in which we were born. Mother, you say I died sinless. That is nothing. I was born in a state. Had I lived, I should have caused you more pain than you can know. I am better here. I was not fit to battle with the world, and they took me from it. Mother, you won't let this make you sad. You must not."

"What can I do to bring you nearer to me?" asked her mother.

"I don't know what will bring me nearer, but I'm helped already by just talking to you... Mother, does it seem strange to you to hear your 'baby' say things as if she knew them? I'm going now. Goodbye."

The next voice to speak through the entranced medium was a guide whom Florence Marryat asked to give a personal description of her "dead" daughter as she then appeared. "Her face is downcast," was the reply. "We have tried to cheer her, but she is very sad. It is the state in which she was born. Every physical deformity is the mark of a condition. A weak body is not necessarily the mark of a weak spirit ... You cannot judge in what way the mind is deformed because the body is deformed. It does not follow that a canker in the body is a canker in the mind. But the mind may be too exuberant – may need a canker to restrain it."

Florence Marryat declares, "I have copied this conversation, word for word, from the shorthand notes taken at the time of utterance; and when it is remembered that neither Mrs. Keningale Cook nor her husband knew that I had lost a child – that they had never been in my house nor associated with any of my friends – it will at least be acknowledged, even by the most sceptical, that it was a very remarkable coincidence that I should receive such a communication from the lips of a perfect stranger."

Her "dead" daughter communicated through this medium only once more. One afternoon, Florence Marryat went to consult her solicitor on a strictly private and painful matter. He gave her advice. The following day, as she sat at breakfast, Mrs. Cook burst unceremoniously into her room. She apologised for her unconventional behaviour, but she said she had received a message from Florence the previous night which the "dead" child had begged her to deliver without delay. The message was, "Tell my mother that I was with her this afternoon at the lawyer's and she is not to follow the advice given her, as it will do harm instead of good." Mrs. Cook added, "I don't know to what Florence alludes, of course, but I thought it best to let you know at once."

At that time, Florence Marryat. had more confidence in her earthly counsellor than her spirit one. She abided by her solicitor's advice and regretted it ever afterwards!

Her conversation with the spirit girl had a great effect upon the mother. "I knew," she writes, "that my uncontrolled grief had been the cause of the untimely death of her body, but it had never struck me that her spirit would carry the effects of it into the unseen world. It was a warning to me, as it should be to all mothers, not to take the solemn responsibility of maternity upon themselves without being prepared to sacrifice their own feelings for the sake of their children."

Florence Marryat was assured, however, that communication between herself and her daughter would remove the "dead" child's depression. Consequently, she seized every opportunity of seeing and speaking with her. She attended various séances, and her spirit child never failed to manifest in different ways, according to the psychic gift of the medium. Florence Marryat says, "Through some she touched me only, and always with an infant's hand, that I might recognise it as hers, or laid her mouth against mine that I might feel the scar upon her lips; through others she spoke, or wrote, or showed her face." Indeed, she never attended a séance at which her daughter failed to notify her presence.

"It seems curious to me, now," writes the author, "to look back and remember how melancholy she used to be when she first came back to me, for, as soon as she had established an unbroken communication between us, she developed into the merriest little spirit I have ever known. Though her childhood has now passed away, and she is more dignified and thoughtful and womanly, she always appears joyous and happy."

Florence Marryat sat a number of times with Arthur Colman, a physical medium whose séances were held in darkness while he was securely fastened and held in his seat. At these sittings, the materialised child would run about the room and mix with the sitters. She played childish jokes on them, just as she might have done had she still remained on earth, a happy petted girl. "I have known her," writes her mother, "come in the dark and sit on my lap and kiss my face and hands, and let me feel the defect in her mouth."

One bright summer evening, on Florence Marryat's birthday, Arthur Colman called on her unexpectedly when she was entertaining some friends. They agreed to hold a séance. It was impossible effectively to darken the room as the windows were shaded only by venetian blinds. These, however, were lowered, and they sat in the twilight. The first spirit visitor was Florence Marryat's child who, saying she had brought a present for her birthday, placed something in her mother's hand. The parent could tell by touching the gift that it was a row of beads and concluded that spirit power had been used to bring a chaplet of beads from her own drawing-room mantelshelf, and place them in her hands as a birthday gesture.

This impression, however, was soon corrected by Aimee, the medium's spirit helper, who said, "You are mistaken. Florence has given you a chaplet you have never seen before. She was exceedingly anxious to give you a present on your birthday, so I gave her the beads which were buried with me." The sitter was asked by the spirit not to let the medium see the gift for the time being. It was not until some months later that Florence Marryat received permission to show this chaplet to Arthur Colman. He immediately recognised it as the one he had placed in the hands of Aimee as she lay in her coffin.

Florence Marryat writes, "But the great climax that was to prove beyond all question the personal identity of the spirit who communicated with me, with the body I had brought into the world, was yet to come." This event occurred at a séance which primarily had been arranged for the benefit of Mr. William Harrison, then Editor of the *Spiritualist*, who had been told by a "dead" woman friend she would do her best to materialise if he would sit with Florence Cook. The room, a small one, was uncarpeted and contained no furniture other than the three chairs provided for the sitters. A black shawl was nailed across a corner of the room, about four feet from the floor. This formed the medium's cabinet.

Florence Cook, who is described by the author as "a small slight figure with dark eyes and hair," wore a light grey dress trimmed with crimson ribbon. The medium sat on the floor behind the raised black shawl which left the lower part of her body still visible to the sitters; the light was dimmed, and the three sitters took their places in the chairs provided.

Before the séance began, Florence Cook told the author that she had been very restless during her recent trances and had acquired a habit of leaving her place in the cabinet and walking out amongst the sitters. The fact distressed her. She asked Florence Marryat if she would direct her back to the cabinet if she should leave it during trance. After some moments, when the medium was heard talking with her spirit controls, the black shawl was raised by a materialised hand, and a feminine figure stood before the sitters. It was impossible in the dim light to identify the features at the distance she stood from them. "Who can it be?" asked Florence Marryat of Mr. Harrison. "Mother, don't you know me?" whispered her spirit daughter. Not having expected Florence to manifest on this occasion, the surprised mother rose from her chair, saying, "Oh, my darling child, I never thought I should meet you here." The girl replied, "Go back to your chair and I will come to you."

Whereupon the fully materialised figure crossed the room and seated herself upon her mother's lap.

"Florence, my darling, is this really you?" she asked, as she held the spirit girl in her arms. "Turn up the light," answered the girl, "and look at my mouth." When the light came on, writes Florence Marryat, "they all saw distinctly that peculiar defect on the lip with which she was born – a defect, be it remembered, which some of the most experienced members of the profession had affirmed to be 'so rare as never to have fallen under their notice before.' She also opened her mouth that I might see she had no gullet... I will not interrupt my narrative to make any remarks upon this incontrovertible proof of identity. I know it struck me dumb and moved me to tears. At this juncture Miss Cook, who had been moaning and moving about a great deal behind the black shawl, suddenly explained, 'I can't stand this any longer,' and walked out into the room. There she stood in her grey dress and crimson ribbons whilst Florence sat on my lap in white drapery." But only for a moment, for directly the medium was fully in view, the spirit sprang up and darted behind the curtain. As she had been asked to do, Florence Marryat then led the entranced medium back to the cabinet. No sooner had she done so, than the spirit girl reappeared. She clutched her mother, saying, "Don't let her do that again. She frightens me." The girl was actually trembling.

"Why, Florence," her mother said, "do you mean to tell me you are frightened of your own medium? In this world it is we poor mortals who are frightened of the spirits." Her daughter whispered, "I am afraid she will send me away, Mother." However, the medium remained quiet and did not disturb them again. Florence stayed for some time longer. "She clasped her arms round my neck, and laid her head upon my bosom, and kissed me dozens of times," writes Florence Marryat. "She took my hand, and said she felt sure I should recognise her hand because it was so much like my own." The spirit girl explained why she had been permitted to show herself with her earthly deformity. "Sometimes you doubt, Mother," she said, "and think your eyes and ears have misled you; but after this you must never doubt again. Don't fancy I am like this in the spirit land. The blemish left me long ago. But I put it on tonight to make you certain. Don't fret, Mother. Remember I am always near you. No one can take me away. Your earthly children may grow up and go out into the world and leave you, but you will always have your spirit child close to you."

Florence remained for nearly 20 minutes at that séance. "Her undoubted presence was such a stupendous fact to me," avers her mother, "that I could only think that she was there, that I actually held in my arms the tiny infant I had laid with my own hands in her coffin, that she was no more dead than I was myself, but had grown to be a woman. So I sat, with my arms tight round her, and my heart beating against hers, until the power decreased and Florence was compelled to give me a last kiss and leave me.

Describing her spirit daughter's appearance, the author says her head was uncovered, and she had an immense quantity of hair, which fell over her shoulders. Her arms were bare, as were her feet. The dress in which she was clothed had no particular shape or style, but seemed to be composed of yards of soft thick muslin which draped her body and fell below her knees. When seated on her knee, the materialised figure weighed about ten stone, and had well-covered limbs. Florence Marryat observed that the spirit girl resembled, in size and appearance, her eldest living daughter. This séance took place when her child had been "dead" for about 17 years. After that séance Florence never appeared to her mother again with the mark on her mouth.

This spirit girl once materialised before Florence Marryat at a public séance three thousand miles from England where her mother was entirely unknown to the medium or the sitters. Florence Marryat had gone to America to fulfil a professional engagement. In New York, she decided to investigate for herself the quality of American mediumship. She therefore chose from a list of mediums in a newspaper advertisement a public materialisation séance that was to take place that evening. The medium was Mrs. M. A. Williams. Florence Marryat writes of the séance, "I took the chair in the front row, exactly opposite the medium's cabinet. There must have been 35 or 40 people present when Mrs. Williams entered the room and, nodding to those she knew, went into the cabinet."

Several spirit forms materialised. When their voices were too weak to be heard by the sitters or when the spirit forms were not sufficiently "built up" to be seen, a chairman, or conductor, who stood near the cabinet, relayed the messages. He addressed Florence Marryat, saying, "I am not aware of your name." "And you will not be aware of it just yet," thought the visitor, wishing, for evidential purposes, to preserve her anonymity. He went on to say that her presence was required by a materialisation in the cabinet. She advanced, but was met by a spirit form unknown to her. He had apparently come to pave the way for another, for, after he greeted her and she had resumed her seat, she was again addressed by the conductor who said, "Here is a spirit who says she has come for a lady named Florence who has just crossed the sea. Do you answer to the description?"

The author was about to say "Yes," when the curtains parted again and her daughter ran across the room and fell into her arms. "Mother!" she exclaimed. "I said I would come with you and look after you, didn't I?

"I looked at her," states the author. "She was exactly the same in appearance as when she had come to me in England – the same luxurious brown hair, and features and figure as I had seen her under the different mediumships of Florence Cook, Arthur Colman, Charles Williams and William Eglinton; the same form... stood before me there in New York, thousands of miles across the sea, and by the power of a person who did not even know who I was. Florence appeared as delighted as I was, and kept on kissing me and talking of what had happened to me on board ship coming over, and was evidently quite au fait with all my proceedings."

Presently, the spirit girl said to her mother, "There's another friend of yours here. We came together. I'll go and fetch him." Like the other spirit forms, she dematerialised before her mother's eyes by sinking downwards, but a moment afterwards she reappeared through the aperture of the cabinet curtains. "Here's your friend, Mother," she said. By her side stood the materialised form of William Eglinton's control, Joey, whom Florence Marryat had last seen in England. "Here were two spiritual beings, *in propria personae* in New York," writes the author, "claiming me in a land of strangers who had not yet found out who I was. I was deeply affected."

Is it not natural that this mother should be touched by her spirit daughter's devotion in accompanying her across the sea to welcome her in a strange country?

"I could fill pages," says Florence Marryat of her spirit daughter, "with accounts of her pretty, caressing ways and her affectionate and sometimes solemn messages. It has been wonderful to me to mark how her ways and mode of communication have changed with the passing years."

The simple child did not know how to express herself when she first appeared to her mother. But with the passage of time she blossomed into a woman, full of tender counsel. Florence Marryat concludes her story: "Only tonight – the night before Christmas Day – as I write she comes to me and says, 'Mother, you must not give way to sad thoughts. The past is past. Let it be buried in the blessings that remain to you.' And amongst the greatest of those blessings I reckon my belief in the existence of my spirit child."

Florence Marryat's remarkable experiences denote the high standard of physical mediumship available in her day. But psychic force continues to flow through present-day mediums. This fact is borne out by the following story of another "dead" child who suffered from a sad physical and mental disability on earth. This little boy returned with convincing proofs of his survival. He, too, was able to comfort his parents with the assurance that he had gained radiant health in the spirit world.

Roy Brandon, a journalist, told the story in a series of articles in a weekly newspaper. A week after his child passed over, the specialist who had attended him informed the father, "Your son is not dead. You can follow his spiritual progress if you wish."

"This astounding statement," writes Roy Brandon in his opening article, "coming from the lips of a doctor skilled in his profession – a well read, much travelled man, on whose word I could absolutely rely – left me staggered. To me, my boy meant more than mere words can express. He was an invalid from birth. We had tended him – his mother and I – day after day for ten long years. A crippled helpless child calls for all the love, all the sympathy, that a parent can express. A few swift, tragic hours, and our boy had been taken from us. I remembered staring unbelievingly at the doctor, and then letting loose a flood of questions."

The father was told that all he needed for an investigation of Spiritualism was an unbiased attitude. The doctor suggested that he conduct his inquiry in secret so that when the evidence came – as come it would – there would be no doubt or suspicion in his mind. It was in a coldly critical state that Roy Brandon began his search for proof of his child's continued existence.

His first sitting was with Helen Duncan. It took place at the house of a friend who was just as anxious as he to obtain evidence. Roy Brandon mentions that the medium's home was 400 miles away. "So far as I am aware," he said, "she had not previously met any of the sitters. She was certainly an absolute stranger to my wife and me." The séance was held under strict test conditions. Not until the sitters had taken their places in front of the cabinet did the medium enter the room for the first time that night. Nobody was introduced. Helen Duncan seated herself in the cabinet, which contained nothing but an ordinary wooden chair.

Albert, her spirit control, was the first to materialise. He drew aside the curtains, which divided the medium from the sitters. "In the red light which illumined the room," writes Roy Brandon, "we saw the spirit form of a man, more than six feet tall, standing upright, separate from the medium, who was still in trance. He selected me to 'test' him. I stood up and touched the spirit form, to find it solid. The hand which he extended to me was warm." Ten other spirit forms materialised. Amongst them was a Red Indian, nearly seven feet in height, wearing a head-dress, who emerged from the cabinet. With the exception of Mrs. Duncan's guides, every spirit who materialised had some definite link with one or more of the sitters with whom they held affectionate conversations.

Then came the thrilling moment for the journalist and his wife. Albert announced that a boy, connected with them both, wished to speak. From the cabinet emerged a small, veiled figure, who showed great excitement. He called, "Mummy, Daddy," before he was overcome with emotion. On this, his first materialisation, he was covered with an ectoplasmic veil. "We did not see his features," records the journalist, "but the mannerisms he displayed were markedly his, and the evidence volunteered by Albert was sufficient to convince us that this was indeed our boy. When on earth, he was highly strung and easily excited. His excitement now made him almost incoherent. He slapped his legs repeatedly to indicate that he now had the use of his limbs, and seemed most anxious to allay the grief which we still felt at his passing."

The spirit child pleaded with his mother not to cry any more "because I am all right now!" Then, throwing his mother and father a kiss in a manner peculiarly his own, he disappeared behind the cabinet. Albert told these parents, "You may not realise it yet, but in the years to come you will better understand what a blessing it is that your boy is on our side of life. He is still receiving treatment over here for his head trouble. You know what I mean. Let me explain more fully. Your boy suffered from an injury to his brain. He was never like other children of his age." The boy's father agreed that this was the case. "I am to tell you," Albert continued, "that although the treatment he was receiving would have helped him, he would always have been an invalid because of his chest trouble." All the evidence provided by Albert was acknowledged by Roy Brandon to be accurate.

At the Brandons' next séance with Helen Duncan, the "dead" boy was able to show his features. "Can you see my face?" he asked proudly. "Yes, old chap," replied his father, "I can see your eyes and nose." But the child was not completely satisfied with this response. "Can you see me, Mummy?" he inquired. "Yes, my dear," said his mother, "I can see your face. You are getting quite clever."

In that small drawing-room, in which 22 people were seated, the "dead" boy ran unhesitatingly to a friend of Mr. and Mrs. Brandon. Without a sign from his parents, he had recognised, among those present, the only other person he knew on earth. "Can you see my eyes, Uncle?" he inquired, as he turned his features towards the red light in order to display them more clearly. The sitter examined the materialised child intently. "Yes," he finally announced, "it is you – there is no doubt whatever about that." With this, the child moved towards the cabinet and, saying he would come another time, disappeared.

Under an assumed name, Roy Brandon booked a trance sitting by telephone with Estelle Roberts, to whom he was a complete stranger. Describing the séance, he writes, "Red Cloud next informed me that I had a child in the spirit world and went on to give me a description of my boy. At this stage, the guide appeared to be in difficulties, due, he stated, to the great excitement of my boy at being able to 'contact' me. In an endeavour to ease the conditions, I volunteered information concerning my son's age, the time that had elapsed since his passing, and the nature of his illness." Inviting the sitter to a forthcoming voice circle, Red Cloud assured him that although, during his son's earthly lifetime, he had been unable to speak, he would hear his child's voice. A month later, Roy Brandon and his wife attended the séance. "There were present on this occasion 20 sitters, among whom were the Earl of Cottenham, Lady Segrave, and Shaw Desmond, the novelist," he writes. "The evidence on this night was astounding. For an hour and a half, voice after voice spoke through the trumpet. Towards the end of the séance, I received a rude shock. A voice, purporting to be my son's, came through the trumpet. It asked for 'Daddy,' and gave the assumed name under which I was sitting!"

A little later the voice said, "Daddy, Daddy... My throat is better now... It worries me when I try to speak ... It was paralysed... Don't grieve for me, Mummy..." Mr. and Mrs. Brandon did their best to encourage the voice. "Finally," writes the journalist, "I asked if he could give us the nickname by which he was known. I strained my ears, but all I heard was a muffled sound from the trumpet, which then fell to the floor."

At once, Shaw Desmond said, "I caught a word that sounded like 'Bunty' or 'Bumpty.' " Lord Cottenham broke in with, "That is what I heard."

"Don't shoot questions at him about his name," said Red Cloud reprovingly. "This boy was ten years of age, and he passed over ten months ago."

Roy Brandon writes, "These details were volunteered by me at the private sitting, therefore, to my mind, they did not constitute evidence. So the sitting ended. My boy's name was Bumpty. Had he given that name through the trumpet?"

I endorse Red Cloud's comment about "shooting questions." This often breaks the line of communication. It is always preferable to let the "dead" provide their own evidence. It is not surprising that the repetition by the spirit voice of the assumed name, given to the medium earlier, came as a shock to the father. In my own long experience of psychic phenomena I have very occasionally come across similar puzzling incidents when, as in this case, there could be no question of the medium's absolute honesty and integrity.

It must not be overlooked that the unconscious mind of the psychic, although dormant during trance, may retain a trace of what has been absorbed during ordinary consciousness. I have heard from experienced spirit guides that, in some cases, it is better to relieve the "congestion" by repeating the erroneous impression in the medium's unconscious mind, and thus enable the channel to be cleared for further communication and evidence. Whether this is the explanation of Roy Brandon's experience I cannot say. But I do know that, whether the investigator is the type who desires to give a false name, or not, the standard of evidence received remains always the acid test of a successful sitting.

A few days after the voice séance, Mr. Brandon went to a public Spiritualist service at Golders Green where the medium, Mabel Challis, told him, "Your boy is here on the platform with me. He seems terribly upset, and says that you have had a disappointment lately. Is that so?" The father replied in the affirmative, whereupon the medium went on, "He says, 'Don't give it up! Please, Daddy, don't give it up!' He has come tonight to give you a little bit of evidence – something that he has never given before. Wait a minute." After a pause, she said quietly, almost in doubt of the message she was receiving, "He says, 'Bumps – tell him, Bumps; he will know what it means.'"[11]

Roy Brandon writes, "Bumps was an abbreviation of my boy's pet name, Bumpty. I had never received this through any other medium. Neither Mrs. Challis, nor any of the hundred odd people present, could possibly have known what it meant."

The father's investigation continued. Under an assumed name, he booked a sitting by telephone with the automatic writing medium, Hester Dowden. "Up to the hour appointed for the séance, Mrs. Dowden and I had never met," he says. "We were total strangers to each other. No one else was aware that I had booked this sitting. Therefore it is patent that the medium could have known nothing whatever concerning me or my mission."

The previous evening, as he sat alone in his own home, the father sent the following thought to his son, "If you can communicate through Mrs. Dowden, will you give me the password, 'F.I.D.'?" These letters represented something intimately connected with his child.

The sitting was, for some time, unsuccessful and the medium was very concerned. She told the sitter she was convinced of the presence of a spirit whose excitement and emotion was causing difficulty. She asked her guide to help the spirit and then, taking the ouija board on her lap, suggested that the sitter ask some questions. Roy Brandon says, "I put forward a number of questions in an audible voice, and without a moment's hesitation the correct answers came through the board."

"Can you give me your name?" was the first question. – "Stanley Thomas," came the reply on the board by means of its alphabetical letters.

"What about your nickname?" – "Bumpty." "Anything else?" – "Yes, F.I.D."

"Can you give me the name of anyone at home?" – "Sister June Dolores and brother Alan."

"How old were you when you passed on?" – "Ten years." "How long have you been on the Other Side?" – "Two years."

(Actually, the boy had passed over one year and nine months previously.)

"There were two things of which you were very fond when you were here. Can you tell me what they were?" – "Yes, music, gramophone."

"What else?" – "Car drives."

"Do you remember what happened on the Sunday before your passing?" – "Yes, I remember well; you took me for a car drive."

"Do you visit us at home?" – "Very often." "What do you do when you come?" "Try to give knocks one on the table."

This reply was confirmation of an incident that had happened several months previously. The parents were alone in the house. They were sitting in the dining-room when they were startled to hear a resounding rap on the table which was beyond the reach of them both.

Bumpty was extremely fond of music. Often, the gramophone was played to him for hours at a stretch. His greatest delight, however, was to go for a ride in the car. On the Sunday before his passing, his father took him for a long drive into the country. It was his first outing for a month. It proved to be his last motor drive on earth.

Summing up the evidence of his sitting with Hester Dowden, Roy Brandon states, "It will be seen that among other things he gave his christian names in full, his nickname, his age, the names of his brother and sister, and the password 'F.I.D.' " He adds, "Some of you who read these experiences may shrug your shoulders and dismiss the whole thing as being so much nonsense. Two years ago, I confess I might have used similar arguments, but, in the light of my experience, I have been forced to change my views."

In a subsequent *Psychic News* article, Roy Brandon told of an experience which occurred at a later Helen Duncan séance, which was held under strict test conditions. 13 spirit forms materialised in all, amongst them the journalist's "dead" child. Bumpty was the second spirit to manifest that night. His face was seen in white light which is usually destructive to physical phenomena. He manipulated a pocket torch so that the beam shone on his features.

"Several times," says Roy Brandon, "the torchlight was flashed about his face. Although it was possible to obtain only fleeting glimpses of the features, I can truthfully say that they bore a distinct resemblance to those of my son. My wife is equally convinced on this point. The critic would do well to remember that Mrs. Duncan had never seen my son during his physical life; nor could she, nor anyone else connected with the séance, have obtained access to any of his photographs. The curious circumstances surrounding my attendance at this séance also call for comment. The Duncan séances are usually booked up weeks ahead. Although on the day prior to this sitting Mrs. Duncan had suggested that I might attend a séance at some future convenient date, no actual date was arranged. Yet, on the following day – the fourth anniversary of my son's passing – I received a telephone call inviting me to sit that same night. The significance of the date, together with the afore-mentioned circumstances, impelled me to cancel a prior engagement and accept the invitation."

Chapter 9

EVIDENCE FROM THE STILLBORN

WE are told by many highly evolved beings on the Other Side that at the moment of human conception the individual spirit identifies itself with the physical organism through which it will express itself during earthly life. The etheric body develops in unison with the now individualised growing physical form. The process of synchronised development continues throughout the prenatal period, and after normal birth. The spark of life, once ignited, can never be extinguished. Many people do not realise the tremendous implications of this fact. Not only do children whose span of physical life measures a few hours, days, months or years survive "death," but also those who never drew earthly breath at all.

Physical birth is not the beginning of life but a natural continuation of the process which began months earlier.

Pre-natal dissolution of the earthly form, at whatever stage of under-development it occurred, does not impair or impede the continued growth of the individualised spirit body which became identified with its earthly vehicle at conception. Thus, when the process of normal birth is prevented from taking place, either through accident or design, the etheric body continues to grow and develop on the Other Side as it would have done if the earthly counterpart had not perished. The immature spirit, projected into the next world through the destruction of the body, is nurtured and cherished by specially qualified spirit beings in much the same way as a prematurely born infant on earth is the recipient of specialised treatment until normality of growth is gained.

Earthly life is but the school which prepares the soul for the larger and fuller existence in the spirit world. When the normal span of years has been reached, the mature individual, ripened by experience, vacates the physical vehicle now unnecessary in the new state of existence. But we, who understand so little of God's purpose, cannot comprehend the Mind which decides to transplant an immature, earthly bloom in the richer soil of the spirit garden. Spiritualists know that when children pass over all the forces on the Other Side are directed towards helping them become accustomed to the new manner of living. When all human efforts have failed to save a young life, we can derive comfort from this knowledge. Life belongs to the Great Spirit, Who alone is capable of creating the vital spark which animates our being. We, who cannot create this force, have not the authority to destroy its mode of manifestation. If, of our own volition, we curtail an earthly life, we do the human spirit a grave injury by plunging it, unprepared and unready, into the next world.

As the spirit body becomes identified with its earthly vehicle long before birth, it follows that the destruction of the physical body, however under-developed it may be, can only be justified if the reason be entirely unselfish. A premeditated abortion, brought about for unworthy motives, is akin to murder.

In our present stage of civilisation we may justify, for one reason or another, the taking of human life. But we know that, if we lived in accord with the teachings of Jesus, such a course of destruction would be avoided. Human evolution has not yet succeeded in superseding the "tooth for a tooth" injunction of the Old Testament by the Nazarene's more tender request that we love one another. We still kill. Our motives in so doing may be in accordance with our ethical and national, if not our spiritual, consciences. Legalised murder is still murder. When humanity is sufficiently evolved, wars will cease and truly civilised methods of settling national and international disputes will eliminate mass destruction. Slowly, very slowly, we move towards a goal of greater humanity. Within many countries today capital punishment has been, or is in process of being, totally abolished. Spiritualists as a body strongly oppose the system of capital punishment. They are aware that the act of projecting a murderer into the next world by the process of another murder – legalised though it be – is not the end of the criminal.

An executed murderer seeking to revenge his "death" may become earthbound by the violence of his own desires to wreak vengeance on humanity. He may obsess a weak-willed, unbalanced human still on earth with the urge to commit a similar crime to the one for which he paid the supreme penalty. Such cases of obsession are well within the knowledge of Spiritualists. Authenticated literature is available on this subject, and on the manner in which earthbound spirits and obsessed humans are helped by those who understand psychic laws. We dwell in an imperfect world. Until a better one is gained through our own efforts, it is often necessary to strike a temporary balance in dealing with existing evils. Our dreams of a

Utopia must, of necessity, lie a little ahead of our waking reality.

But the vision of a more highly evolved and truly civilised community must not be allowed to grow dim because it cannot immediately be fully realised. By practical application of the knowledge that man survives death, we will one day learn to live in accordance with the natural laws we know to be true and unchanging. We will refrain from curtailing the allotted span of years of any individual, whether the physical vehicle be still in embryo form, or whether it be a mature adult whose life on earth has already registered many years.

Immature spirits who pass on without having drawn earthly breath present special problems to those on the Other Side who are charged with their care. Such problems do not arise in the case of children who lived, if only for a few moments, after birth. These children have inhabited for a short time the world of matter to which they belong. They have claimed their heritage.

But the spirits of stillborn and incompletely formed infants pass over without having established their first link with the world in which they were conceived. Yet they are children of the earth whose spirits became individualised through material circumstances. They belong to the world of matter, but the process of normal birth has been prevented by the early dissolution of their bodies.

In *The Nurseries Of Heaven*, by Miss H. A. Dallas and the Rev. G. Vale Owen, there is an extract from the latter's automatic script received from a spirit communicator on the subject of stillborn children. The clergyman was told, "These children come here asleep, and you will realise that their first awakening is that process here which answers to birth on earth. They have never breathed the atmosphere, nor seen the light, nor heard any of the sounds of earth. In brief, none of their bodily senses have been exercised in the way for which they were prepared by their natural formation. The organs of these senses are, therefore, nearly, but not quite, perfect in their structure. Moreover, the brain has never been called upon to interpret their messages. And so the child of earth lacks earthly qualities empirically, while having them potentially...

"The problem, therefore, which they have to solve who take these children in hand is not a small one. For it is necessary both that the organs be dealt with so that a natural progress may attend the child, and also that the brain receive its lesson. In the case of an infant a few minutes old, this connection between the brain and the organs of sense has been established and can be used in the maturing of those faculties dependent for their exercise on those organs. But a stillborn child brings not that connection, and it has to be made on this side. Once that is done, the progress is merely a matter of orderly development on the same lines as that of ordinary children.

"To this end several means are pressed into use. There is the relationship between the child and his parents, and especially between him and his mother. He is brought into contact with her in such a way that he experiences what is nearly as possible equivalent to birth. By this process he is made to feel his separation from her bodily and his individualisation as a separate and complete entity. This is achieved not by his taking a body of flesh, but by his being brought into intimate association in his spiritual body with the spiritual body of his mother. This does not effect so perfect an inception of contact between brain and organic faculties as does a natural birth, but it does establish in a definite way the relationship of earthly parenthood, and from that time the child is kept in touch with his mother in order that he may, as he grows up to maturity, be as others, so far as it is possible to compass this. Still there is always some little difference between such children and those others who have been born on earth. They are lacking in some of the sterner virtues and, on the other hand, they are more spiritual in their personality and outlook. But as earthborn children progress in spiritual development, and stillborn children develop their knowledge of earth by contact with their mothers, and later with their other relatives, so the difference is minimised until they are able to associate on quasi-equal terms of loving friendship, and so help in the mutual giving of what each lacks."

Evidence of the individual survival of stillborn children has been obtained again and again by parents who had never suspected their continued existence. Such evidence is particularly valuable to the sceptical mind which cannot throw off the telepathy bugbear. Sometimes, details concerning their earthly links supplied by those who never breathed on earth have to be confirmed by the sitters. There are occasions, too, when parents who have practically forgotten the incident of the birth of a stillborn infant are reminded of the event by the spirit child who has returned with incontestable evidence of Survival. The memory of a premature parturition or of a stillborn child may easily become clouded by the passage of years, particularly if a family of children has been brought up since the incident. Then, the "death" of a beloved member of the family may start the parents on a quest for information about the child's survival. Sitting with a medium, they may find, to their astonishment that not only does the recently mourned child manifest, but they receive additional evidence of the survival of a stillborn infant whom they have forgotten, but who has not forgotten them.

Mr. H. T. Whorlow, of North London, describes in *Psychic News* how he and his wife attended a public Spiritualist meeting for the first time. They were impressed with the service and decided to continue their psychic investigations at home. They invited two neighbours, Mr. and Mrs. Randall, to join them in a sitting for table phenomena. They sat with no result for an hour and a half, and were about to abandon their efforts when the table moved. By the prearranged alphabetical code of table tilts, a spirit message was received from one who declared she was Geraldine, the daughter of Mr. and Mrs. Randall.

"We have no dead daughter," said these nonplussed sitters. Despite the spirit communicator's insistence that she was their child they affirmed that this was untrue, and the séance was concluded.

The following morning Mr. Randall arrived at the Whorlows' house in some haste to give them his news. He told his friends that when he and his wife had talked over the events of the séance, they both remembered that a stillborn child had been born. Moreover, they now recalled their intention, before the event, to have the baby christened Geraldine should it be a girl. Their spirit daughter had taken the name they wanted to give her if she had lived on earth.

When Mr. F. S. Comer sat with the well-known medium, Horace Leaf, his guide described a beautiful 11 year-old spirit girl. She had very little, if any, contact with earthly life and was the daughter of Mr. Comer's sister, Ethel. The sitter said he knew of no child belonging to his sister who answered to the description, but the spirit communicator assured him that if he made inquiries he would ascertain the accuracy of the statement. Consequently, Mr. Comer wrote to his sister, Ethel, who replied, "You were too young to know at the time, but my first child was a stillborn girl. She would have been 15 this year if she had lived."

A similar incident occurred to the medium Fred Jordan Gill. When he first inquired into Spiritualism, before he developed his own psychic powers, he went to a voice séance. At that period, there was considerable doubt in Mr. Gill's mind as to the genuineness of the particular medium's phenomena. In this uncertain frame of mind, the sitter was addressed by a spirit who gave his name as George. "I am your father," he declared, "and I have your brother with me." The sitter replied, "That is ridiculous. If you are my father you know very well I am an only son." The sitter was now convinced that his doubts about the medium were justified, and that the séance was fraudulent. But the spirit voice insisted that his wife had been delivered of a six-and-a-half months' child who had not lived. He named the year and the month in which the event had occurred. Still unconvinced, Mr. Gill returned home after the séance and asked his mother whether such an incident had ever taken place. Not only did his mother confirm every statement made at the séance, but she told her son she had purposely kept the knowledge of this premature birth from him. Indeed, with the exception of her husband, nobody had been told of the event.

In the *Proceedings* of the Society for Psychical Research is Mr. J. Rogers Rich's record of a sitting with the famous Victorian medium, Mrs. Piper. The medium's control said that a child was constantly beside him and in his surroundings. It was attached to him and had much influence over him. "It is a blood relation, a sister," affirmed the control. This he denied, replying that he never had a sister and never heard of one. The answer came: "I know that you were never told of it. The birth was premature, the child dead, born some years before you were. Go and ask your aunts to prove it."

He questioned a member of the family and the information was confirmed. He writes, "By the time I came into the world the affair had been forgotten and there had never been a reason for informing me of the circumstances, proving that I had in no way had any intimation of it, and that this communication could not be explained by thought-transference or the like."

The Rev. Lionel Calway wrote a series of articles in *Psychic News* describing how, through various mediums, he obtained remarkable evidence of the survival of his "dead" wife, Mabel. She not only proved her continued existence but, to the joy of her husband, gave evidence that the child, stillborn a short while before her own passing, had survived. A few months after his wife's "death," this clergyman called on Annie Brittain, the well-known medium. "She did not know I was coming," he affirms. "She knew absolutely nothing about me. She did not know my name, and I was not wearing anything to indicate I was a parson." He describes his first sitting with Mrs. Brittain as "the most extraordinary hour I have ever spent in my life." He received at this séance 22 definite points of evidence! The medium told him she could not understand why the "dead" woman repeated the name of Michael. But Mr. Calway knew. He declares, "We hoped the child would be born on St. Michael's Day and intended to call him Michael – there is no one either in Mabel's or my family of that name. After her awful agony, her only reference to what she had gone through was, 'No baby, no Michael.' She said it with such a wistful smile, so I had to be brave and smile too. I had to consent to the child being destroyed to save the mother's life – and it was a girl. She never knew. She thought the child was a boy."

Referring to the "dead" woman at his second sitting the medium said, "She has a boy of her own in the spirit world. The child was not actually born, but he cost her her life. The baby is with her now and is growing." Annie Brittain went on to say that the child was reunited with the mother when she crossed to the Other Side. The medium was told by the "dead" woman that the baby's limbs "are all right now."

"It must be remembered," writes the clergyman, "that Mrs. Brittain did not know who I was, and Mabel had no idea what had actually happened. Yet here she was, nearly four months later, telling me the child was alive and the limbs, which had been severed from the body when the poor little mite was destroyed, were sound again. How truly wonderful!"

During these earlier sittings, his wife persisted in speaking of her spirit child in masculine terms, despite the fact that the infant was a girl. Later, she referred to the child's true sex. She had longed for a son and had never been told on earth that a daughter had been born. On this point, the Rev. C. L Tweedale, a Spiritualist clergyman with much experience, wrote to Mr. Calway, "It is very interesting to see how the mother's earliest desire for a boy had persisted. But now she realises and knows. It is one of the most touching and pathetic cases I have ever come across."

At a séance with J. J. Vango, Mabel told her husband that she and her child were always together. Her voice softened as she declared, "She is in my care, so that she will get to know you. I should not like it to be otherwise."

At another séance, with Elizabeth Cannock, Mabel reiterated her previous statements through other mediums that she was glad she and the little one were together. She was preparing a home on the Other Side, she added. By the time he joined them, the baby would be grown up. They would be so happy together when they were united. She referred to the baby's transition by saying she now thought it all for the best. The child had been spared all worldly anxiety and sorrow.

A woman whose unborn child had passed with her fully materialised at one of Helen Duncan's séances and showed her spirit infant. The mother who "died" during her early married life, materialised in a gown of gleaming white material.

The séance, held under rigid test conditions, was described in *Psychic News* by Roy Brandon, whose own son, as already recorded, also showed his features in the white light of a flashlamp. When the medium's control materialised, he told Miss Jeannette Strom, one of the sitters, "I have a lady here for you. She passed to our side soon after her marriage." Giving further evidential details, he added, "Earlier this evening I overheard your conversation in which mention was made of 'cheesecloth' and 'gauze'. I want you to take particular notice of the dress worn by this lady.

"It is certainly not cheesecloth!" She manipulated a flashlamp, directing its beam of light over her face and dress. Roy Brandon declares, "As the white light shone on her features and gown the sitters were moved to murmurs of amazement and admiration. Judged by its sheen, the gown was satin."

The spirit was immediately recognised by Miss Strom, who was told by the "dead" woman that she was showing herself in her wedding dress. She spoke in quick cultured accents. When the sitter said she was looking "more beautiful than ever," the spirit answer was, "You see, my dear, I have no make-up on!"

"Have you got your baby?" asked the sitter. "Yes, here with me," was the instant reply as, moving swiftly into the cabinet, she returned a few seconds later with an infant in her arms.

Miss Strom's signed statement was included in Roy Brandon's description of that remarkable séance. Here it is:

"I have had the most amazing experience of my life. Tonight, I was privileged to see the materialised spirit form of Agnes Sakoshansky, a Russian Jewess, who came to this country when she was a very young girl. A refined, cultured young woman of rare beauty, she was a very dear friend of mine. I was in close touch with her right up to the time of her passing, which occurred shortly after her marriage. She passed with her baby unborn. Her features were so clearly defined in the white light that anyone who had known her could easily have recognised her. The charm of manner, the voice, and every gesture of the materialised form were characteristic of Agnes. It is true what she said about her bridal gown. *She was married in white satin.* When I spoke to her about her baby, she immediately replied, 'I have the baby with me.' She went straight back into the cabinet, and only a second or two could have elapsed before she returned with the infant in her arms. I would take my oath in a witness box that the spirit form I saw and spoke with was Agnes Sakoshansky."

Mrs. Edith Wynne Mitchell, of Shrewsbury, says in a letter to me: "My grandson, who never lived on earth, was seen and drawn by Frank Leah, the psychic artist, who got most evidential items from him. The drawing is very much like his earthly brother, whom he helps with his studies." Mrs. Mitchell, and her married daughter, Norah, called one day at the Spiritualist Community, then housed at the Grotrian Hall, London, and asked whether they could have a sitting with Frank Leah either on that day or on the following one. The secretary said it would not be possible, as these were not his attendance days. Mrs. Mitchell and her daughter were most disappointed and begged the secretary to telephone Frank Leah to ask him whether he could change his usual arrangements and give them a sitting.

While they were talking, Frank Leah himself entered, much to the secretary's surprise. "What brings you here today?" she asked. He replied that he had been psychically told he was wanted at the Grotrian Hall. Then, almost immediately, he walked over to Mrs. Mitchell's daughter and, drawing her a little aside, told her there was a spirit boy with her. She said that she knew of no such child. "It is your own child, but he has never lived on earth," replied Frank Leah. This information was correct for, some years previously, she had a miscarriage at an early stage of foetal development. "You also have a boy still on earth," continued the medium, who gave the approximate ages of the living and the "dead" boys.

After entering the séance room with his sitter, he drew the likeness of the child who never breathed on earth but whose growth had continued in the spirit world. The boy would have been about 11 years of age had his early parturition not occurred. It was at this age that he showed himself to the psychic artist. But Frank Leah was puzzled as to why the boy appeared to him dressed in an Eton suit and why the surroundings of Winchester College were psychically conveyed to him. He asked the sitter what the spirit was trying to indicate by these symbols. His mother understood. She had decided that, if a boy was born, he was to be educated at Winchester. The spirit boy also told the artist that he bore the same name as his ancestors – which is Michael. When the drawing was completed, it showed a distinct likeness to the sitter's earthly son, who was then about nine years of age. The artist, of course, had never seen him. "It was our first introduction to Frank Leah," declares Mrs. Mitchell, who adds that neither he nor the secretary of the Spiritualist Community knew who they were or where they lived.

At séances, Michael has told his relatives that there are wonderful colleges of instruction in the spirit world. Paul, his earthly younger brother, is considered at school to be a brilliant and advanced child for his age. He has been clairvoyant since his very early years and he says that his spirit brother helps him with his lessons. If Paul finds any difficulty in mastering a particular problem, he tells his spirit brother about it before retiring for the night. Inevitably, the problem is simplified in his mind on the following morning. At one time, Paul found mathematics most difficult. After he asked Michael to help him master the subject he made great progress, and, says Mrs. Mitchell, "he came out top in his examinations for mathematics."

Chapter 10

EXCEPT YE BECOME...

THERE are child guides and controls whose special qualifications bring them into direct contact with the material world. They are the spirit messengers whose labour of love is to provide mediums with evidence of Survival for those who mourn. In their close relationship with their earthly instruments these guides acquire a wide and sympathetic understanding of human behaviour and reactions. They are acquainted with mankind's suffering, sorrows and disappointments. These spirit children give unstinted service to all who come within their influence.

It is sometimes asked why child guides never seem to grow any older and continue through the years of their association with their mediums to talk in childish tones. Spiritualists are asked why these guides do not grow to maturity, since they affirm that children do grow up on the Other Side. The reason the childlike personality is retained in the case of guides and controls is a simple one. Children have simplicity of outlook. Because of their inexperience of life's problems and difficulties their minds are fresh and unbiased. The conventional behaviour adopted by the adult world has yet to be acquired. The young usually say, with complete frankness, what they think. They accept conditions and appearances at their face value.

When evidence is to be conveyed from the Other Side, it is necessary for the messages to be transmitted as accurately as possible. Spirit children are particularly well suited to pass on messages without distortion and misinterpretation. They do not suffer from adult inhibitions or self-consciousness. They are untroubled by doubts and considerations as to whether they are correctly transmitting the messages they are charged to carry. It is for these reasons that children who have passed on are particularly successful in giving evidence of their survival to their loved ones. Although children normally grow to maturity in the spirit world, those who have chosen to act as guides and controls voluntarily retain their youthful personalities in order that their childlike qualities, so helpful in transmitting messages, may continue to be utilised. Were they to relinquish their voluntary service of comforting the bereaved they would gravitate to their rightful sphere of consciousness in the spirit world.

I am acquainted with many of these young spirit guides. They have varied personalities, but two great qualities is common to them all. I have yet to know a child guide who does not radiate love, or whose aim is other than to comfort aching hearts.

One of the most lovable of these spirit children is Poppet, who first manifested through Lilian Bailey about eight months after the medium had developed trance phenomena. Lilian Bailey says of these early spirit manifestations, "I was controlled by a power which could only express itself in a very high-pitched tone and in an entirely foreign tongue." Being then in the immature stages of her now splendidly developed psychic powers, Lilian Bailey could not understand how such a personality, unable to speak English, could possibly be of service to the bereaved. She had no desire to encourage this unknown control to continue to manifest through her own mediumship. One day, Lilian Bailey was entranced in the presence of a man, an accomplished linguist. Poppet's strange, high-pitched speech was understood at last. The visitor later told the medium that he had been addressed in perfect Hindustani. The voice was that of a child, he said, who told him she had waited a long time for the opportunity of making herself understood. She wanted to learn the English language and had implored him to get Lilian Bailey's consent for her young daughter to act as tutor. Poppet spoke of the profound importance of her medium's future psychic work, and the necessity for Lilian Bailey to understand their relationship in this connection.

Lilian Bailey was somewhat disconcerted when she learned that her strange foreign control wanted to learn English from her little girl. Her mediumship was still rather new and perplexing, and she thought a closer contact with psychic conditions might make her young daughter nervous until she was better acquainted with the whole subject. But after further consideration, she rather diffidently told her daughter of the spirit's request. To her surprise, Dorothy was absolutely thrilled with the idea. She wanted the lessons to begin at once. Some weeks elapsed, however, before the "dead" child and the living one spoke to each other.

It happened one morning when Dorothy had gone to her mother's room and curled herself up at the end of her bed. "Almost immediately," says Lilian Bailey, "I found myself falling into trance. Fearing to dismay Dorothy I managed to say, 'It's the little girl,' before I was completely controlled." The child afterwards told her mother what transpired at this impromptu "sitting." Said the living girl, "The funny little voice kept giving little laughs and squeals. Then I laughed and she laughed. Then she patted me and I patted you, Mummy, as I didn't know what else to do. I pointed to myself and said 'Dorothy,' and the funny voice repeated 'Dolsfry.' Then I pointed to things in the room and called them by their names. The voice said the same as I said, as nearly as it could. I pointed again to you, Mummy and said, 'My Mummy.' The voice said, 'My Mummy, too.' Then it all went quiet and you came back."

This, the children's first meeting, was the beginning of a great friendship which endures to this day. "Dorothy is now a young woman," says the medium. "But the voice of the little spirit girl remains the same. She continues to refer to herself as 'My' instead of 'I', for that is the way she first learned to talk when Dorothy described 'My house, my dollie, my books.' After a while the two children understood each other very well. Naturally, Dorothy wanted to know her spirit friend's name. It proved to be one that the English child could not pronounce. The difficulty was quite a stumbling-block in their acquaintanceship until, one day, the 'dead' child spoke of somebody in her own world who always began, 'Now, my poppet;' when he addressed her. 'I like that name,' she said, and it was agreed between them that Poppet was an easier name to use than the foreign one which Dorothy could not pronounce. So Poppet she became and as Poppet she lives in our surroundings. She has become one of the dearest members of our family. The love that exists between her and Dorothy is inexpressible."

After their first meeting, conversations between the two children became more and more facile. Once, Dorothy told her beloved spirit friend, "We will always be own sisters for ever and ever." This delighted Poppet, who immediately replied, "Yes, own sisser Dolsfry." And even today, when Poppet wishes to acquaint Dorothy of her presence, she will say, in the direct voice, "Own sisser Dolsfry," before she gives the rest of her message.

I must agree with Lilian Bailey that Poppet has never completely mastered English. Her grammar remains amusingly unconventional.

The last time I talked with her, I asked whether she was pleased about a certain incident. "Oh, I'm delightmented!" she declared.

In the early days of Lilian Bailey's mediumship, her husband could not accept the case for Spiritualism. He was distinctly sceptical of his wife's psychic gifts. Knowing her great integrity of character, he could not, of course, doubt her honesty, but he believed that part of her subconscious mind was impersonating a child. Even when Poppet materialised for him at one of Helen Duncan's séances, he was still unable to accept her reality. One day, when Lilian Bailey and her husband were sitting alone by the fire in their home in Crewe, the medium was controlled by the spirit child. Mr. Bailey asked Poppet to furnish him with proofs of her separate individuality. "I shall be in London in a few days' time," he said. "If you are, as you tell me, a quite separate person from my wife, will you let me know, when I return home next Saturday, what I was doing at seven o'clock the day before?" Poppet agreed to give him this proof, but stipulated that he should not tell his wife about the pact.

At the time of the conversation with Poppet, Mr. Bailey had no idea what he would be doing the following Friday, the day of the test. Indeed, he deliberately put the conversation out of his thoughts so that there should be no question of telepathy between his wife and himself.

The following Friday, it happened that Mr. Bailey met a man whom he had not seen for a long time. His acquaintance invited him to dine at his home near Romford. They entered the house together. His host's little daughter, who was just about to be taken upstairs to bed, ran forward to greet her father. Then, seeing Mr. Bailey, the small girl thrust into his arms the doll she was holding. As she did so, he heard the clock in the hall strike seven. The chimes reminded him of the pre-arranged test with Poppet and mentally he noted what had just taken place.

The following day he travelled home. He did not tell his wife where he had spent the previous evening. Later, when Lilian Bailey was entranced by Poppet, he asked the spirit child, "What was I doing on the night of our agreed test?" "At seven o'clock you were nursing Barbara's dolly," she replied.

"Who is Barbara?" he inquired. "That is the name of the little girl where you went for dinner," she told him.

The experiment proved to be a greater success than he had dared to anticipate. Neither he nor his wife knew the child's christian name. She was always called Baby. When Mr. Bailey asked her father, "What is your little girl's real name?" he replied, "Barbara." This test convinced Mr. Bailey of the spirit child's separate identity and established a firm friendship between them. When he is away from home, he often "speaks" to Poppet and, if he asks her mentally for help, she always responds.

One of his friends, a stranger to his wife, suddenly became extremely ill and was hurried to the nearest hospital. On his way to inquire how this man was progressing, Mr. Bailey mentally asked Poppet to accompany him to the hospital to see whether she could do anything to help the sick man. The medium was entranced when her husband arrived home and Poppet instantly told him, "My went with you to the hospital. The man will get better. His head is bad, but he will get better." Although the sick man's life was despaired of, he made a complete recovery when a cerebral operation was performed. He is now in good health.

"I'm only a mite," Poppet will sometimes inform her earthly friends. But so large is the heart of this spirit mite that she is in truth a great influence in the lives of all who are privileged to possess her friendship.

Poppet's early history has been conveyed to her medium. When on earth she was a cripple and an outcast. She had received no love from her parents and after considerable hardship she passed to the Other Side at the age of four. This child who had been denied affection in the material world found in the Beyond the love she craved. As a flower opens to the sun, so her spiritual evolution expanded under the influence of the love now showered upon her in the Beyond. In gratitude and happiness she was stirred by the desire to radiate the affection she had found by serving those on earth who needed comfort and help. To fulfil this mission satisfactorily it was desirable that her now highly evolved spirit should reassume the personality of the child she had been when she first passed over, yet still retain the spiritual power her evolution had acquired. It is this great psychic force which enables her to remain closely linked with her medium, the earthly channel through which she operates. Lilian Bailey states, "It is the power of love which enables my little Poppet to stay so close to the dense vibrations of earth. Love was the foundation stone of her return to earth and her work. She has helped many dear children to return to their mothers and fathers.

In fact, to help anyone and in any way is the main joy in Poppet's life."

Lilian Bailey says that the most striking thing about Poppet is her natural, childlike behaviour. "She is a real little girl," says her medium, "not a ghostly apparition floating around in a flimsy garment. She has proved dozens of times over that children after physical death act in exactly the same way as they do on earth. They are not wafted into a superior state of life that suddenly transforms them into angelic beings."

To illustrate her point, Lilian Bailey relates the following incident. When Dorothy was 15 she was presented with a gold wrist watch. She loved it, of course, and when Poppet controlled her medium she was very thrilled with the sight of Dorothy's birthday gift. Rather wistfully she said, "My never did have a clock in my life, so can My have it for a whole day to look after it, Dolse?" The medium's daughter, who could not quite understand what having the watch for a whole day meant to her spirit friend, replied, "Of course you may have it."

A week later, on a Sunday morning, Dorothy raced downstairs to her mother and exclaimed, "I was putting my watch on when I saw it just disappear!" The medium could not quite accept her daughter's account of the incident. She felt the child's imagination was running riot. She went upstairs and searched high and low for the watch, moving and sweeping everything that might have hidden it. When she had changed every garment Dorothy was wearing, she was finally satisfied that the watch was certainly lost. As the day wore on the incident receded from her mind.

Some friends arrived in the evening and suggested a table sitting. Dorothy sat curled up in a big easy chair by the fire, rather bored with the proceeding and trying to read. Suddenly the table moved in her direction and hoisted itself almost on to her lap. Then the following message from Poppet was spelled out by table tilts: "My has got watch, it stop at ten. It come back tonight." The medium did not let her daughter out of her sight after the receipt of the message. When Dorothy's bedtime arrived, her mother accompanied her upstairs to her room. She opened the bedroom door and switched on the light. Simultaneously, another more powerful light overwhelmed them for a moment. "We entered the room," declares Lilian Bailey, "and Dorothy executed a little squeak of excitement, for there, on the eiderdown, lay the watch. It hands had stopped at ten o'clock.

It was very hot as though it had been clutched for a long time in a warm little fist. Poppet had kept the 'clock' for a day, as she had been told she could by Dorothy. But I rather imagine that the fact that it had stopped ticking troubled her a little."

Relating this experience reminds Mrs. Bailey of another incident which greatly amused her. It was an exploit one could expect from a little girl with a taste for bright colours. One lovely summer evening, the medium was upstairs alone in her room. Feeling at peace and in harmony with the world of nature, she gazed out of her window, which overlooked some fields. She was conscious of Poppet's presence, but paid no particular heed to the fact, for the spirit child was often with her. "Poppet must have been waiting for an opportune moment to manifest more closely," says the medium. "My abstracted calm, as I gazed across the fields, must have given her the chance to control me. The next thing I remember was finding myself sitting on a chair, still looking out of the window. As I glanced down, however, I was amazed to find that I had a piece of wide, flame-coloured ribbon draped across me. I had last seen the ribbon neatly folded in a drawer! Now, pinned on to this wide band was every conceivable kind of brooch and pin I had ever owned. On my hands were all the rings, good, bad and indifferent, that my daughter and I possessed. Bead necklaces were wound around my arms and neck. It must have taken some time for all these trinkets to be found and attached to me."

Lilian Bailey was so intrigued that she went over to her mirror and studied the general effect, which, she says, "was awful." In addition, she was startled to observe that her face was covered with a thick coating of powder. Her lips were heavily reddened, and there were dabs of red on both cheeks. She says, "Although I had to laugh at my grotesque appearance, I was extremely annoyed in case such a thing happened again in different circumstances. Afterwards, Poppet explained to Dorothy that she thought Mummy would be so pleased to see herself so beautifully dressed up. 'My did like doing it so much!' were her words. Here, in this spirit child, was the human little girl's love of dressing up. I was sorry afterwards that I had been cross with her, for it had given her so much fun."

Some years ago, Lilian Bailey owned a beloved cat named Topsy. Because the cat was expecting some kittens, she was being specially cared for by the whole family. One night she insisted on remaining out of doors. All efforts to get her to come into the house were unavailing. There was nothing to be done but leave Topsy in the garden. The household that night consisted of the medium, her daughter and a housekeeper.

"About two a.m.," says Lilian Bailey, "we were awakened by Poppet's voice calling each one of us loudly by name. She said, 'Get up, get up. Topsy has got four little babies under the lilac tree. They is wet and cold and will be deaded if you not get them.' We all heard her, but as can be imagined we were not, for a moment, unduly anxious to spring out of our warm beds and go down into a cold, wet garden. Dorothy sleepily said, 'I'm sure there must be a mistake, Poppet. The kittens aren't coming yet.' Truly, Dorothy had no authority for saying this, for she did not really know. However, Poppet's insistent voice drove us into dressing gowns and slippers. Armed with a torch, we sleepily filed downstairs and out into the garden. There, under the dripping lilac tree, was poor Topsy, with four half-dead kittens. She was crying piteously. How thankful we were that we had gone! We soon had them all tucked in a nice warm basket, where they revived. If our spirit companions will go to such endless trouble to save four new-born kittens, how much more would they attempt for us if we would but co-operate with them?"

After Poppet had helped Philip Clarke prove his survival to his parents – this story has been told in a previous chapter – a firm friendship was cemented between the two spirit children. Poppet often speaks of "my friend Philly" for whom she has considerable admiration. She thinks he is a clever little boy. Lilian Bailey tells a rather amusing story about their companionship. One morning, about one o'clock, the medium awoke with a start to discover her bedroom lights were switched on. Somewhat alarmed, she decided to go to her daughter's room to ensure that all was well. As she made her way through the landing and the hall of the house, she was astonished to see that all the lights were burning. She found Dorothy sleeping peacefully, but her room was also illuminated by the electric light. Lilian Bailey's concern increased. Her husband was away from home and she feared that somebody had broken into the house.

"Walking warily," she says, "I made my way to my housekeeper's room and told her there was a man in the house – I wonder why we women always think it's a man! My housekeeper rose in wrath, ready to deal with a hundred such intruders. She, too, was convinced that something was out of order, as we had seen that all the lights were switched off before we retired. The thought that spirit power of any kind was responsible for the burning lights did not enter my head. I never accept the idea that friends on the Other Side are always in evidence. I know this is not so. Well, we both toured the house, I having secured for myself a weapon of defence – the oak stair rod from the top stair. I am often amused at the thought of the comic pair we must have made. We found nothing wrong – apart from the fact that every light in the house was blazing. Windows and doors remained secured and fastened, as we had left them.

"We decided to go back to our beds, turning off each light as we passed. Finally, we went into Dorothy's room to make certain all was well with her. As we entered her room we heard a terrific thump which sounded like a chair falling over in my own bedroom. 'Goodness,' I said, 'that is where the wretched burglar has been all the time, in my room!' All our courage oozed, and we locked ourselves in Dorothy's room. She had awakened by this time. We decided, all three of us, to get into her bed, and here we spent the night. The next morning, full of courage again, we unlocked the door and went along to my room to view the scene of the crime. We found three books on the floor, and the bookcase was in great disarray. Otherwise everything was as usual."

Lilian Bailey goes on to say how, a little later in the day, Poppet spoke. Her voice was very subdued when she said, "My is very sorry to have given you fear. Philly Clarke told me he knew all about electric and My said My had the psychic power if he would show how to do it. My made his hand solid and he turn on the light downstairs. But the light make the psychic power go and Philly say if he turn it off in box" – meaning the switch-box in the hall which controlled all the house lights – "the light would go off. But they all come on instead and My not know what to do."

Her story made them all realise Poppet's dilemma, and her medium said she could not be cross about it. Poppet told them that as their minds had been in such a perturbed and flurried state she had not been able to control her medium and calm their fears. That is why she had disturbed the books in the medium's bedroom, hoping the performance would suggest her presence to their minds and allay their anxiety.

"This story proves how little death changes the mind of a child," says Lilian Bailey. "I wrote to Mrs. Clarke and asked her if her little son Philip had been interested in electricity when on earth. She replied that Philip was always fixing new lights and devices and had been tremendously interested in electricity.

"Many are the things Poppet has done," concludes the medium. "We often hear her feet racing over the corridors upstairs. Her high-pitched laugh comes to us, her voice tuning in with ours. Yes, and in dangerous and difficult times, we hear her say, 'Don't have fear, My will look after you.' We have much for which to thank God, but Poppet's love and companionship is, to us, His greatest blessing."

The coloured control of Louisa Bolt, the well-known voice medium, is another spirit child who has done much to prove Survival. Ivy has a most distinctive, mischievous giggle. I was present at a remarkable materialisation séance held by Louisa Bolt when we heard Ivy's characteristic laugh emanating from the closed curtains of the cabinet. The next moment she stood, fully materialised, before our eyes. Describing this séance, my husband relates how he knelt before the spirit child, holding in his hands a toy piano which she played. "She was just my height kneeling," he says. "I could see her black face, her white teeth, her thick lips and her long, pink tongue, which she insisted on showing to everybody present."

On another occasion I was present at a voice séance when Ivy promised Marcel Poncin, a gifted French artist, that she would visit his home on the following day and try to impress him to paint her picture. She achieved her purpose. The following day, the artist had a strong urge to paint the portrait of the child he had never seen. Within a few hours, the portrait was finished and he experienced the sense of exhaustion which always follows the completion of his inspirational paintings.

A few days later, Ivy manifested at her medium's voice séance and told the sitters that Marcel Poncin had painted her picture, a fact he had not told Louisa Bolt. Although delighted with her portrait, Ivy expressed disappointment that the artist had omitted to include a favourite bow on her hair. When Marcel Poncin learned of Ivy's regret, he repaired the omission and the spirit child was made happy. The picture now hangs in Louisa Bolt's séance room. Most people who see it comment on the striking brilliance of the eyes. The explanation was provided by a spirit communicator at a subsequent voice séance. Ivy had lived in the Southern States of America in the bad old days of slavery. She suffered cruel treatment and actually had her eyes burned out. In her new life on the Other Side, the "dead" child was compensated for the agonising destruction of her earthly vision by becoming the possessor of spirit eyes of exceptional beauty and luminosity.

It is regrettable that Bertha Hirst's ill-health has prevented her from continuing her public mediumship. Her child guide, Rosie, an expert communicator, has been the means of drying the tears of many sorrowing parents. For many years now, I have known this little spirit, whose generous nature has always been at the disposal of those who needed help and comfort. Rosie's simplicity of utterance contains deep truth and knowledge. More than one self-styled materialist has been affected by her wisdom.

Gladys Osborne Leonard's child guide, Feda, is well-known for the work she has done with her medium in proving Survival to scores of famous people.

It is sometimes asked why so many of these spirit children who act as guides were members of coloured races when on earth. The dark-skinned races, who lived close to nature, had, and still possess, great psychic power. Indians in particular were great masters of psychic laws, and their ability to communicate with ease has. rendered them invaluable in helping the "dead" to prove their survival.

Frank Decker, one of America's most famous voice mediums, has as one of his controls a boy named Patsy, who, when on earth, used to sell newspapers. In the spirit world this boy has continued to indulge his gamin wit and lively sense of fun. His pert "wisecracks" keep the sitters at Frank Decker's séances in good humour. Nervous tension amongst newcomers to a physical séance can ruin a potentially good sitting. Patsy's cheerful personality and amusing repartee usually puts all the sitters entirely at their ease. Patsy has been the means of furnishing proofs of Survival to scores of sceptics. He has provided them with outstanding psychic phenomena. So amazing are some of his exploits that they must sound almost incredible to those who have had no experience of the wonders of the séance room.

In the height of one summer I was present at a voice séance held by Frank Decker in New Jersey, U.S.A. The temperature of the cellar in which we sat registered 95 degrees. But the humid atmosphere, usually so deleterious to physical phenomena, did not subdue the flow of Patsy's witticisms. Owing to the intense heat, my husband had left his coat in a room two flights above the cellar. In one of the pockets of his jacket was an envelope which contained four picture postcards we had bought that afternoon at the New York Metropolitan Museum. When Patsy spoke to us that evening he indicated that he knew all about our purchase. He did more. His voice was silenced for a few moments. Then once again we heard his vivacious chuckle. "Hold out your hand," he said to my husband. Then, placing something in the sitter's upturned palm, Patsy proudly declared, "I have brought down the picture of Joan of Arc. I like your choice." Now although the medium had no knowledge of our visit to the Museum, we had bought, amongst other cards, a reproduction of Bastien-Lepage's painting which depicts Joan as she stood listening to the voices of her spirit inspirers. When the séance was over and the lights were turned on, we confirmed that Patsy had indeed brought us from the room upstairs the one postcard with a psychic significance. Later, my husband went up the two flights of stairs, and examined the envelope in which he had put the four cards. There were now only three, as we had anticipated!

Almost a score of spirit voices were heard at this physical séance. Each proved his or her identity. Describing this remarkable séance my husband writes, "Name followed name in quick succession, with Patsy 'chipping in' all the time with additional proofs to sceptics having their first experience of a voice séance. Usually the voices started softly, but quickly became loud enough to be identified by those who had known the speakers on earth. Patsy took particular delight in having fun with the sceptics. He forced them to remember forgotten incidents and names. To show Patsy's control over laws not yet understood by science, he played a tune on a harmonica which was inside one of my pockets. This was done while my hand covered the pocket, so that Patsy had no physical contact of any kind. The psychic phenomena exhibited at that séance were very varied, for later Patsy showed us his own spirit light, a soft ball of phosphorescence which appeared with surprising rapidity in different parts of the room."

Once whilst his medium was asleep in an adjoining room, Patsy fully materialised and talked on the telephone to some of his earthly friends. This was done in the presence of Mr. Joseph De Wyckoff, a well-known American business man. The story of this remarkable manifestation has been described by Dr. E. F. Bowers, one of the people who talked with Patsy on the telephone.

"This experience is unique in the history of psychic annals," says the doctor in *Psychic News*. "There is no possible way of explaining this amazing experience, except to declare – with the usual sangfroid of those who disbelieve, detest, or deny the phenomena of Spiritualism and the implications – that three people are deliberately not telling the truth, or that they are all suffering from identical hallucinations – something entirely unknown in psychiatrical symptomatology. These three people are my wife, Joseph Dc Wyckoff and myself, all of whom are honest, God-fearing people. Oh, yes, another participant in this demonstration I nearly forgot – the telephone operator of the American Telephone and Telegraph Company, who received the strange call, and put it through. She would probably have been stupefied with amazement or paralysed with fear had she known the identity of the person whose call she was transmitting. There is also the butler who answered the phone in De Wyckoff's home in Ramsey, New Jersey, and who was thunderstruck when De Wyckoff disclosed to him next day the identity of the person to whom he had been talking

Dr. Bowers describes how, on this memorable night, the telephone bell rang in his apartment at Riverside Drive, New York City. Not wishing to disturb her sleeping husband unnecessarily, Mrs. Bowers rose from her bed and lifted the receiver. Patsy's voice is unmistakable and unforgettable to those who have spoken with him. You can imagine Mrs. Bowers's momentary surprise when she heard his voice address her. "Hello, Ouise," he said. "I might say here," the doctor writes, "that Patsy makes it a uniform practice to address almost everybody who comes to Decker's séances by their first name – whether they be millionaire, dowager, dignified corporation lawyer, captain of industry or stenographer. He has the most photographic memory for names and incidents that only the most proficient of hotel clerks ever seems to acquire. My wife, of course, has spoken with Patsy dozens of times during the five or six years she has been intermittently attending Decker's séances.

Patsy joked with Mrs. Bowers for a minute or two, telling her that the telephone operator who had put him through had addressed him as "Ma'am!" – his youthful voice might easily be mistaken for a female one. Mrs. Bowers awakened her husband, who spoke with Patsy for a minute or two, telling the spirit boy how delighted he was to talk with him in such an unexpected way. Patsy said, "Wait a minute. I'll put Joe on and he'll tell you all about it." Mr. Joseph De Wyckoff then said to Dr. Bowers, "I couldn't wait to tell you of the most phenomenal demonstration I have ever witnessed in all my life. I am so thrilled I can hardly speak." He went on to say that he had visited Frank Decker in his apartment that night but had stayed so late that he decided to remain in town. The medium gave him a "shakedown" in his studio bed in the adjoining room.

Shortly after one o'clock, Mr. De Wyckoff was awakened from a deep sleep. Someone was shaking him by the shoulder. In the fairly bright illumination from a street arc lamp shining into the window, he saw a shape, dressed in a sort of messenger boy's trim fitting uniform and wearing a white cap. For a moment he was startled. Then he heard Patsy's familiar voice saying, as though in reproach, "You're not afraid of me, are you, Joe?" Mr. De Wyckoff immediately regained his composure on hearing himself addressed by the spirit friend he knew and loved so well. He answered, "Why, Patsy, my dear boy, how could I ever be afraid of you?" Patsy, well pleased with his reassurance, told him that his medium was in an excellent condition that night for the production of psychic phenomena. "And we're going to show you something you never saw before," he went on. "Now you close all the windows, so you don't catch cold. Pull down the shade and shut out as much light as you can. Put on your robe and sit up in bed and you'll see something." Patsy then moved swiftly across the floor and disappeared into Frank Decker's room.

Mr. De Wyckoff did everything as instructed by the spirit boy. He looked into the medium's room and was interested to note that he was in a deep trance and breathing stertorously. Presently, from the medium's room, which Patsy and his spirit helpers were evidently using as a "cabinet" to conserve and consolidate the ectoplasm, a feminine form floated towards him. Patsy's voice shouted from the adjoining room, "It's Madame Pav-a-lo-va, Joe." The spirit boy accented every syllable of the dancer's name and as Dr. Bowers comments, added one for good measure. "She wants you to sing some Russian songs and she'll dance for you," continued Patsy. Mr. De Wyckoff, who speaks many languages, began a little song used as a dancing tune by the peasants in the Ukraine.

As he sang, the fascinating, graceful figure of the spirit dancer began to swirl round the room. The form was covered in drapery.

The swift turning of the moving figure disclosed, however, the beautifully formed limbs and feet of the dancer who, during her earthly existence, had been seen by Mr. De Wyckoff a score of times in various capitals of the world. The dancing figure disappeared and Sir Arthur Conan Doyle, whom Mr. De Wyckoff had known intimately on earth, next spoke to him. Later, a spirit giving her name as Lucille Weston, who said she had been a concert singer before her "death," sang "Annie Laurie" in beautifully modulated tones.

Finally, Patsy said to his medium's guest, "Joe, come over here and sit on this couch, near the 'phone. I want to telephone your wife." The spirit boy was told it was unlikely that Mrs. De Wyckoff would be at home that night. Nevertheless, Patsy insisted on telephoning, saying, "It'll be good practice." Then the materialised boy lifted the receiver and gave the operator the telephone number of Mr. De Wyckoff's home in Ramsey, New Jersey. The butler's voice could be heard as he answered the call. The spirit inquirer was told that Mrs. De Wyckoff was "not at home." The boy replaced the receiver and appeared to be lost in thought for a moment. Then, with some delight, he announced, "I know. We'll call 'Doc' Bowers" – his somewhat disrespectful nickname for the doctor. "Do you know his number?" asked Mr. De Wyckoff? "Yes," answered Patsy, and for the second time that night, the spirit boy lifted the telephone receiver, placed it to his ear and talked into the mouthpiece. As the voice of the operator was heard answering the call, Patsy half-turned towards his earthly friend, saying, with some disgust, "She called me Ma'am," as though, boy-like, he resented the belittlement of his masculinity. The operator put him through to Dr. Bowers's home, little realising that the caller was a visitor from another world, a "dead" newspaper boy.

Those who sit with Helen Duncan are acquainted with Peggy, a spirit child who frequently materialises. Some years ago, Mrs. Hazeldine, of Newport, Fifeshire, asked Dr Montagu Rust to, attend her sick child. Despite his medical skill, Peggy "died" at the age of three and a half. But neither her mother nor Dr. Rust had seen the last of her, although her physical body was buried. Many times since, they have seen her fully materialised form and spoken with her, for Peggy has become the bright, vivacious little control of Helen Duncan. Peggy shows herself as a perfectly formed child. Her diminutive figure is in distinct contrast to the medium's other control, Albert, a "dead" Australian, whose masculine voice is very different from the Scottish child's treble. Peggy is an expert, experienced communicator. She sometimes puts in an appearance at other mediums' physical séances, where her distinctive voice is easily recognisable to those who know her.

At good materialisation séances, I have watched this spirit child execute a dance, keeping excellent time with her tapping feet. Sometimes she will sing a favourite song. I have seen her, in good red light, come some distance from the cabinet and fondle one of her earthly friends. This spirit girl is usually full of vitality and childish fun. At one Helen Duncan séance, two of my acquaintances received evidence from their "dead" child, Yvonne, who materialised before them. Just before the séance ended we all heard Peggy, behind the cabinet curtains, playing with something which sounded like a ball. "Are you playing with a ball, Peggy?" asked one of the sitters. Her answer was to throw something amongst us, saying pertly, "Here it comes; here's the 'ball'." We found she had thrown a tangerine amongst us – undoubtedly it was a pre-war sitting! Later, we learned that the fruit had been brought by psychic power from the home of Yvonne's parents, five miles away from where the séance was held. "How did you do it?" my husband asked Peggy at a materialisation séance we later attended. "I didn't do it at all," she answered, "that would be stealing. Yvonne took it, and it was her house." Nevertheless, I feel pretty certain that Peggy helped her!

Lili Alani, known as Topsy, the splendid spirit control of Pamela Nash, passed to the Other Side in her eighth year. Norman Swaine has recorded the touching story of this child in his *Autobiography Of Two Worlds*. Topsy's earthly life reads like a second *Uncle Tom's Cabin*. Through a series of misfortunes, her parents left the happy environment of their South Pacific home, and went to Brazil where their child was born into slavery. She became separated from her parents and was destined never to meet them again in her earthly existence. The youthful slave became the victim of the cruelty of a white overseer, whose vicious behaviour installed in the lonely girl a fierce and bitter resentment of white folk. She suffered such tortures that she prayed she would never grow up. Her plea was answered and she passed to the spirit world. The love and understanding she received on the Other Side aroused in her the desire to compensate for the intense hatred of the white races bred through earthly hardship and suffering. In the spirit world, she learned the true value of love and forgiveness. She elected to return to try to comfort those who suffered. Topsy chose, as her earthly instrument, Pamela Nash, through whose mediumship she continues her mission of bringing solace to aching hearts.

These, then, are some of the child guides and controls who have come back to help prove Survival. In many instances, these spirits knew little but misery and suffering in their short earthly lives. Yet, because on the Other Side they learned the joys of service, they became eager to assist in spreading the knowledge that there is no death.

Chapter 11

WHY THEY COME BACK

MOST "dead" children have the ability to communicate successfully with this world. It may be asked why young ones who have recently passed over desire to return to the troubled earth since their new environment is one of brightness and joy. If you are a bereaved parent, the question is superfluous, for you have the answer. "Dead" children return to earth because love calls them and will not let them go until a mother's tears have been dried, and a father's heart comforted by this reunion. "Dead" children come back to prove their survival to those who previously believed them gone for ever. They return to the séance room of their own free will to share their new experiences and adventures with the loved ones they have left behind. They come back to keep in touch with all the interests that held them on earth. They still want to know how their earthly relatives and playmates are faring. The séance room is a place of sacred but joyous reunion where natural law operates and enables the gossamer veil that divides the two worlds to be lifted.

It is perfectly natural that "dead" children still retain their interest in the world they have left. Have no fear that the time they spend with you disturbs their happiness on the Other Side. These bright young spirits lose nothing by their reunion with earthly relatives and friends. On the contrary, compassion, sympathy and the desire to comfort sorrowing hearts are qualities that enrich the soul and unfold the spiritual nature of a child.

There are "dead" children who return to this world for other reasons than reunion with relatives. They may be impelled to come back because of something left undone before their transition. They may need assistance that only earthly individuals can render.

We have been told that the psychic power which generates in a séance room is seen by the "dead" as a beacon of light. Spirit children who need earthly help are led towards this psychic beam. And, if the conditions are good, such children can manifest in the séance room and make their presence known. They are often unknown to the mediums and sitters when first they return. Later they frequently become regular visitors to the circle which first attracted them.

It was in this way that "Jimmy Sparrow" became attracted to

Lady Caillard's circle. A ten-year-old slum child was run over and killed by a motor lorry in the East-end of London. Although in the spirit world this neglected boy had truly found "heaven," compassion brought him back to this world – compassion for the sparrows he used to feed. He was afraid they would go hungry without him.

The "dead" child manifested about ten days after his passing at Lady Caillard's home circle through the voice mediumship of Louisa Bolt. Through the trumpet came an unknown boy's voice, which, in cockney accents, ejaculated, "Bli'me, where am I? Is this a palace? I say, I've got the wind up, I 'ave. Does the King live 'ere?"

Lady Caillard assured him that it was her home. "Bli'me!" repeated the voice. "Ain't it lovely 'ere? The boss said I could come. My name's Jimmy. I'm in a lovely place now. I ain't 'ungry no more. The only thing is about my sparrers – they ain't being fed now. I say, Missus, can you feed my sparrers?" Lady Caillard promised she would look after the birds whose welfare so concerned him. "Ain't that a bit of all right?" said Jimmy. "I'm 'appy now."

Several times after that first visit, "Jimmy Sparrow" – as he became known – spoke through Louisa Bolt's voice mediumship. He was so grateful for what was being done for his "sparrers." On earth he used to share his food with them, even though there was little of it. The sparrows were his friends, all he had to love, for his parents drank too much and had no interest in him. Jimmy's language, when first he spoke at the circle, was not very edifying. He came back as he had passed on, using the colloquial slang and habitual bad language he had heard in his home environment. But one day he said to Lady Caillard, "Missus, I ain't going to swear no more. I go to school now, and they tells me I mustn't swear. I'm so 'appy now. I'm awful glad I'm 'dead.' No one cared for me before. They are ever so kind to me 'ere. Do you know I've got a collar and tie now? I say, Missus, why are they so good to me 'ere?" He was told, "Because, Jimmy, you loved your sparrows here and love means everything. Now you are going to have all the love you ought to have had on earth."

Jimmy made great and rapid progress in the spirit world. He was an expert communicator, almost from the first. When my husband visited Lady Caillard's voice circle, "Jimmy Sparrow" announced his intention of speaking at his own voice circle the next time it met. The "dead" boy said he would try to prove his identity. When subsequently our own séance was held, the medium was not told beforehand of my husband's visit to Lady Caillard's circle.

Soon after the medium was entranced, a boyish cockney voice came through the trumpet. "Jimmy," it announced. "Which Jimmy?" we asked. "Bli'me!" came the reply, confirming that the little boy had kept his word. With typical gamin wit Jimmy commented on the room, the furniture and other objects. He spoke of his beloved "sparrers" and his happiness in the knowledge that their needs were being met. Finally he announced, "I must go now, my wind is getting short."

The following day he manifested through Louisa Bolt's voice mediumship and told Lady Caillard he had kept his promise to my husband. Incidentally, as neither she nor the medium had been told about Jimmy's success in fulfilling his promise, he had provided an added test to the one arranged.

Children who have had little or no contact with this world sometimes come back to learn the value of contrast between their own spiritual lives and those of earthly individuals. This experience gives them an understanding of inequalities of existence and develops in their nature qualities of love and compassion.

In *The Dead Have Never Died*, an American lawyer, Edward C. Randall, records how a neglected waif, who had passed over in infancy, was brought back to earth to gain experience. A spirit teacher told the "dead" girl's story. "We taught and carefully guarded and schooled her," he said, "in the pure conditions of our sphere, until she approached womanhood. But she had no contrasts, therefore she could not judge of the relative purity and delights of her environment. In order that she should be able to enjoy her home and the glories of our world, it was necessary for her to have a knowledge of earthly conditions." The spirit teacher was therefore instructed to conduct the child back to earth from time to time. At first, she could hardly endure earth's gross conditions. "She could not understand how people could exist in such dark, crude elements," said the spirit communicator. "But as I led her along from one condition to another, over the road she would have gone had she remained on earth for the ordinary allotted period, I said to her, 'Had you lived your time in the body, you would have been in the condition in which you see these people.'

I also told her that they would look gross to her when they reach the spirit state, but that in course of time they would improve enough to assume the state of purity and peace that she enjoyed."

The spirit child was conducted through the homes of the rich and cultured; she saw the children of the poor and ignorant. "We tarried," explained the spirit communicator to Edward C. Randall, "until my little charge thoroughly learned the different environments of children on earth, and the great contrasts between their homes, daily life and schooling, and those in spirit life. This child had never known anything but innocence and purity, and she was far removed from the ordinary conditions of the childhood of earth. It was long before she could, in any degree, recognise it as a reality."

"Dead" children often retain affection for certain of their earthly toys. Invisible to the non-clairvoyant sight, spirit children sometimes return to their old surroundings to renew acquaintance with their favourite possessions. It is usually the worn-out battered playthings that hold pride of place in a child's affections. We have learned from spirit communicators that a "dead" child may be distressed, when returning, to discover that a favourite, decrepit doll, or a maimed, semi-bald teddy bear has been removed from the familiar surroundings.

Sometimes these children bring other playmates with them when they return. Their spirit friends may never have breathed in our world, but have been brought from the Other Side to become acquainted with the joys that earthly children experience. It is necessary that a spirit child, who is to become a guide or control of a medium, should understand the mentalities and reactions of children who have sojourned in the physical world. Only by such understanding can a guide successfully interpret a message and help a child who has recently passed on to give evidence of Survival.

The natural psychic faculties of children often become atrophied in later life. Youthful supernormal experiences fade from the memory as the years advance. Many adults have forgotten the psychic experiences of their childhood. Others, upon reflection, are able to recall these events. I have known Mrs. A. J. Farr for the better part of my life. Yet it was only by a chance conversation that a recollection of her spirit playmate was disclosed to me. The name of her companion was Lucy. Mrs. Farr can recall her demeanour and appearance so clearly that even today she remembers her long, flowing hair, as well as the dress, with a blue sash tied around her waist, that she wore. Her memory of the games they played is undimmed. Lucy's reality was accepted without question. The fact that she did not belong to the physical world had no disturbing effect on the mind of the earthly child. She took her spirit friend entirely for granted. There was no more doubt of her existence than of all the other children in her environment. Mrs. Farr cannot now explain why she never mentioned her spirit playmate to her mother. Possibly she may have known her parent would be unsympathetic.

Many mediums retain the memory of the spirit friends of their youth. "From my earliest childhood," says Edith Clements, "I have always been conscious of the presence of other people who were apparently not seen by those with whom I might be conversing. I have always had 'unseen' boy and girl playmates, but my parents used to laugh at me because they thought it was pure imagination on my part. I could never make them understand I really had child playfellows."

Christmas time is usually one of the happiest seasons for children in the material world. Often, months beforehand, the young make their simple, but so important, plans for Christmas. They prepare elaborate secrets and surprises for their parents and friends. Their excitement grows as the season of good will approaches. Whether the purely religious festival is celebrated or not, Christmas is usually a season of happiness and joy for the young. In normal circumstances Christmas is holiday time, a vacation period for children and parents alike. It is a season when devoted families are reunited, when adults cast off business worries and difficulties and recapture the carefree attitude of youth, so that they may join wholeheartedly in the children's celebrations. The Christmas tree adds to the excitement of giving and receiving presents. Joyful memories of this time of the year are implanted deeply in the hearts of the average children. They are memories linked with parental love and home associations.

Although in the spirit world happy festivals are also held for the little ones, is it not perfectly understandable that the thoughts of "dead" children turn to their mothers and fathers at Christmas time? Is it not equally natural that, as the season approaches, the loving thoughts of parents go out to the young ones who have passed over? It is in the séance rooms that they meet again, to recapture and renew their Christmas associations, and exchange personal messages of love and good will.

In normal times, Spiritualists hold Christmas séances expressly for the benefit of "dead" children. A decorated tree, laden with gifts, is generally provided by the sitters. Do you think this is foolish? Why should we present toys to spirit children who cannot take these earthly gifts away with them when the séance is over? Have we not affirmed, too, that "dead" children have everything for their happiness in the spirit world? Such questions may naturally cross your mind. Let me explain. The young are no less human because they have passed over. Their characters and personalities are unchanged. They still experience the same joyful reactions to exciting surprises. That is why we, on earth, do our best to give spirit children a happy time when they return to their earthly relatives and friends at the joyous season. To these Christmas séances, too, come "dead" children who, in their physical lives, yearned for toys they were never able to possess.

It may be difficult for the sceptic to believe that a "dead" child actually retains the etheric counterpart of the material toy he or she chose at a Christmas séance. The duplicate of the gift is reassembled in the spirit world where it continues to delight the little one. An etheric, or astral counterpart of a physical object may be likened to a thought-impression, since, in a mental world, a thoughtform is tangible and real. Even on earth, material designs are created by the process of mental imagery. The very words you are now reading are products of thought-forms which have been translated into material symbols. They are physical expressions of mental impressions. Since material objects are products of mental imagery, it should not be too difficult to adjust our minds to the idea that physical objects have non-physical counterparts.

I have attended a number of Christmas séances held by gifted mediums. At these physical séances I have heard scores of "dead" children talking and laughing excitedly as they made their choice of toys from the Christmas tree. Paper parcels have been unwrapped by little fingers, toy trumpets have been sounded, tops spun, mechanical toys worked, amidst a babel of excited comments from "dead" children. These Christmas parties are not quiet affairs! The "dead" children's excitement is every whit as intense, the joys as profound, the thrills as natural as the normal reactions of any children at an earthly party.

After the Christmas séances, the presents are usually sent to children's hospitals, or distributed amongst the little ones whose worldly circumstances are not flourishing. The repercussions of these spirit parties can go still further. A "dead" child named Margaret Hambling told, at a séance held at the Stead Bureau, that the toy given to her at a previous Christmas séance established a link of friendship between her and an earthly child who later passed to the spirit world. The toy chosen by Margaret was sent, after the séance, to a sick girl. "This child had very little to brighten her life," said Margaret. "I found out how much I could help her. I saw how patient she was, where I had always been impatient on earth. Then she came to this side and we are now great friends."

Another spirit girl, choosing a doll at this same séance, told the sitters that the doll was destined to be given to a little earthly girl then lying in hospital. The "dead" girl explained that, during sleep, the sick child would visit her in the spirit world, where a closer link of friendship would be forged between them. Thus, not only does the same earthly gift bring happiness to a "dead" and a living child, but it may establish an alliance which is of mutual benefit to the two children.

Some of the gayest Christmas parties imaginable used to be held by Mrs. A. E. Perriman, that gifted voice medium who has herself now passed to the spirit world. No doubt she has met again some of the "dead" children who, year after year, were warmly welcomed at her Christmas parties. Perhaps because the medium's control, Belle, was herself a child, she could so well understand the reactions of the spirit children. Belle would act as hostess or "usherette in chief" to the little ones. When she thought a "dead" guest had lingered long enough near the Christmas tree, the little control would ring a bell which hung on it. The tinkle of the bell was a signal to the spirit child to make room for the next young visitor who would be anxiously waiting his or her turn to receive a toy. Usually there were so many gifts on the laden tree that the surplus toys would be piled up all around it.

The medium was not in trance most of the time and was able to join the sitters in their conversation with the spirit children. No trumpets were used at Mrs. Perriman's séances. The young spirit guests distinctly and clearly reproduced their earthly voices.

The first voice to be heard at one of these parties belonged to a small girl. "I'm Betty Chester," she declared. "Please can I take a dolly?"

"Certainly, you may," answered a sitter.

"I'm Jimmie Tasker," came the voice of a boy. "I should like a motor car." Frank Hobson wanted a different variety of toy. Then Rosie, a small girl, asked if she could have "the pink dolly." At this stage a little diplomacy was used by Belle and the sitters, for another child wanted the same present! However, finally appeased, they made way for yet another "dead" child. This little girl fervently desired a toy "pinnano," as she called it. When she was told the piano was hers, she proceeded to strike the notes with more good will than good execution.

Because of the medium's powerful physical gifts, the spirit children were sufficiently materialised to handle the toys. A spirit boy named Desmond followed the little pianist. He spoke with a marked Lancashire accent. He chose, as his present, a toy trumpet which, he affirmed, was the same shape as his father's pipe. "Show me the trumpet," said one of the sitters. "Your eyes cannot see," answered Desmond – for the séance was held in darkness. But the "dead" boy took the trumpet to the sitter who had spoken so that he could feel the shape of the toy. This action seemed to be the signal for other toys to be placed on the laps of various sitters, the spirit children describing the kind of gifts they were passing to and fro.

Meanwhile, the voice of a small girl plaintively demanded, "Can I have the mummy dolly?"

"Yes," she was told, "you can take the mummy dolly." A laugh was raised when she continued guilelessly, "Then if I can have the mummy dolly, may I have her three children dollies, too?"

We listened to the voices of these "dead" children, urging each other to choose their presents. "Come on, come on," they cried excitedly as we heard them moving the branches of the Christmas tree – a sturdy one, fortunately. Meanwhile, trumpets were sounded, whistles were blown, concertinas and toy pianos were played. When a sitter put a record on the gramophone, the voices of the spirit children enthusiastically accompanied the melody. Then a little girl named Peggy Rowland said she would like to dance for us. Soon, we saw a psychic light, spherical in shape, move across the floor. "Can you see my feet?" demanded the voice of Peggy. "Yes," we answered, for now the globular shape had become a pointed shaft of light moving gracefully and rhythmically, indicating that Peggy was on her toes.

Dozens of children spoke in the direct voice that night before the séance came to an end. When the lights were switched on, we saw the disordered room, strewn with toys and strips of paper. The Christmas tree was practically denuded of the presents it had borne. Many of the sitters still held the toys that the spirit children had passed to them during the séance.

Would that all those who believe their children are gone for ever could attend one of these happy Christmas parties. The parents would realise that "dead" boys and girls have not lost their capacity for enjoyment, and remain as human and alive as before their passing.

Chapter 12

"THY SERVANT HEARETH"

TIME-HONOURED records have provided instances of psychic ability in children. In the Old Testament we read how the child Samuel, whilst in the charge of the priest, Eli, was composed for sleep one night when he heard his name called. "Here am I," he answered and ran to Eli, thinking the priest had summoned him. "I called not," said Eli, "lie down again." Yet a second time the voice spoke his name, and once more the child hastened to Eli saying, "Here am I, for thou didst call me." The priest answered, "I called not, my son, lie down again."

It was not until the child had been addressed for the third time by the spirit voice that it became evident he was hearing clairaudiently. And, obeying Eli's injunction, when the voice called his name again, Samuel answered, "Speak; for thy servant heareth."

At that time, even Eli believed that the spirit voice came direct from God. Today, we consider that Samuel was probably addressed by a highly evolved spirit who found in the young psychic an instrument through whom messages from the Other Side could be delivered to Eli.

The course of history was changed when, in her thirteenth year, the psychic powers of a French country girl blossomed. She has become renowned as Joan of Arc. Whilst standing in her father's garden, Joan clairaudiently heard a voice. She looked in the direction whence the sound came, "from the right towards the church," as she afterwards described its location. There she beheld a radiant spirit being who, with gentle words of wisdom, revealed to the simple girl the mission she was to fulfil. Throughout the short span of earthly years that followed her first psychic revelation, the Maid faithfully carried out her promises to her guides. So human in her weaknesses, so superhuman in her spiritual strength and knowledge, Joan went to the stake confident that her spirit counsellors would sustain her during the fiery ordeal and receive her spirit when it was released from physical bondage.

The Roman Catholic Church, through whose instrumentality she suffered the "death" of an unrepentant heretic, afterwards rehabilitated her. Finally, she was canonised as a saint of "the Catholic Church of which she was always a submissive child…" surely an ironic sequence of events.

The "miracle" of Joan's aptitude for leadership, her military genius, her "supernatural" qualities, her prophecies, and all the contradictory elements in her behaviour continue to perplex both historians and theologians. Only those who are conversant with psychic laws know the one answer to the whole case. "Saint" Joan of Arc, a village girl from the Vosges, was a medium – that is all.

We respect the great psychics of the past. But supernormal manifestations are no more sacred because they bear the stamp of antiquity or historical importance than are psychic phenomena of the present day. The Great Spirit had no message for the world of yesterday that He has not made equally available to the modern age. Those whose clairaudient ears are attuned still hear spirit voices. Those whose inner sight is opened still see clairvoyant visions. The implication of the messages from Beyond remains the same because spiritual truth is consistent and unchanging.

We are not in a position to judge or assess contemporary history, since we ourselves are living it. Yet I have little doubt that amongst the younger generation of today are those destined to help build a better world because of the revelations they are receiving from the Other Side. Supernormal perception in children is not an abnormality. It is a perfectly natural faculty which should be fostered and encouraged. Alas, only too often, such qualities are misunderstood by ignorant or unsympathetic parents. Fortunate is the psychic child whose parents encourage the gifts which will bring solace and joy to sorrowing hearts.

The sensitive reactions of most mediumistic children render them extremely susceptible to the conditions of their environment. They suffer intensely if their supernormal faculties are not understood.

When they disclose a supernormal experience, these children are sometimes scolded, by well-disposed but uncomprehending relatives, for telling untruths or being "too imaginative." They begin to feel a sense of shame in being different from others around them and they cease divulging their psychic experiences. Sometimes, in this way a perfectly normal and God-given faculty becomes atrophied or stifled.

How inconsistent are some parents in their attitude to the young! They encourage their children to accept without question the authenticity of "Father Christmas." Indeed, a male parent may even feel aggrieved if, one Christmas Eve, his child awakens unexpectedly and recognises Daddy in the role of Santa Claus!

In the toy department of a popular general stores I heard some parents trying to convince their sensitive-looking child that a genial but somewhat seedy-looking individual, dressed in a tawdry robe and wearing false whiskers, was actually "Father Christmas" who had arrived that day with his team of reindeer. I must admit the little boy looked very unconvinced. It is probable that if the same child described to his parents a bright spirit he had seen, clad in raiment far superior to that worn by the shoddy impersonator at the stores, he would be told, "You must have been dreaming." Many children are informed that, while they sleep, their guardian angels watch over them through the night. But supposing a child does really see his guardian angel, who is none other than his own spirit guide. "You mustn't make up stories, dear," says his mother when he relates his psychic experience. "What ideas that child gets into his head!" she may say to her husband. "I'm sure he doesn't mean to tell untruths. It's just his vivid imagination. Perhaps he got too excited today. I had better give him a dose of medicine."

"Like the vast majority of children," writes Margery Lawrence, "I came into this world with a very definite consciousness of the Other Side and the beings that inhabit it. But, as I grew older, and found that the things I saw and heard and innocently retailed to my elders were laughed at or else flatly described as 'lies,' in time I learnt to say nothing about my 'other world' contacts. And, as I grew older still, and became interested in things like frocks and fun and flirting, my early sensitiveness became temporarily obscured, as so often happens."

The recollections of the youthful experiences of many mediums are not happy ones, mainly because their supernormal faculties were misunderstood by their parents. Estelle Roberts received her first psychic manifestation when she was eight years of age. She was playing a game with her sister in a third floor room of a house in Isleworth, Middlesex. Suddenly, the window darkened as though a thunder cloud had cast a shadow there. Estelle looked up and beheld at the window a knight clad in shining armour. In his hand he held upright a glistening sword. His visor was thrown back, and his features were clearly visible to the astonished girl. The most astounding thing of all was that he appeared to be suspended in mid-air. Fearing that the apparition would frighten her sister, she cried out, "Oh, don't look, don't look!" Childlike, her sister promptly turned her eyes to the window and ran screaming from the room. The whole psychic manifestation then disappeared as suddenly as it had appeared. Describing this happening in the *Sunday Pictorial*,

Estelle Roberts declares, "That was my first experience of seeing a spirit. I didn't know what it was or what it meant. But it made such an impression on my childish mind that, although I have since seen and spoken to thousands of spirits of all kinds, all ages, from all generations, my recollection of the knight in armour has never for one moment been blurred or confused."

The immediate effect of this vision was not a pleasant one for Estelle. When her sister ran in fear from the room, their father rushed upstairs. Estelle told him of the apparition. He scolded her for being naughty and said she must have seen a bat! Meanwhile her sister had fainted. When she was revived, she, too, told her father of the knight in armour. And she also was chided by her disbelieving parent for making such a fantastic claim.

Estelle Roberts says that this, her first supernormal experience – which her sister also shared – was an indication of the mediumistic work which later absorbed all her energies. Not until she was in her fifty-first year did she see the same shining figure of the knight. This time the spirit visitor disclosed his identity. "It is a name," writes the medium, "you would know instantly if I could tell you."

In her schooldays Estelle was neither particularly brilliant nor very stupid. She was an average girl for her years – with one outstanding exception. She constantly heard spirit voices. "They were talking to me all the time," she writes. "The other children called me a dreamer. Little they knew that, when I seemed too abstracted to take notice of what they said, I was listening to conversations far more fascinating. My parents, good sound Church people, deliberately suppressed my psychic tendencies. I do not blame them. They knew nothing about Spiritualism. Neither did I. They attributed my apparitions and voices to imagination."

Edith Clements is another gifted medium whose youthful psychic faculties were misunderstood by her parents. In fact she received medical treatment for the "complaint" of clairvoyance! Nobody in her surroundings understood the psychic powers of the child. In *Psychic News*, Edith Clements writes of the psychic manifestations of her childhood, "My mother sometimes told her friends of my strange ways and remarks about the things I saw. They came to the conclusion it was because I was such a delicate child and so thought it best to humour me!"

After her brother "died" as the result of an accident, Edith gave her mother a shock when she insisted that she had seen him after his burial.

The medium thus describes the events that immediately followed the accident: "A policeman arrived in the early hours of the morning when everybody was sound asleep. The constable's sharp knock aroused me, and, although our bedrooms were at the back of the house, I rather startled my parents by exclaiming that it was a policeman knocking and that something had happened to my brother Harry. My father found this to be correct when he interviewed the officer, who advised my parents to go to the hospital to see my brother.

"Several weeks elapsed, and my poor mother was recovering from his tragic death, when I suddenly 'saw' my brother before me, looking exactly as he did before his 'death.' I was simply terrorstricken at the vision and rushed screaming into my mother's arms, telling her we must have buried the wrong man. 'Harry is not dead,' I said, 'because I have seen him!'"

Thoroughly alarmed by the child's behaviour, the mother immediately took her to the doctor. Poor little Edith was promptly ordered to be kept in bed in a darkened room, and a bottle of soothing medicine was prescribed.

The childhood experiences of another well-known medium were more fortunate than those of Edith Clements. Grace Cooke saw clairvoyantly when she was seven years old, but she belonged to a family of Spiritualists who understood her gifts and were able to help her develop them. The little girl was not at all disturbed the first time she saw a "dead" individual, for her father had often spoken of her spirit mother. Grace thought it perfectly natural and normal that she should see those who had passed over. Her budding mediumship was fostered and encouraged and, when she was 13, she was entranced by an African girl named Lulla. This same control still manifests and helps the medium in her clairvoyance.

T. E. Austin, another medium, began, at the age of four, to talk with someone unseen by the rest of the family. When his mother asked him to describe his invisible friend, he gave her an accurate description of his brother who had "died" before his own birth. The psychic child had never been told by his family about this brother, of whom there was no photograph in existence.

Writing in the *North Mail and Newcastle Chronicle* a contributor states that her grandson, a child of five, clairvoyantly saw his great-grandfather who passed over many years before the boy's birth. The writer tells how her grandson, who was paying her a visit, had just been put to bed when he suddenly jumped up and pointed to a photograph of her father which hung in the room. "See that man, Grandma," he said. "Well, after you had gone downstairs last night, he came and told me you were his little girl." Thinking the child's imagination was running riot, she asked him whether the man was the same size as the photograph-about eight inches high. "Oh, no," answered the little boy, "he was a very big man." The contributor declares, "My father was six feet two inches, and died 35 years before this child's father was even born."

Psychic faculties sometimes function in the sleep state. In the early hours of the morning, a seven-year-old Edinburgh boy awakened his mother, Mrs. Warrington, telling her he had dreamed that his brother was drowned. The mother hastily dressed herself and travelled to Granton, where her elder son was camping. Upon her arrival at Granton, she met a woman who told her the bodies of two boys had just been removed from a salt water quarry. One of the drowned boys was Mrs. Warrington's son. He had met his "death" in the manner indicated in the "dream" of his younger brother.

Mediumship is often hereditary. A ship's officer, who writes under the nom de plume of "Jazon," tells in *Psychic News* of his son's clairvoyant powers which began to function when he was little more than a baby. "Jazon junior, aged two years," writes the officer, "was playing one day on the hearthrug of my home in Barry. From where he sat he could not see the roadway through the window, which in any case was eight feet above the ground. My mother-in-law, a well-known South Wales clairvoyant, Antoinette, was sitting in the room sewing, and no one else was present at the time."

Suddenly, the child looked up from his play and said, "Man." His grandmother asked, "Where?" The little one pointed to a corner of the room by the fireplace. His grandmother clairvoyantly saw the spirit form of her own guide. He stood smiling at the two psychics, the child and his grandmother.

A few minutes later, the little boy exclaimed, "Anuzzer man," and pointed in another direction. Again his grandmother saw clairvoyantly the form of a massive Indian, complete with his trappings and feathered head-dress. The tall figure rather scared the little child, who ran to his grandmother's side for protection.

The boy's father arrived home a few weeks later. One morning, in his parent's presence, the child dragged a large encyclopaedia from the bookcase and began to look at the pictures. "Suddenly," writes Jazon, "he came staggering to me, the large open book almost as much as he could carry. Pointing to a picture, he said, 'Man of de fedders.' He had found a large coloured plate depicting three Sioux Indians with their feathered head-dresses. Immediately his young mind had seen the resemblance in them to the Indian he had seen clairvoyantly some weeks before.

"Can the shallow-minded sceptics who are so ready to cry 'Fake' and 'Fraud' as the only explanation of clairvoyance, raise these cries to explain this episode? Could they accuse their own innocent babes of such fraudulent precocity that would permit the staging of such a fraud by a two-year-old? It is inconceivable and positively absurd even to think that a child so young could plan such a deception, and support his first actions by the pretence of fording a picture, indicating and agreeing with what had evidently frightened him before. Rather it is more reasonable to take the natural and easiest explanation, that the child really saw the spirit forms. 'I did hear the voice,' said the child Samuel. 'I did see that Indian,' said little Jazon in effect as he pointed to the picture."

Clairvoyant descriptions given by children strongly support the case for Survival. Sometimes a child, little more than a baby has, in an unconcerned manner, addressed a "dead" relative, of whose passing it has been kept in ignorance, being considered too immature to understand the meaning of death.

Camille Flammarion's *Après la Mort* contains an account written by Madame Anne E. Carrere. She states that her husband promised that if he passed over before her he would return and provide, if it were possible, evidence of his survival. "Our family," she writes, "was composed of my husband, myself, and my daughter, who had been left a widow very young, with three small boys, the eldest of whom was five, the second three and a half, and the third two and a half. During the sad period of my husband's last illness, some friends had taken the children, from whom their grandfather's death was concealed. The youngest of the three, Guy, was at table with our friends at the hour of the funeral, when he suddenly sat up in his chair exclaiming: 'There is Grandpapa outside the window! Look!' And so saying, he got down from his chair and ran to meet him.

"Next morning, he was playing in a room next to mine and I heard him suddenly laughing and shouting joyfully, 'Grandpapa! My Grandpapa!'" She went into the adjoining room and found the little boy clapping his hands with joy as he laughingly said, "Look at Grandpapa, how fine he looks dressed all in white. And he has shining clothes!"

Hearing the noise the child made, Madame Carrere's sister-in-law and the servants came into the room. They were amazed at his exclamations. They asked him whereabouts in the room he saw his grandfather. The little boy seemed astonished that they were unable to see what was so tangible to him. He exclaimed in surprise, "There! Don't you see him?" His grandmother writes, "His eyes were fixed on a point in space at the height where a man's face would be; then we saw his eyes follow something that was rising in space, and he exclaimed, 'Ah! Now Grandpapa has gone away.'"

Not only, as Madame Carrere points out, was this child only two-and-a-half years of age, but he had no idea of the meaning of death.

F. W. H. Myers records in his classic, *Human Personality And Its Survival Of Bodily Death,* the touching story of a child who, after the "death" of his infant brother, persistently spoke of the baby's presence. The children's mother states that when her baby "died" at the age of eight months, Ray, her two-and-a-half-year old son, was then in perfect health. But every day that followed the infant's passing, this boy, little more than a baby himself, would say, "Mamma, Baby calls Ray." He would come running to her from his play, repeating, "Mamma, Baby calls Ray all the time." He would awaken her from sleep saying, "Baby wants Ray to come where he is; you must not cry when Ray goes, Mamma, you must not cry, for Baby wants Ray."

"One day," says the mother, "I was sweeping the sitting-room floor, and he came running as fast as he could through the diningroom, where stood the table with Baby's high chair, (which Ray now used) at the side. I never saw him so excited, and he grabbed my dress and pulled me to the dining-room door, jerked it open, saying, 'Oh, Mamma, oh, Mamma, come quick; Baby is sitting in his high chair.'" His mother followed him to the room, but as soon as Ray opened the door he said, "Oh, Mamma, why didn't you hurry? Now he is gone; he laughed at Ray when he passed the chair, oh, he laughed at Ray so nice. Ray is going with Baby, but you must not cry, Mamma."

Ray soon became very ill. Neither nursing nor medicines were of any avail. He "died" two months and seven days after his baby brother's passing.

Chapter 13

THE GIFTS OF THE SPIRIT

THROUGH the mediumship of a timid girl in her early teens, Abraham Lincoln was encouraged to issue his famous Emancipation Proclamation of 1863 which abolished slavery. The young medium who helped to change the history of the New World was Nettie Colburn.

Lincoln never publicly declared that he was a Spiritualist, but neither did he deny the fact. After his election to the Presidency, an article was published in an American newspaper stating that Abraham Lincoln was a Spiritualist. The information was based upon the statements of a well-known New York medium named H. B. Conkling, who claimed that the President had sat with him on numerous occasions. When the newspaper article was brought before Lincoln's notice, in the hope that he would contradict the affirmations, he merely replied, "The only falsehood in the statement is that half of it has not been told. This article does not begin to tell the wonderful things I have witnessed."

Nettie Colburn, whose mediumship had functioned ever since she was a small child, gave her first sitting to Abraham Lincoln at the White House. She recalls the occasion in *Was Lincoln a Spiritualist?*, a book she wrote in later years, after she became Mrs. Maynard. She tells how, upon being introduced to the President at the White House, she was shy and awkward, until he eased her embarrassment by his kindly manner. He asked her questions about her mediumship, and told her he had already heard good accounts of her psychic ability.

"While he was yet speaking," says the medium, "I lost all consciousness of my surroundings and passed under control. For more than an hour I was made to talk to him, and I learned from my friends afterwards that it was upon matters that he seemed fully to understand, while they comprehended very little, until that portion was reached that related to the forthcoming Emancipation Proclamation.

"He was charged with the utmost solemnity and force of manner not to abate the terms of its issue, and not to delay its enforcement as a law beyond the opening of the year. He was assured that it was to be the crowning event of his administration and his life; and that, while he was being counselled by strong parties to defer the enforcement of it, hoping to supplant it by other measures and to delay action, he must in no wise heed such counsel, but stand 'firm to his convictions and fearlessly perform the work and fulfil the mission for which he had been raised up by an overruling Providence.'

"Those present declared that they lost sight of the timid girl in the majesty of the utterance, the strength and force of the language, and the importance of that which was conveyed, and seemed to realise that some strong masculine spirit force was giving speech to almost divine commands."

When the young medium regained normality, she was standing before the President. He was leaning back in his chair while, with arms folded on his breast, he gazed intently upon her. Nettie was childishly confused at the situation, and did not remember immediately the circumstances in which she found herself. Then, recovering herself, she heard one of those present say to Lincoln, "Mr. President, did you notice anything peculiar in the method of address?" The President glanced up quickly at a full-length portrait of Daniel Webster – a former Secretary of State. "Yes," he replied, "and it is very singular, very!" Another person, a Mr. Somes, asked, "Mr. President, would it be improper for me to inquire whether there has been any pressure brought to bear upon you to defer the enforcement of the Proclamation?" Lincoln replied, "Under these circumstances that question is perfectly proper, as we are all friends. It is taking all my nerve and strength to withstand such a pressure."

"At last," writes the medium, "he turned to me and, laying his hand upon my head, uttered these words in a manner that I shall never forget, 'My child, you possess a very singular gift; but that it is of God, I have no doubt. I thank you for coming here tonight. It is more important than perhaps anyone present can understand.'"

A short time after his first sitting with Nettie Colburn, President Lincoln abolished slavery with his famous Emancipation Proclamation – an act which freed men's minds, as well as their bodies, from narrow prisons of ignorance and prejudice.

Lincoln had many subsequent sittings with the young medium who had been used by the spirit world to give him courage and tenacity of purpose in the face of much opposition. On one occasion she was entranced by the spirit of a Dr. Bamford, who advised the

President to visit the front during the Civil War. The "dead" man pointed out that a very precarious state of affairs existed at the front, where General Hooker had recently taken command. He affirmed that the army was completely demoralised, the men refusing to obey orders or to do their duty. A general retreat was threatened. The position described by the doctor was a great surprise to everyone at the sitting, except President Lincoln, to whom the grave words were addressed.

"You seem to understand the situation," said Lincoln, "can you point out the remedy?"

"Yes," answered the doctor, "if you have the courage to use it."

"Try me," answered the President, with a smile.

The spirit declared that the remedy was simple. "Being so simple," he said, "it may not appeal to you as being sufficient to cope with what threatens to prove a serious difficulty. The remedy lies with yourself. Go in person to the front; taking with you your wife and children; leaving behind your official dignity, and all manner of display.

"Resist the importunities of officials to accompany you, and take only such attendants as may be absolutely necessary; avoid the highgrade officers, and seek the tents of the private soldiers. Inquire into their grievances; show yourself to be what you are, 'The Father of your People.' Make them feel that you are interested in their sufferings, and that you are not unmindful of the many trials which beset them in their march through the dismal swamps, whereby both their courage and numbers have been depleted."

Abraham Lincoln answered quietly, "If that will do any good, it is easily done." The spirit replied that it would be a successful undertaking. "It will unite the soldiers as one man," he asserted. "It will unite them to you in bands of steel. And now, if you would prevent a serious, if not fatal, disaster to your cause, let the news be promulgated at once, and disseminated throughout the camp of the Army of the Potomac. This will stop insubordination and hold the soldiers in check; being something to divert their minds, and they will wait to see what your coming portends."

Abraham Lincoln at once said, "It shall be done."

In the conversation that followed the spirit told Lincoln that he would be re-nominated and re-elected to the Presidency. Abraham Lincoln smiled sadly, "It is hardly an honour to be coveted," he said, "save one could find it his duty to accept it."

When, after the séance, one of the sitters asked him whether the conditions were truly as bad as had been described by the spirit, the President said, "They can hardly be exaggerated; but I ask it as a favour of all present that they do not speak of these things." He went on to say that he had just received messages from the front which depicted the state of affairs to be pretty much the same as the "dead" doctor had described. "We were just having a Cabinet meeting regarding the matter," he said, "when something, I know not what, induced me to leave the room and come downstairs when I found Mrs. Lincoln in the act of coming here. I felt it might be of service for me to come; I did not know wherefore." As he made this statement, he leaned forward in his chair with bowed head. Then, looking up suddenly, he said, "Matters are pretty serious down there, and perhaps the simplest remedy is the best. I have often noticed in life that little things have sometimes greater weight than larger ones."

And so, once again, the wise counsel from the spirit world given in trance by a young, inexperienced girl, was acted upon without delay by Abraham Lincoln. He visited the Army of the Potomac, where he was received with great enthusiasm, as the spirit doctor had prophesied. The situation was saved.

In her book, the medium recalls her last interview with Abraham Lincoln. He referred to the fact that he was being warned by psychics of a plot to take his life. He found it difficult to absorb the warnings, saying to Nettie Colburn that he did not think there was a knife or a bullet made that could reach him. "Besides," he went on, "nobody wants to harm me." At these words, a feeling of unaccountable sadness overcame the girl and she replied, "Therein lies your danger, Mr. President your over-confidence in your fellow-men." A look of melancholy shadowed his face as he answered quietly, "Well, Miss Nettie, I shall live till my work is done, and no earthly power can prevent it. And then it doesn't matter so long as I am ready – and that I ever mean to be."

A few weeks later, the President was assassinated. His work on earth was ended, but in the spirit world, like another famous American opponent of slavery, "his soul goes marching on…"

Since his passing, Abraham Lincoln has returned many times to this world, utilising the same channels of spirit communication he had himself so often used on earth. Through different mediums, he has displayed his continued interest in the fellow-men for whose betterment he worked so unceasingly during his lifetime. Before Hannen Swaffer sailed for America on one of his visits, Abraham Lincoln spoke to him at our home circle. "I was one," he said, "who understood this truth, who could retire from the clash of political things and obtain the guidance of the spirit in my hours of torment and conflict. I freed the slaves. You are helping to put an end to slavery, too. I was opposed by all the reactionary forces who could not understand that wrong was wrong, no matter how long it had been upheld... Everything which hinders freedom must be swept away."

At a séance held in America, Lincoln impinged his likeness on a psychic photograph taken on the anniversary of his birthday. At the same séance, he controlled a medium through whom he confirmed his previous message to Hannen Swaffer delivered in England. Lincoln left on record an inspiring trance address before he left the medium.

The walls of the White House have enclosed many a séance given by the young medium, Nettie Colburn, to America's most honoured President, Abraham Lincoln. The spirit world was ever ready to sustain him in his hours of trial. Words of counsel and encouragement helped him perform his great tasks. Because America is passing through dark days as I write these words, I cannot believe that Abraham Lincoln is far from his beloved people. I do not doubt the presence of his noble spirit guiding and counselling another great President of high moral principles and dauntless courage. In his arduous labour to preserve the threatened liberty of the people of his country, I cannot doubt that President Roosevelt is beyond the influence of his great predecessor, Abraham Lincoln, who so dearly prized the right of the common man to be free.

The psychic career of Cora Tappan, one of Spiritualism's greatest trance orators, began at the age of 11, when she was unexpectedly entranced.

It would appear that the Other Side was determined to establish modern Spiritualism through the instrumentality of children. Cora's mediumship developed only a short time after the Fox sisters discovered their ability to communicate with the "dead."

In her home in Wisconsin, U.S.A., Cora was sitting alone in a garden arbour, preparing on her slate a composition for her school mistress, when she was suddenly controlled. She regained normality to discover that her slate was covered with unfamiliar handwriting which took the form of a letter beginning, "My dear Sister." The child ran to her mother with the slate, declaring, "Someone has written all over my slate while l was asleep." The mother read the message. It was a communication from her sister who passed over when they were both children. The letter referred to scenes of their childhood and ended with her sister's signature. Cora's mother was profoundly moved by this communication. She kept the slate, but made no particular comment to her daughter who, childlike, dismissed the incident from her mind.

But a day or two later, whilst sitting by her mother's side, Cora was again entranced. At first, her mother thought the girl had fainted, and tried, without success, all kinds of restorative measures. Then, observing that Cora's hand was moving, her parent thought of the earlier communication. She brought a slate and placed a pencil in the hand of the entranced girl. Soon the mother read, "We are the spirits of your departed friends. We will not harm your child, but we have found a method of holding converse with the earth."

This incident was the beginning of Cora's mediumistic activities. She developed trance speaking, clairvoyance and psychic healing. For a period of four years, Cora was controlled by a "dead" German physician. Through the entranced lips of the child, unacquainted with any language but her own, the spirit spoke in his native tongue, in French and in Italian. They found the "dead" doctor was fully experienced in every branch of the medical profession. From her village home in Lake Mills, Cora visited the sick who desired the ministrations of her spirit medico. Fully controlling the young medium, the physician examined his patients, prescribed for their ailments and often healed them by making psychic passes.

A carpenter who lived in the village received an injury to his finger, which rapidly swelled and became highly inflamed. After several days of excruciating pain, his medical attendant lanced the finger to the first joint. Gangrene developed and the carpenter implored his wife to send for Cora. His request was refused, for his wife believed that Spiritualism was unholy. The doctor also refused to have anything to do with such a suggestion. Nevertheless, the young medium was awakened from her sleep by the "dead" physician, who caused her to arouse her father and bid him accompany her to the carpenter's house. Together they called on the sick man, whom they found in the utmost agony. His own doctor sat by his side, unable to alleviate the pain which for three weeks had been increasing in intensity. Cora, now completely controlled by the "dead" physician, asked the earthly doctor for his case of instruments. The request was definitely refused by the owner, who hastened from the house, declaring that if his patient "died," he would not be responsible. But he left without his instruments. The entranced girl unbound the sick man's hand and arm. Then, having selected a suitable instrument for the operation, she proceeded to cut out the gangrene from the patient's finger. When the wound had received complete and skilled attention, the hand and arm were re-bandaged. Magnetic passes were made and, before the medium left the house, the patient was sleeping peacefully.

For two weeks the carpenter received a daily visit from the young medium. At the end of that time he was better. He regained the use of his hand, only the joint of the finger remaining a little stiff.

Although the psychic occurrences which took place in the presence of the two Fox sisters a few years previously created something of a sensation, trance speaking was still unknown. Cora was the first medium to exercise this psychic faculty. It was not at first realised how important was this development of her mediumship which permitted the "dead" to prove their survival by speaking through the lips of a living instrument. Cora Tappan, a simple child, raised amongst rural surroundings, was, within a few years of the discovery of her gift of trance oratory, to confound enormous New York audiences by her impromptu eloquence. By the time she was 16, the now famous young medium had travelled throughout the United States, delivering learned lectures to scientists and theologians. Without previous preparation, Cora was able, under spirit influence, to answer the most elaborate and highly involved questions put to her on matters of history, science, moral and religious ethics.

One of the most remarkable cases of spirit control that has ever occurred is that of Mary Lurancy Vennum, a young medium who was controlled for nearly four months by a "dead" girl. When the spirit finally left the medium, Lurancy's sick body was completely restored to health. The case, a classic in the history of Spiritualism, is known as the "Watseka Wonder." The details of the occurrence are fully substantiated by reliable and authoritative witnesses. The story begins in Watseka, Illinois, U.S.A., when Mary Lurancy Vennum, a child of 13, began to fall into cataleptic trances. She would lie in a state of complete rigidity for hours, as though her body was already dead. Whilst in this condition, her mind seemed to function on two planes of existence at the same time, and she would describe the spirit people with whom she was associating whilst her physical body lay inert. This cataleptic condition did not come to an end for about two months.

Then, nearly two months later, Lurancy began to suffer excruciating pains, which would rack her body at intermittent periods throughout the day. This condition lasted for two weeks. Then her former trances were resumed and her clairvoyance functioned again. Meanwhile, the unfortunate girl became subject to obsessions. It was thought by many of her relatives and friends that she was insane. The Methodist minister at Watseka was anxious to get her admitted into an asylum. Naturally, the girl's parents were averse to their child being condemned to such a fate. When some local Spiritualists, Mr. and Mrs. A. Roff, interested themselves in the case, Lurancy's parents agreed to have the obsessed girl examined by a medical practitioner who was a Spiritualist. She was controlled, in the presence of Dr. E. W. Stevens, by a spirit entity of low intelligence, who at length left her body, which then collapsed on the floor.

By skilled magnetic action, the experienced Spiritualist doctor was soon in communication with the sane, serene mind of Lurancy, now free of obsessing influences. She answered Dr. Stevens's questions rationally and with understanding. She declared she was "in heaven" and said she was sorry she had allowed spirit entities of low intelligence to control her physical body. The doctor suggested that she should seek the co-operation of a spirit of high evolution for this purpose. She appeared to be only too anxious to comply with this suggestion.

Declaring that there were many "dead" individuals in her environment who would be glad to help her, Lurancy said that Mary Roff, in particular, was anxious to co-operate. Now Mary was the "dead" daughter of Mr. and Mrs. Asa Roff, who had introduced Dr. Stevens to the Vennums. Mary had passed to the Other Side 12 years previously. In her earthly life she had suffered from the same kind of attacks as Lurancy. And so, Mary Roff agreed to take control of Lurancy's body in order to protect her from the influences of the unreasonable entities who had formerly controlled her. Thereafter, the "dead" girl, tenanting the body of the living one, went to live with the Roffs as their daughter – as indeed she was. The action caused bitter hostility from some of the local bigots. The Methodist minister, the Rev. B. M. Baker, told Mr. Vennum, "I think you will see the time when you will wish you had sent your daughter to the asylum." A relative, encouragingly informed Lurancy's father, "I would sooner follow a girl of mine to the grave than have her go to the Roffs and be made a Spiritualist."

From the very beginning of Mary Roff's control of the living girl's body, a remarkable change took place in the physical condition. Gone were the cataleptic fits and the wild, ungovernable moods. It must be pointed out that, before their interest in Lurancy's case, Mr. and Mrs. Roff were comparative strangers to the Vennums, the two families having lived in completely opposite limits of the city. In her new home with the Roffs, the girl seemed perfectly happy, recognising everybody and everything that Mary had known in her earthly existence. She referred to incidents that had occurred in Mary's life many years previously. Yet she recognised none of the relatives of the Vennums, and had no knowledge of any of the friends or neighbours whom she had known before Mary Roff took control.

Once, when the girl saw, for the first time, a head-dress that belonged to Mary Roff, she said, "Oh, there is the head-dress I wore when my hair was short." Another time, she said to Mrs. Roff, "Where is my box of letters?" The box she asked for contained letters and odd souvenirs belonging to Mary. While she was looking through the box with delight, recognising different relics of the past, the girl said, "Why, here is the collar I tatted. Why did you not show me my letters and things before?" The collar had been worked by Mary Roff before Lurancy Vennum had even been born. Almost every day that passed, some evidence of Mary Roff's continued tenancy of Lurancy's body was provided. Not once, during the whole period of time she lived with Mr. and Mrs. Roff, did an incident occur leading them to doubt the reality of their "dead" daughter's presence. Lurancy Vennum's earthly body was a perfect vehicle for spirit control. Often, the Roffs held a séance, when other "dead" individuals manifested for a short time.

At one of these séances, Lurancy Vennum came back and manifested through her own physical body vacated by Mary RoffLooking wildly round the Roff's séance room she said, "Where am I? I was never here before." After a few minutes, Mary Roff returned. Once the "dead" girl told the Roffs that her brother Frank would have to be watched carefully during the coming night. He was then in perfect health, but at two in the morning he was attacked with a spasm and congestive chill. Taking charge of the situation, Mary Roff said, "Send to Mrs. Marsh's for Dr. Stevens." She was told that the doctor was not there, but she insisted, and when Mr. Roff went to Mrs. Marsh, he found the doctor was there. He had arrived, unannounced, the previous evening. Meanwhile, the "dead" girl had taken complete charge of the case. The doctor afterwards declared that her brother's life had been saved by her prompt action and ministrations.

On one occasion when the Roffs were holding a séance with a Dr. Steel and other friends, Mary released her control of Lurancy's body and entranced Dr. Steel, giving definite proofs of her identity.

All this time, the physical condition of Lurancy Vennum's body continued to improve. Finally, it was restored to complete health and Mary announced that soon Lurancy would be coming back. She stated the time and date when the change would be effected. She visited neighbours and friends, bidding them farewell. It was arranged that Mary's sister would be present when the change occurred and then take the returned Lurancy, first to Mr. Roff's office, and next to her own parents' home. After an affecting scene, Mary promised that, although she would soon be leaving her earthly home and friends, she would often return from the Other Side and manifest her presence whenever she could. She would be with them in times of sorrow and they would feel her closeness to them. The "dead" girl still seemed loath to go, and her sister had already started for Mr. Roff's office before the change was made. For a moment Lurancy spoke, and offered to retire again to enable Mary Roff to have a few more moments with her earthly relative. So Mary returned and accompanied her sister until they reached their father's office. The final change took place at the time predicted, and Lurancy Vennum returned permanently to her own physical body. She declared she felt as though she had been to sleep, yet she knew this was not so. Lurancy addressed Mr. Roff with the deference of any well-behaved young girl in the presence of an adult of slight acquaintance. But when she met her own parents and her brothers, she greeted them with warm affection and gladness.

Such is the remarkable history of Mary Lurancy Vennum. She loaned her body to a spirit who, after four months' tenancy, restored it to her, completely cured of all former ills. Mrs. Vennum stated that her daughter was now "perfectly and entirely well, and perfectly natural." She went on to say, "Lurancy has been smarter, more intelligent, more industrious, more womanly and more polite than before. We give the credit of her complete cure and restoration to her family, to Dr. E. W. Stevens and Mr. and Mrs. Roff... We firmly believe that had she remained at home she would have died, or we would have been obliged to send her to the insane asylum... Several of the relatives of Mary Lurancy, including ourselves, now believe she was cured by spirit power and that Mary Roff controlled the girl."

A number of American newspapers commented on this remarkable case. They all accepted the facts, although they did not profess to understand the implications.

Eight years after this remarkable experience, Mr. Asa Roff was asked to give a history of the case to date. He stated that for four years after the event, Lurancy continued to live with her parents. Then she married and moved to Kansas. He wrote, "She has never had any occasion for a physician since she left us, never having been sick since then. Neither has there been a return of the old symptoms – no pain, no fits." To demonstrate that his daughter continued thereafter to remain under the care of unseen helpers, her father said, "At the birth of her first child she was entranced. Her eyes were turned heavenward, a beautiful smile played over her face. The work of deliverance went on painlessly, and not until the new soul voiced its presence did she show any sign of consciousness of what had occurred." When she was informed that her baby had been born, she seemed overjoyed to know that spirit assistance had prevented her from experiencing the agony of childbirth.

When such occasions were possible after Lurancy's marriage, a séance with Mr. and Mrs. Roff would be arranged. Then, once again controlling the body of the girl she had helped to cure, Mary Roff would talk for a brief spell with her beloved parents.

Lewis Carrol did not devise stranger adventures for his own "Alice in Wonderland" than those that have actually occurred to Alice Bell Kirby, of Louisiana. This 13-year-old medium recently became a sensation overnight when the physical phenomena which occurred in her presence became publicised by American newspapers and radio features. It only needed the presence of this girl in a room for tables to move by themselves and a piano to slide across the floor. The young medium and other sitters have been levitated. Whilst blindfolded, Alice answered written questions. In her presence, the whole room frequently vibrated and furniture rattled.

Mr. Eric E. Montgomery, a Spiritualist who has studied this girl's physical phenomena ever since it began, gave, in the *Journal of the American Society for Psychical Research*, an account of an astounding séance he attended, when a table was levitated in broad daylight in the open air. Alice was demonstrating her psychic powers to seven people in her home, when the table she was using "walked or bounced" on to a porch, then came down the steps and moved across a lawn at the back of the house. From there it travelled 200 yards across a meadow to a barn and up a sloping drive to the second storey of the barn.

Then the young medium said, "Sit me down." The visitors watched the girl being lifted by an unseen agency more than two feet in the air, turned round, and then gently seated on the table which slid across the floor with Alice perched upon it.

At another séance, at the house of a friend, not only was Alice levitated, but also James, the ten-year-old son of one of the sitters, was also raised from the ground. Alice took the boy by the hand and together they were lifted to the top of a table. The same magnetic force once lifted Alice to the top of a table which had been placed upon another one.

At a subsequent sitting which Mr. Montgomery attended, Alice Bell Kirby was blindfolded by a man who submitted 12 written questions. The young girl rewrote and correctly answered the questions. She told the investigator his correct age and the number of children in his family. She quoted correctly how many were boys and how many were girls, and gave their ages. She also told him the number of his wife's brothers and sisters, and their ages. She told him which of them were on earth and which of them had passed over. All the other sitters were then asked to go out of the room. Alone with Alice, the investigator held her hands whilst the girl was raised in the air by psychic power and placed upon the top of a table. After this investigator had left, another séance was held during which the table slid right across the floor to one of the walls. It then raised itself into the air as high as anyone could reach. Compelled by the same psychic force, it appeared to float, and then to be pulled back across the room before it came down again.

In one corner there was a piece of furniture covered with small articles. Many of them were transferred to the sitters' laps. While this was happening Mr. Montgomery felt concerned because nothing had been placed in his hands. The next moment, something nudged against his hands on the table. It was the largest vase in the room!

Wishing to test the medium, an investigator took Mr. Montgomery's watch from his pocket. He altered the hands and placed the watch on the table, asking the unseen powers that it should be rewound and correctly set again. All the sitters clasped hands round the table. They heard the watch being rewound and afterwards found it had been reset to the correct time.

At another sitting when eight women were present, a spirit voice asked them to remove their rings and pile them on the table. The lights were put out, but, in the dark, every ring was correctly placed on the hand of its owner.

Thousands of people have witnessed the psychic phenomena which takes place in this girl's presence. Mr. Montgomery says that she sits more to please her friends and guests than to become famous. She discovered her mediumship at the age of ten. She had been playing dominoes, when, tired of the game, she and her friends experimented with a table, copying her mediumistic grandmother. Alice found, at this, her first sitting, that the table would move with no apparent cause. Then the other physical phenomena began to occur.

There have been many cases publicised where phenomena of the furniture-moving and crockery-breaking type have occurred in the presence of young people during their puberty. The disturbed psychic powers of a child, going through this stage of life, sometimes attracts spirit entities of an undeveloped and prank-loving order who are responsible for causing this distress and discomfort. Sometimes an experienced medium has been asked to help overcome these disturbances. Usually, with the aid of the medium's spirit guides, the disturbances have abated.

In the Victorian age, when materialistic beliefs were more prevalent, the remarkable mediumship of Florence Cook, a girl of 15, first convinced the renowned scientist, Sir William Crookes, that Survival could be demonstrated under strict scientific conditions. Although many of his colleagues did not share his views on Spiritualism, honours and distinctions continued to be showered upon Sir William after he had freely reported his convictions. Throughout a long lifetime, he never deviated from his affirmations concerning spirit communication. He never concealed his knowledge, based on the evidence he received through the channels of mediumship. In 1898, Sir William received the greatest distinction that can be conferred on a scientist. He was elected President of the British Association, a position he held for three years. Later still, he became President of the Royal Society.

When Florence Cook first called on the scientist and asked him to test her psychic powers, this young girl may not have been aware that she was to become one of the most famous materialisation mediums in the world. It was largely due to the remarkable cooperation between the medium, her guide, Katie King, and Crookes that the scientific tests were so successful.

Many and varied were the experiments carried out by Sir William to prove the separate and distinctive individuality of Katie King. At times she fully materialised in the glare of electric light and revealed herself as a lovely young woman who had temporarily assumed the flesh-and-blood appearance of an earthly individual. So powerful was Florence Cook's mediumship that white light did not destroy the phenomena. In electric light, Crookes took 44 photographs of the materialised girl. For this experiment, five complete sets of photographic apparatus were used. These cameras, of different sizes and structure, were all operated at the same time, but from different angles. One of the most amazing spirit photographs in existence shows Sir William Crookes, the earthly scientist, standing arm in arm with the "dead" girl, Katie King.

"During these photographic experiments," writes Sir William, "Katie muffled her medium's head up in a shawl to prevent the light falling upon her face. I frequently drew the curtain on one side when Katie was standing near, and it was a common thing for the seven or eight of us in the laboratory to see Miss Cook and Katie at the same time, under the full blaze of electric light... One of the most interesting of the pictures is one in which I am standing by the side of Katie; she has her bare foot upon a particular part of the floor. Afterwards I dressed Miss Cook like Katie, placed her and myself in exactly the same position, and we were photographed by the same cameras, placed exactly as in the other experiment, and illuminated by the same light. When these two pictures are placed over each other, the two photographs of myself coincide exactly as regards stature, etc., but Katie is half a head taller than Miss Cook, and looks a big woman in comparison with her."

"But photography," writes Sir William Crookes, "is as inadequate to depict the perfect beauty of Katie's face as words are powerless to describe her charms of manner. Photography may, indeed, give a map of her countenance, but how can it reproduce the brilliant purity of her complexion, or the ever-varying expression of her most mobile features, now overshadowed with sadness when relating some of the bitter experiences of her past life, now smiling with all the innocence of happy girlhood when she had collected my children round her, and was amusing them by recounting anecdotes of her adventures in India?"

Sir William had no fear in introducing his own children to the natural phenomena of Spiritualism! Apart from his scientific experiments, Katie was a familiar and welcome guest in his own home circle.

Dr. Gully, a well-known medical man, was also photographed whilst he was timing the pulse of the materialised Katie King. Sir William measured the differences in height of the guide and the medium when they stood together. He also testified that Katie's neck was perfectly smooth to the sight and to touch, while on the medium's neck was a large blister, which was distinctly visible and rough to the touch. Several marks on the medium's face were absent from her guide's. Katie's ears were unpierced, while Florence Cook wore ear-rings in her perforated ears. Katie's complexion was fair, the medium's was very dark. Their hands were of different shapes and sizes. The medium had very dark brown hair. The lock of hair which the scientist was once permitted to cut from Katie's luxuriant tresses was a rich golden auburn.

When, on one occasion, Crookes tested the pulse-beat of the materialised Katie he found it to be beating steadily at 75. After the séance, the medium's pulse was going at the usual rate of 90. Katie's heart-beat was more steady than Florence Cook's, and, when tested, the guide's lungs were found to be sounder than her medium's. Florence Cook, at that time, was under medical attention for a severe cough.

Once, replying to the suggestion that he might have been the victim of a fraud, the scientist replied, "To imagine that an innocent school-girl of fifteen should be able... successfully to carry out for three years so gigantic an imposture as this, and in that time should submit to any test which might be imposed upon her, should bear the strictest scrutiny, should be willing to be searched at any time, either before for after a séance, and should meet with even better success in my own house than at that of her parents, knowing that she visited me with the express object of submitting to strict scientific tests – to imagine, I say, the Katie King of the last three years to be the result of imposture, does more violence to one's reason and common sense than to believe her to be what she herself affirms."

The time came when Katie's work with her medium was to terminate, for another guide was due to take her place. Sir William bade a moving farewell to the guide who had done so much to help him proclaim to the world his Spiritualistic knowledge. Katie had asked Florence Cook to provide a large basket of flowers and ribbons, which she distributed to her earthly friends at this last séance.

In her account of the final materialisation, Florence Marryat writes, "Mine, which consists of lilies of the valley and pink geranium, looks almost as fresh today, nearly seventeen years after, as it did when she gave it to me." The flowers were accompanied by a little note of farewell written by the materialised spirit.

Sir William Crookes, too, records the moving farewell scene. After conversing with him for some time, the "dead" girl walked across the room to her medium. "Stooping over her," writes the scientist, "Katie touched her and said, 'Wake up, Florrie, wake up! I must leave you now.' Miss Cook then woke and tearfully entreated Katie to stay a little time longer. 'My dear, I can't; my work is done,' Katie replied. 'God bless you!' She then continued speaking to Miss Cook... For several minutes the two were conversing with each other till at last Miss Cook's tears prevented her speaking."

Following the guide's instructions, the scientist went forward to support the sobbing medium. When next he looked about him "the white-robed Katie had gone."

When the honour of Presidency of the British Association was conferred upon him in 1898, Sir William Crookes, in his presidential address, said, "Upon one other interest I have not yet touched – to me the weightiest and farthest-reaching of all. No incident in my scientific career, is more widely known than the part I took many years ago in certain psychic researches. Thirty years have passed since I published an account of experiments tending to show that outside our scientific knowledge there exists a Force exercised by intelligence differing from the ordinary intelligence common to mortals... I have nothing to retract. I adhere to my already published statements. Indeed, I might add much thereto."

And, in 1917, two years before his passing, the famous scientist made this statement in regard to spirit communication: "I have never had any occasion to change my mind on the subject. I am perfectly satisfied with what I have said in earlier days. It is quite true that a connection has been set up between this world and the next."

Physical phenomena were at their best in that Victorian era. In those days, when to see was to believe, it was deemed necessary by the Other Side to concentrate their powers in producing psychic the phenomena that could be seen, heard and touched. Those were days of wonderful physical phenomena, where fully materialised spirits manifested under the most ordinary and commonplace conditions. They were seen in daylight, and were sometimes able to walk about, unrestricted by the usual séance-room conditions.

The days of materialisation beliefs have largely disappeared. Scientists have themselves destroyed the case for materialism that they once supported. New facts have now been discovered and the honest worker in the field of science must follow truth and abandon that which is outworn and discredited.

In view of our increased knowledge of non-physical realities, the spirit world has ceased to concentrate so largely on purely physical phenomena. There has been a decline, for example, in the number of materialisation mediums, and an increase in the number of psychics specialising in mental phenomena. The quality of mental mediumship has improved tremendously since the days when a schoolgirl revealed to a scientist that life after death is an indisputable fact that can be demonstrated.

Chapter 14

BETWEEN TWO WORLDS

THE loss or weakening of one or more of the physical senses often develops other faculties. With the loss of sight, the sense of touch frequently becomes more acute, while increasing deafness may bring another more latent sense into fuller use.

In a similar fashion, bodily illness and the resultant lessening of the physical capabilities, often brings to the surface latent psychic faculties.

When death is imminent, and the physical powers are at their lowest ebb, we may develop clairvoyance, even though psychic vision never found expression during a vigorous and healthy lifetime. The fine, gossamer veil which divides the two worlds becomes increasingly transparent to the ones who stand on the threshold of a larger life. Those about to pass through the curtain of death may clearly see and recognise some of the spirit friends who have come to welcome them to a new life of renewed strength and vitality. Children, in common with adults, often become psychic as their earthly span of life draws to an end.

Children's death-bed testimony to the reality of the spirit world has particular value. In numerous cases, such children are not members of a Spiritualist family, and know nothing of the case for Survival. It cannot, therefore, be put forward that they are merely repeating, consciously or unconsciously, the things they have learned or overheard concerning psychic phenomena. Yet dying children have, on many occasions, indicated their knowledge of the presence of individuals unseen by others in the same room. The descriptions they have given so spontaneously and innocently have tallied in all respects with Spiritualist knowledge.

Daisy Dryden, daughter of a Methodist minister, passed to the Other Side at the age of ten. During her last days, her psychic faculties awakened. So detailed and explicit were the death-bed revelations of the child that her mother recorded her utterances. A full account of Daisy Dryden's dying experiences is given in the *Journal of the American Society for Psychical Research.*

Daisy Dryden passed over as a result of enteritis following typhoid fever. Although two weeks before her "death" she appeared to be on the road to recovery, the child herself insisted that she was not going to stay on earth.

Three days before her passing, when her father was reading aloud from the Bible, the child broke in to say that she hoped to return after her "death" to console her parents. She added, "I'll ask Allie about it." (Allie, her younger brother of six, had passed to the Other Side about seven months previously.) After a short silence, Daisy said, "Allie says I may go to you sometimes; he says it is possible, but you will not know when I am there, but I can speak to your thought."

Recording Daisy's final days on earth her mother states, "During this time she lived in both worlds, as she expressed it. Two days before she left us, the Sunday School superintendent came to see her. She talked very freely about going and sent a message by him to the school. When he was about to leave, he said, 'Well, Daisy, you will soon be over the dark river.' After he had gone she asked her father to explain what he meant by 'the dark river.' He tried to explain it, but she said, 'It is all a mistake; there is no river; there is no curtain; there is not even a line that separates this life from the other life... It is here and it is there. I know it is so, for I can see you all, and I see them there at the same time.'"

Daisy's mother goes on to say that, when asked to tell them something about the appearance of the other world, the child answered, "I cannot describe it; it is so different, I could not make you understand." While the mother sat by the bed, clasping her daughter's hand, Daisy looked up wistfully and said, "I do wish you could see Allie; he is standing beside you." Involuntarily her mother turned her head, but Daisy went on, "He says you cannot see him because your spirit eyes are closed, but that I can, because my body only holds my spirit, as it were, by a thread of life." Mrs. Dryden asked, "Does he say that now?" The dying child replied, "Yes, just now." Wondering how Daisy could be talking to her brother when there was not the slightest sign of conversation between them, Mrs. Dryden asked, "How do you speak to Allie? I do not hear you or see your lips move." Smiling, the girl answered that they talked with their thoughts.

"How does Allie appear to you?" asked her mother. "Does he seem to wear clothes?"

"Oh, no, not clothes such as we wear," replied the child. "There seems to be about him a white, beautiful something, so fine and thin and glistening, and oh, so white, and yet there is not a fold, or a sign of thread in it, so it cannot be cloth. But it makes him look so lovely."

What the dying girl actually saw was, I expect, the spirit raiment of her brother.

When Daisy's sister sang to her from a hymn book about "angels and their snowy wings," the dying girl exclaimed, "Oh, Lulu, isn't it strange? We always thought the angels had wings! But it is a mistake; they don't have any."

"But they must have wings, else how could they fly down from heaven?" asked her sister.

"Oh, but they don't fly, they just come," said Daisy. "When I think of Allie, he is here."

Once, when Mrs. Dryden asked her sick child to explain how she saw her spirit visitors, Daisy replied: "I do not see them all the time, but when I do, the walls seem to go away, and I can see ever so far, and you couldn't begin to count the people. Some are near, and I know them; others I have never seen before."

Mrs. Dryden writes, "The morning she died she asked me to let her have a small mirror. I hesitated, thinking the sight of her emaciated face would be a shock to her. But her father, sitting by her, remarked, 'Let her look at her poor little face if she wants to.' So I gave it to her. Taking the glass in her hands, she looked at her image for a time, calmly and sadly. At length she said, 'This body of mine is about worn out. It is like the old dress of Mamma's hanging there in the closet. She doesn't wear it any more, and I won't wear my body any more, because I have a new spiritual body which will take its place. Indeed, I have it now, for it is with my spiritual eyes I see the heavenly world while my body is still here... Now my life here is at an end, and this poor body will be laid away, and I shall have a beautiful body like Allie's.'"

Begging her mother not to cry, the child, whose awakened spiritual consciousness had given her wisdom and knowledge beyond her years, went on, "It is much better for me to go now. I might have grown up to be a wicked woman, like so many do. God knew what was best for me." Then, asking her mother to open the shutters so that she could look out at the world for the last time, she said, "Before another morning I shall be gone." Her father supported her frail body as she gazed out of the window. "Goodbye, sky," she said. "Goodbye, trees. Goodbye, white rose.

Goodbye, red rose. Goodbye, beautiful world. How I love it, but I do not wish to stay!'"

That evening, she looked at the time and remarked, "It is halfpast eight now; when it is half-past eleven Allie will come for me... When the time comes, I will tell you." She bade farewell to her sister Lulu, whose bedtime had arrived, saying, "Good night and goodbye, my sweet, darling Lulu."

Her mother writes, "At about quarter-past eleven, she said, 'Now, Papa, take me up. Allie has come for me.' After her father had taken her, she asked us to sing. Presently someone said, 'Call Lulu,' but Daisy answered promptly, 'Don't disturb her, she is asleep.' Then, just as the hands of the clock pointed to the halfhour past eleven, the time she had predicted Allie was to come to take her with him, she lifted up both arms and said, 'Come, Allie,' and breathed no more."

The mother concludes her moving account of Daisy's passing in these words: "There was a solemn stillness in the room. We could not weep, and why should we? We could only thank our Heavenly Father for the teachings of her last days, those days rendered sacred by the glory of heaven which illumined them. And as we stood there, gazing on the face of the dear one, we felt that the room must be full of angels come to comfort us, for a sweet peace fell upon our spirits, as if they had said, 'She is not here, she is risen.'"

Now there is nothing that Daisy Dryden said on her death-bed that was not entirely consistent with Spiritualistic knowledge of psychic laws and life after death. Yet, this little girl was the daughter of a minister. She had been trained in her father's beliefs and doctrines. Her parents were unacquainted with Spiritualistic knowledge. Indeed, at the time of Daisy's passing in 1864, modern Spiritualism was in its early days. Yet, from their dying child, they heard and accepted the same psychic facts, the same truths that are propounded today by mediums throughout the world.

Recently, another child's death-bed psychic experience has been described in *Psychic News* by a medical contributor. He relates how, when he was senior medical student at a well-known infirmary, a little girl was received in his ward. She was dying from an incurable spinal disease.

Winnie was a lovable child who endeared herself to all the staff on account of the courage, patience and gratitude she displayed during her last difficult weeks. She was compelled to lie prone on her back for her body was wasted. "As the weeks passed," writes this contributor, "mobility of arms and legs became practically impossible, so much so that she had to be fed by a nurse. This fact is important in view of what follows. We were a hard-boiled lot of undergrads, with a deal sight more of the material than the spiritual in our make-up, so that 'cases,' let them be never so bad, were simply 'cases' to us all. With Winnie, however, it was different. One felt almost awed and dumb in the child's presence, for there was certainly more spiritual than material in the composition of this little patient."

One morning, when he was "writing up" a case in the main ward, a nurse beckoned him, saying, "You might come and see Winnie. I think we should send for her parents." The senior medical student went at once to the small private room where Winnie lay. The child was talking in feeble tones to the house surgeon, but she at once greeted the newcomer with a smile. As her respiration and pulse slowed down gradually, it became obvious that death was very near. Twice, her medical attendants thought that all was over, but the little patient rallied again.

"Then," continues the writer, "the miracle... Winnie, lying flat on her back, who had moved neither hand nor foot for weeks, suddenly opened both eyes to a most unnatural extent while staring fixedly at the ceiling. We onlookers unconsciously raised our heads ceilingwards in order to see what the child found so interesting. We saw the ceiling and nothing else."

With fixed bright eyes, the dying girl held out both arms. Her hands curled over something invisible to the onlookers, whilst she slowly rose to a sitting position. In that posture, she called, in a strong voice, "Oh, Ganma, dear Ganma, I'm coming!"

"Just as slowly as she had risen," says the writer, "she returned to the prone position, giving us all the impression that she had been raised slowly by some unseen entity, then gently allowed to fall back quietly on the bed."

And so Winnie passed to the Other Side.

"It is perfectly obvious," concludes the writer, "that the poor wasted muscles were quite incapable of performing the (to us) wonderful feat which the dying child achieved. It transpired later that 'Ganma' was her grandmother, who was devoted to the child and who had passed over about a year previously."

So objective was a psychic manifestation afforded to a child who lay dying in a ship's cabin, that it was seen by the doctor who attended her as well as by four other people in a different part of the ship. The story, recorded by Professor Bozzano in *Discarnate Influence In Human Life*, was told by the medical officer, Dr. W. T. O'Hara.

During a voyage to Yokohama, a small girl, who was travelling alone to relatives in Japan, was entrusted to the captain's care. The child, an orphan, was so charming and intelligent that she soon won the hearts of the ship's whole personnel. When the ship entered the China Sea, the little girl fell seriously ill with tropical fever. She grew rapidly worse and it became evident that her earthly end was approaching.

While the doctor sat by the child's bedside, he became conscious of a supernormal condition in the room. Then, although it was not near morning, the cabin grew slowly brighter until it was as bright as full dawn. The light seemed to converge in flickering, uncertain waves of blue, white and golden rays, which gathered directly over the child. These rays remained for a moment and then disappeared, leaving the cabin in darkness, except for the light from a shaded night lamp. The little girl's pulse still beat softly. She looked up at the doctor; her fingers closed over his hand as she said, "Oh, look! How beautiful!" Dr. O'Hara writes, "She turned her eyes upward, and looking, I saw, close to the ceiling, straight over her head, a blurred, misty, luminous globe, like a distant light diffused and glowing in a heavy fog. This grew slowly, almost imperceptibly, as before, until it hung, a quivering sphere of bluish-white wavy light. It was more nearly like the St. Elmo's fire that clings about the ends of the spars in a heavy electrical storm than anything else with which I can compare it."

"See," said the dying child, "Oh, see!"

The doctor continues, "Slowly, so slowly that I did not notice it at first, the ball of light descended until it seemed to envelop her face and hair, giving the peaceful pleased look on her face a glory and radiance such as we think of the angels having; the sweetest and most heavenly vision I ever saw or ever expect to see. As it lay for a moment wavering about her pillow, I felt the child's hand grow tense in mine, her body trembled slightly, and she made a feeble effort to raise her head as she cried out falteringly, 'Oh, Mamma, Mamma, I see... the way... and... it is... all bright... and shining!' And as the voice died in a low whisper, the light rose rapidly, dissolving and disappearing as it reached the ceiling; the curly head lay quietly back among the pillows; there was the faintest breath of a sigh, a nervous flutter of the muscles, the fingers of the hands relaxed, the pulse was lost and she lay very still and white, as I knelt beside her couch alone with death."

The doctor mechanically looked at his watch. It was 2.30 a.m. He placed the child's hands across her breast and rose to his feet as the door opened and the captain entered, followed by the first and second mates and two other officers. The captain stepped to the side of the bed and placed his hand on the child's forehead, saying, "I thought so!" Then he added, "Doctor, I don't believe in ghosts and spirits and that sort of thing. I don't think there are any of us here who do, but these men and myself have just seen something that was very queer; and it was so real and plain that there is no mistaking that we did see it. There was a ball of blue fire, just like the St. Elmo's fire in a thunderstorm, that appeared right over our heads in the smoking-room, and when we looked at it the thing floated straight across the room to the door. There it hung for a second, turned in this direction and disappeared. When it had gone I said right away: 'Boys, that little girl of ours is dead.'"

This globe of light, seen by six people in two different sections of the ship, must have been guided by an invisible intelligence. It was seen by the doctor and the dying child. Before it turned in the direction of the child's cabin, it was seen in the smoking-room by the officers, amongst whom was the captain in whose care the little girl had been entrusted.

The dying girl had recognised her "dead" mother when she looked in the direction of the shimmering mass. Was the psychic manifestation, seen by all the others objectively, the spirit of the child's mother who had come to fetch her daughter and, at the same time, indicate this fact to those who had grown to love the little girl?

Chapter 15

COUNSEL FROM BEYOND

THERE are highly evolved spirit guides who have elected to return to this world to give humanity the benefit of the wisdom they have accumulated during their progress through earthly and spiritual lives. These great teachers often view our problems from a different and wider aspect than the worldly point of view. They are not bound by orthodoxy, by creed, custom or prejudice. The purity and the simplicity of the truths they propound clarify our vision and help us in our groping towards the light of understanding.

Many of the advanced spirit guides return to this world wearing a cloak of anonymity, since their true status might overawe some of us, did we but know their names. Because the Indians were, in their prime, masters of psychic knowledge and power, it is not surprising that a number of spirit guides use the "personality" of a "dead" Indian while they work with mediums. In such a category is Silver Birch, the guide of the home circle of which I am a member. This evolved spirit once said, "I had to come in the form of a humble Indian to win your love and devotion, not by the use of any highsounding name, but to prove myself by the truths I taught."

"By their fruits shall ye know them," declared the teacher of simple truths, Jesus of Nazareth. And it is by his service to this world that Silver Birch, a humble Indian, is known to the many thousands who hold him in esteem. Silver Birch has been questioned on various aspects of child survival. When a member of the circle asked what happened to children who passed on as a result of bombing, Silver Birch replied:

"The period of recuperation and recovery is longer in the case of children, but they learn much more quickly once the adjustment is made. This interregnum period, which is a kind of twilight of the soul, is not painful – I do not want to give that impression – it is a process of recovery. The spirit has to learn to express itself in its new body, and that expression is dependent on the experience it has. Obviously, in the case of children the experience is more limited. That is why the period of recuperation is longer. And, in their case too, to show how the law provides, I would like to say that if they come alone and their mothers are still on earth, then the ones who take charge of them are those whose strong maternal instincts were never expressed in your world, but now can be devoted to the care of the new life which is gradually awakening and unfolding in our realm."

"In our world, children adapt themselves very quickly to new conditions," remarked a sitter.

"That is purely physical," said Silver Birch. "We are dealing with the spirit now, with the spirit conditioning itself in the world of spirit, which is vastly different from the physical world in many respects and very similar in others. You must understand it is all a question of awareness. Awareness supplies the key. You hear me always speak about knowledge as the priceless gift of the spirit. It is a world of the mind where we live, and little minds have to be prepared for it. There is another aspect which is not really germane, and that is a law of compensation, which outworks itself in the case of children who, while deprived of earthly experience, are not stained by earthly faults."

"They are not improved by earthly virtues, either," remarked a sitter.

"That is the compensation," said the guide, "that souls who are deprived of earthly experience do not have to pay the price for earthly faults which would have developed."

"Does that equally balance?" asked a sitter.

"That is not a question which can be generally answered," said Silver Birch. "It depends on each individual soul. I am only pointing to the law of compensation."

"If the earthly wrong were inherent in the individual, would it not develop on the Other Side?" Silver Birch was asked.

"I do not agree with your question," he replied. "Earthly wrong is not inherent in the individual. Give an example of what you mean.

"Suppose a child, had he continued to live on earth, would have been greedy," said the sitter, "would he not develop greediness just as easily in the spirit world as if he were still here?"

"You must try to get the whole subject in its proper perspective," said the guide. "Once realisation comes in our world, the feet are placed on the paths of advancement. Until then, there is scope for the exercise of all undeveloped qualities. Until then, you dwell in those grey spheres where there is a simulacrum of the desires you wish to have gratified. But once you awaken, the mere fact that you have awakened means that you have said farewell to all the desires to gratify what belongs to the undeveloped side of your nature. That is why I say, 'Put the question in its proper perspective.' If you are still greedy, it means you have not yet awakened, so you can satisfy that greed."

"But the characters of little children would be undeveloped," commented a sitter.

"The point I was trying to establish," said the guide, "was that they would arrive in our world immature because they had lacked the earthly experience to equip the soul. But also they would not be stained by the faults which had developed, unfortunately, in adult life, and to that extent the law of compensation would work, and they would not have to remove those blemishes from their characters."

"Didn't they come here to do wrong, so they would learn to do right?" asked a sitter.

"No, you do not come here to do wrong in order to learn to do right," said the guide.

"But we were not sent here to be plaster saints from the moment of birth, were we?" the sitter persisted.

"No," said Silver Birch, "but there is a difference between coming here to wreak malice and to be extremely selfish, and coming here as raw material and becoming a finished product."

"Isn't the difference explained in terms of doing wrong?" asked the sitter.

"Yes, but I do not like very much the terms you use," said the guide. "I do not visualise the supreme and sublime development of the human soul as being towards a plaster saint, as you call it, neither do I conceive that the purpose of earthly life is to breed a race of criminals who will commit crimes until they learn that crime is wrong. No, the number of those who do wrong callously, deliberately, with premeditated forethought, is comparatively small compared with the vast numbers of those who inhabit your world. The really evil person is fortunately in the minority. Most of the crimes, if crimes they can be called, are caused by ignorance, by wrong training, faulty education, belief in superstition."

"If a child were greedy on earth," said a sitter, "would he not still be greedy for a little time in the spirit world, and from that point of view would have earthly experience?"

"Do you mean, if the child were naturally greedy, it would still pass with desire ingrained in its consciousness?" asked the guide.

"Yes, that is quite possible. But then the life it had lived, if it were a young life in your world, would not have given it much opportunity for that greed to grow, and it could easily be corrected. There is all the difference between an incipient greed which has hardly been expressed and a selfish greed that has lasted for 50 or 70 years and has constantly been satisfied and has grown upon its own appetite."

The next question was from a member of the circle who wanted to know whether families killed together in an air raid would continue to remain together in the next world.

"It all depends," said Silver Birch, "and I answer very carefully because I do not wish to hurt anyone's feelings. It depends on whether they want to be together or not. You must realise that in the world of spirit the tie that binds is the tie that wishes to bind and that there are many families held together in your world by a bond which is soon dissolved by death. If the family possesses a community of interest, if there – is a natural attraction of love, of affection, or even of friendship, the ties that bind will not be severed. It is just like marriage. There are many in your world who are tied only by a physical bond. Their spirits are divergent. There is no unity between them. Death provides an unbridgeable chasm. But where there are those whose spirits are married too, then death will bring them even closer together."

"At what time before physical birth, as far as you know, does the spirit enter the body?" Silver Birch was asked. This was his reply:

"As spirit, *you* have always existed because spirit is part of life and life is part of spirit. *You* have always existed. Because you are part of the Great Spirit, which is the life-force, *you* have never had a beginning, but you as an individual, as a separate conscious individuality, must begin somewhere even in the stream of life. When conception takes place, the cells of the male and female meet and provide a vehicle for a particle of the life-force to begin to express itself through a physical body. The life-force is unexpressed until there is a vehicle through which it can manifest. That is what the earth parents provide. From the time the cells have coalesced and formed their union, the tiny particle of spirit has naturally attached itself and begins its expression in your world of matter. And I hold that that is the dawn of consciousness. From that moment it begins its conscious individual life. Thereafter it will always be an individual entity of its own."

"Through no fault of their own innocent babies are born into the world victims of hereditary, venereal and other diseases," began the next question. "This does not seem quite fair, as it is not the fault of the child that it has inherited such a disease. Can you say something about that?"

"Those who talk of unfairness are still thinking in terms of bodies, of a world of matter, and not of an infinite life," the guide answered. "The spirit does not suffer from venereal disease. The spirit is not crippled or misshapen or bent. The spirit is not suffering from any hereditary traits or any of the acquired characteristics of the parents. These do not change the individual, although they do affect the body through which the spirit manifests on earth. Whilst you can quite possibly argue that, from the earthly point of view, looking at life solely from a material standpoint, the one who is born into a diseased body has a much worse time physically than the one born into a healthy body, those opinions do not hold in regard to the spirit which is behind the body. You will not automatically be poorer in spirit because your body is diseased, and richer in spirit because your body is healthier. Indeed, it can be argued that your spirit will be richer because you will have learned the many lessons of pain and suffering which are all part of the equipment of the spirit in its essential evolution."

Here a sitter interjected, "But it would always be better for the body to be born free from disease."

"Of course," was the spirit rejoinder. "It would be better that your world were free of slums, but slums are caused by part of that self-same free will which could enable your world to be a paradise on earth. If you have free will, then you must allow for its misuse and its correct use."

Thinking of all the children who never reach physical maturity, a member of the circle said to Silver Birch, "In the next world we know that children grow up to become adults; but what about those guides who remain children for many years on earth, and also children who have been 'dead' for 18 or 20 years who still return as children?"

"I will come to the defence of the Topsies who never grow up," replied the guide. "Your hard, bitter world condemns those who go on being children, and claims all the time that it loves the innocence of the child. Yet it objects to them when it chooses to persist in that form of evolution solely to help them. The advantages are very easy to understand. The child does not suffer, from the inhibitions of the grown-up. It has a naturally fresh outlook on life. It is not beset by the many problems that perplex adults and therefore is the best channel for communication. The child can naturally perform this task because it has not so many of the intolerances and prejudices of the grown-up people to conquer.

"It starts off as a fresh, radiant being, willing to help, and is not troubled by all the problems that belong to the adult life. Because it is not worried by them, it can quickly hold on to those elusive vibrations that make for the success of spirit communication. But that child personality is only a personality voluntarily adopted in a large number of cases with a sole desire of aiding your world. If at any time it chooses to surrender its task, it can return to a higher sphere, there to take up its thread of the larger consciousness in which the child had lived. Do not condemn them, they are most lovable instruments of the Great Spirit whose only desire is to serve, a service they give willingly and freely because they think they can help those who are hurt or crushed by your world.

"In the case of the ordinary child who comes back after many years still as a child, this is done for recognition. When you are concerned with identification, you must remember that children would not be recognised unless they showed themselves in the form and with the characteristics and habits by which they will be known to their parents. But that is only a picture drawn for the medium to transmit. It is like the television thrown on the screen. The medium sees the picture that is thrown on to the screen of her mind and transmits it. With a voice medium, it is the same, except that instead of the process being a visual one, it is an oral one, moulded out of the ectoplasm. The voice which is moulded reproduces, as far as conditions allow, the voice the child had on earth."

"How would a child who had been brought up to be cruel to animals be treated on the Other Side; would it be given animals to look after?" was the next question. The guide replied:

"We would have to undo the earthly teaching by showing how animals have rendered great service throughout many years. The child would be taken to the varying animal spheres to see what they are really like when they are allowed to have contact with those who love them and understand them. Gradually, the false teaching would be shed as greater knowledge came to the child.

And it would be shown that the effects of cruelty are not only to be observed on the animals, but on the one who performs the act."

Another sitter introduced her question by saying, "Many people when they pass on have no knowledge of the after-life. They are in a sort of daze and do not know that they have passed on. Does that apply to children, or do they accept the new life instinctively?"

"It depends on the child's knowledge," Silver Birch replied. "If it has not been too tainted with the ignorance and superstition of your world, then its natural understanding, based on its natural psychic powers, will enable a natural appreciation to occur."

"Did the Great Spirit intend that some human beings should die before they fulfilled their plan of life?" was the next question.

"The plan is always that you should enjoy a full expression on earth so that you shall be equipped for the greater life of the spirit," said the guide. "If fruit drops from the tree before it is ripe it is sour. All life that is forced to quit its body before it has achieved its maturity on earth is unprepared for the world of spirit."

"If a child dies of an accident, was that intended by the Great Spirit?" the guide was asked.

"That is difficult to answer, because always I have to say 'yes,' with qualifications," was the spirit answer. "The whole of life is controlled by law and the Great Spirit is responsible for law. But law works through human beings. Ultimately everything comes back to the responsibility of the Great Spirit. You can argue that if you do something wrong you are not responsible because the Great Spirit made you like that. But that is fallacious reasoning. It is true to an extent that He ultimately is responsible for the whole universe, because His power created it and His intelligence endowed it, but you have your intelligence. You have the power of reasoning. If you choose to put your head under a train it is no use blaming the Great Spirit."

"Will you explain 'infant prodigies'?" was the next query.

"There are three kinds," said Silver Birch. "Some are incarnated souls with a memory of past experience to help, others are mediums subject to spirit influence, albeit unconsciously, and therefore receptacles of much learning, wisdom, knowledge and truth from our world. In the third category are the geniuses who are the advance guards of evolution."

A sitter referred to the case of infant prodigy, the famous violinist, Florizel von Reuter. His mother had, before her son's birth, implored the "dead" musical genius, Paganini, to influence her child to become a great violinist. Paganini responded to the mother's plea.

"That is the mediumistic category," said Silver Birch.

"Did his mother's plea make him a medium?" asked a sitter, "or was her request the channel which enabled Paganini to attach himself to Florizel von Reuter?"

"The psychic power was there just the same," answered the guide. "Had he not been psychic it could not have functioned. There are many people who are psychic without being mediumistic. They have all the powers of the soul, the psyche, but they do not express it in conscious communication with our world. They are unconsciously influenced. That is the secret of inspiration."

On one occasion, a member of the circle asked Silver Birch, "Of what use is the earth life of all the countless millions of babies who perish at, or soon after, birth by infanticide or otherwise?"

"As long as people judge eternal principles by material standards they will never understand these things," the guide answered. "The wisest of your wise ones do not see beyond earthly knowledge. When the light of spiritual knowledge reaches them through their evolution, then they will see the plan which is, as yet, not revealed to them. They see through a glass darkly, and so they do not understand. Would you attempt to judge the life of a schoolboy only by the years that he goes to school, and ignore that greater life which starts beyond his school? There is a greater life than the one in which you live – a world of beauty, a world of colour, a world of love, a world of labour, a world where every sincere desire finds expression, where every creative impulse can express itself, where everything that cannot be fulfilled in your world is able to realise itself. Until you have seen this world, you cannot criticise the Great Spirit."

"In our world," said a sitter, "some children are born in a slum atmosphere of drink, mental, moral and physical filth, and are faced with a life of hard, monotonous labour, while others grow up surrounded by beautiful things and have a delightful preparation for life. How is the unfairness of such cases taken into account?"

"The soul registers its own evolution," answered the guide. "People in your world judge always by material standards and not by the expression of the soul. To all, whether born in high or low estate, come opportunities for service, for the soul to find itself and to express its own divinity. That is the only standard of judgment.

All things in your world, judged by a material standard, seem to produce inequalities, but the true compensation is the compensation of the soul, which learns to express itself through all difficulties."

"But surely," commented a member of the circle, "it is easier for a soul to express good motives when surrounded by a good environment rather than in surroundings where sin, hunger and everything that is low predominate?"

"I do not agree with you," replied Silver Birch, "because I see that nearly always the great souls of your world have been born of low estate. All the great masters of your world have come from low estate. The more difficulties that the soul has to struggle against, the greater the soul can become. It is in the struggle against circumstances that the soul comes into its own. Try to judge not from without but from within."

"Knowing that abortion is wrong, what is the spirit world's view of birth control?" Silver Birch was then asked.

"You have been given free will and a conscience to distinguish between that which is wrong and that which is right," was the spirit rejoinder. "It always depends on the motive. Say that once. Say it a hundred times. What is your motive? It is that which counts, nothing more."

"But does the restriction of births interfere with the law?" interjected the sitter.

"Where a spirit has to be born into your world, it will come through those who will not prevent its entry," insisted the guide. "The law is supreme. If it is part of your evolution that through you there is to come into your world a spirit, a new life, then you would not prevent it, because you would not desire it."

"Then, if it was to be, you would want it to happen," said the sitter.

"Yes," answered the guide, "because you would have reached that stage in evolution where it was necessary that the influence of a new life should be brought into your life."

"Is that necessarily a higher evolution?" he was asked.

"No, it is not high, it is not low," said Silver Birch. "I must make a distinction between those who seek only to enjoy the lust of the body and to prevent the consequences. With that I do not agree, because the motive is one of selfishness."

"But if one had an idea it was not advisable, from the child's point of view, what then?" was the next question.

"It always depends on the motive," came the reply. "You cannot cheat the law. The law is registered on your soul. Every act, every thought, every idea, every desire is registered for ever on the aura of your soul. It can be read by those who have the eyes of the spirit. The motive of everything you have ever done in your world of matter is known by those who see with the eyes of the spirit. Your soul is naked before them."

Chapter 16

LOVE FINDS ITS OWN

CHILDREN grow and develop in the spirit world until they reach womanhood or manhood. In contradiction to earthly life, the spirit body does not begin to deteriorate after maturity, but remains at the height of its vigour. In the next world, as in the temporal one, it is the spiritual evolution of the individual which imparts true beauty. Imagine, then, the radiant personality of an evolved spirit being.

I expect you have noticed, as I have, that there are people in this world whose beauty emanates from within themselves and has nothing whatever to do with their cast of features or physical appearance. A life of selfless service to humanity has endowed such individuals with a subtle, indefinable beauty which arrests our attention and compels our admiration. Be their physical features ever so commonplace, I know few people of highly evolved characters who do not bear the stamp of true beauty upon their countenances.

Untouched by worldly temptation in the spirit spheres, your child will grow in loveliness and grace. In course of progress, the stillborn boy will attain vigorous maturity. The tiny girl, whose eyes you once closed so sadly will, in the Beyond, eventually manifest the full glory of her womanly charm. "But how," you may ask, "shall I know my own when I too pass over? How shall I be able to recognise my little daughter, grown to womanhood in the spirit world?" First of all, she will know you. Ever since her passing, she has visited the beloved ones in her earthly home. It makes no difference that, until recently, you had no knowledge of spirit return or psychic laws.

Your child has been with you on countless occasions, whether you knew it or not. She has seen the passage of years take their toll of your features. Her spirit has not been restricted by earthly limitations. Although you may have travelled to the ends of the earth, she will never have lost sight of you, as long as love and remembrance operated. When you pass over, possibly she will come forward to greet you in the company of a "dead" relative who knows you both. After all, if force of earthly circumstances separated you from your baby daughter until she attained womanhood, a similar re-introduction from a mutual friend or relative might have to take place.

Another method of spirit recognition is when a child, using her or his psychic power, temporarily reassumes the youthful earthly appearance.

There are other ways by which you may know your own when you pass on. During sleep, it is possible that you have visited the spheres whilst your physical body lay dormant. Temporarily realised from four-dimensional captivity, you have enjoyed, for a while, the companionship of your beloved. Alas, upon awakening, the remembrance of the astral experience has failed to register through the earthly consciousness. But the spirit, the larger personality does not forget. Upon passing over, you may well recognise scenes and individuals familiar to you in your astral visits during sleep.

Soon after her small daughter's "death," Mrs. C. Fisher, a medium now living in Australia, awoke one morning fully conscious of the fact that, whilst her earthly body slumbered, she had been reunited with her spirit child. Her little girl discussed her new life and gave details of her spirit environment. "Each night after that," writes the mother, "I fell asleep quickly with the conscious knowledge that I was going to spend my sleep state with my child. In consequence I received consolation and happiness. She was delighted to meet me and I was thus more easily reconciled to the great parting which so recently had taken place. I had the consolation every morning of knowing that my daughter was just as much alive as she had ever been, and nothing but our own desires could keep us apart.

"How few mothers, who have lost their darlings, realise the existence and blessing of this wonderful manifestation of God's goodness in providing a place where we can, in our sleep state, still continue to mother our loved ones! Instead, these parents fret and mourn, and the little one frets and mourns too, for a child responds to a mother's craving. Isn't that child part of herself?

"It is just as natural to visit a loved one on the Other Side during sleep as it is for a mother to get out of bed to see if her babies are covered in their cots during a cold night. Few mothers have awakened to the conscious realisation that they spend a great deal of their sleeping hours with their departed children."

There are, in truth, many ways by which you may know each other again. You might recognise your child by means of the purely spiritual bond which unites you. Spiritual ties do not necessarily exist between parents and children. But when true love, sympathy and understanding reign in a family, there is not only a physical relationship but a more lasting, and infinitely deeper bond.

In every desirable case, parents are always given the opportunity of reunion with the children who passed over before them, even the ones who never breathed on earth. I say "in every desirable case" with reason. An unloved, unwanted child, neglected in earthly life by delinquent parents, would have no link with them after leaving the physical world. Neglected or ill-treated children find, on passing over, the happiness and affection denied them in the earth world. They become the charges of spirit individuals whose chosen vocation is to help these children to obliterate painful and deleterious memories of the past from their minds.

Naturally, then, the young who lived under harmful hereditary influences are not encouraged to return to their earthly homes, unless such an experience is deemed necessary for their evolutionary progress in the Beyond. Even in this world, in humanitarian countries, children are legally removed from the influences of cruel or vicious parents. Still, children passing over in such circumstances are the exception and not the rule. Reunion between families takes place whenever affection still exists. The physical link of relationship is already forged. Whether the tie is to be maintained and strengthened on the Other Side must depend on mutual desires. Love is always the deciding factor. It is the only permanent bond.

Perhaps the perfect reunions in the spirit world are between those who loved one another on earth, and who possessed knowledge of Survival and spirit communication.

When Spiritualists pass on, they have no difficulty in finding their own children, since they have never, at any time, been lost to them! There are no barriers, even temporary ones, to prevent immediate recognition and reunion. No explanations are required, no gaps to be filled in by those who have been in constant communication through channels of mediumship. Again and again, the little ones have returned to earth and given details of their progress and experiences in the spirit world.

At home circles, they have had intimate and happy talks with their earthly relatives. The parents have marked the gradual expansion of their "dead" children's knowledge and mental capacity. The children have spoken of their spirit teachers, of the lessons they have learned, of the games they have played. The earthly parents have, in return, related such incidents in their own lives as would have been discussed if the little ones had still remained in their physical environment. The home ties, in such cases, have never at any time been severed.

Mr. R. H. Saunders, a well-known Spiritualist, describes in *Psychic News* how he kept in close touch with his six children who were still-born. "For the past 25 years," he says, "I have followed their careers in the kindergarten, the schools and the colleges of the Spheres, and know of their work and recreations. I have seen and heard them on hundreds of occasions."

He states, "My wife, who found it difficult to accept the truth of Spiritualism here, spoke with me ten days after her passing and said, 'I am sorry I did not take my stand by your side. There was something in my nature that prevented it. When I came here and saw my six dear children whom I had regarded as lost waiting with open arms to receive me, I was overwhelmed with joy. I found I had often been over to see them during sleep, and I knew them all'"

As Silver Birch stated, "dead" children usually reveal themselves in the séance room at the age at which they passed over. Even though, on the Other Side, they have progressed towards maturity, the child-like aspect of themselves is a reality while they manifest in their earthly environment. Time is a reality, but it has more dimensions than our material standards can measure. Our artificial measurement is but a convenient and necessary means of registering events. The recorded time of the day and date is circumstanced by the particular part of the globe we inhabit. Stretching the long arm of coincidence to its limit, I give, as an example, the hypothetical case of a New York citizen and an Englishman having a short conversation by means of the trans-Atlantic telephone. During their talk, they are informed that an infant has just been born to each of their wives. Because American and British time differs by a number of hours, the birth certificates of the children,' born simultaneously, might bear different dates.

Writing of the Japanese assault on Wake Island in the Pacific, and referring to the bombing of Pearl Harbour, Donald Wilhelm in *The American Legion Magazine* says, "Sunday, December 7th at Pearl Harbour was Monday, December 8th here, for Wake is just west of the international date line." Thus, in one hemisphere, the same event took place on two different dates!

When we want to listen to a broadcast from the United States, we must make allowances for the difference between their times and ours. "Last night" in Australia is "today" in Great Britain. As I write, "Double British Summer Time" is in operation, which means we have put our clocks forward and are living, so to speak, two hours in the future!

"Unborn Tomorrow and dead Yesterday," wrote Omar Khayyamm of humanity. In the vastness of eternity, the terms past, present and future cease to bear their earthly significance. Time is measured by the progression of the soul towards spiritual perfection. Our puny physical lives, from the cradle to the grave – and beyond – actually register in a further dimension, which we can call "space-time."

Those who passed long ago as children to the Beyond merely conform to our material approximation of time when they return in the child-like aspect of themselves. Nevertheless, this aspect is real while they are manifesting in earthly vibrations. Many experienced Spiritualists, however, have witnessed the growth of their children at recurring materialisation séances. This is what a contributor to *Psychic News* says of her experience at Helen Duncan's séances: "I have watched my daughter's materialised form grow from girlhood to beautifully developed womanhood."

It will not be a problem to this mother to know how to recognise the child whose spirit appearance is already familiar to her.

Chapter 17

BEYOND THE VEIL

THE ethers body might be described as a perfect reflection of the physical one since, as has been pointed out, it does not reproduce any physical discrepancy or disablement. The spirit body of an aged, weak human remains young and vigorous, but it is unable to reflect this vitality through the decrepit earthly vehicle. A scratched, worn-out gramophone record cannot reproduce the true quality of the voice it so accurately registered when the disc was new. Similarly, imperfect mental conditions in an individual are not reflected by the spirit, the real ego.

The brain is a purely physical part of the body. Discrepancies of the brain or other bodily organisms may prevent the mind from registering truly or, as we say, sanely. However expert a typist may be, however agile her fingers, the manuscript she types will be imperfect if the keys are faulty or damaged. Likewise, the greatest musician in the world could only render a distorted melody if the strings or keys of his musical instrument were out of tune, damaged, or incomplete.

The mind of an individual is unable, during earthly life, to register accurately through the medium of an impaired brain. Once released by death from physical bonds, the earthly disability ceases to handicap the expression of the true personality. Those who, in their earthly existence, suffered from any deficiency which prevented a true expression of their individualities, pass to the spirit world with inexperienced, untried characters. Their minds are sound and completely adequate, but are "out of condition" through lack of earthly exercise. Such individuals pass over comparatively unsullied by worldly conditions. Their inherent qualities have yet to be tested and proved in their new existence. Their mentalities, for the first time, are able to register accurately through their perfectly equipped spirit bodies. They are free to express their true selves and to assume their responsibilities as human individuals. Rich experience of living lies ahead of them. They pass over poorer for lack of worldly experience, but purer in spirit since they have not succumbed to, or been subjected to, human weaknesses. The law of compensation strikes an equal balance.

In this world, the very young are usually assisted in their first hesitant steps until they have mastered the use of their inexperienced limbs. Individuals who were deformed or disabled on earth find themselves, on first passing over, in much the same position as an earthly child. Those who were lame have to learn to use their completely healthy etheric limbs. People who were totally blind during physical existence pass to the next world with newly-awakened vision. But their eyes have to become accustomed to variations of light. They must learn to recognise objects already familiar to those who possessed physical sight. They must learn to appreciate the significance of size, width, depth and distance in order to assess visual values. In the spirit world, scenes of beauty and splendour will unfold before their wondering gaze. They will behold mighty mountains. They will examine minute objects of beauty. They will see, for the first time, richness of colour in flowers and foliage. They will learn to use their new-found sight to the greatest advantage in order that the fulness of their lives in the spirit world may not be impaired or retarded.

Those who were deaf during earthly life have to acquire an appreciation of sound and an evaluation of notes previously unregistered by their physical senses.

Children who suffered physical deformities and discrepancies are in much the same position as adults when first they pass to the next world. But they learn to use their new faculties easily and rapidly.

Bodily sickness has many effects. Long illness may reduce the usually bright and alert mentality of a child to lethargy and inertia. Since the etheric body is so closely associated with the physical counterpart during earthly life, certain physical conditions may have a transient effect on the spirit body when it first passes over. A child who was heavily drugged to alleviate suffering, or whose mentality was deranged during illness, or who suffered from a long wearisome disease, or who underwent severe operations, would, in the next world, require remedial treatment for the temporarily affected etheric body. Such a child would, almost certainly, undergo a restful convalescence to enable the spirit body to recover from the resultant conditions of the earthly illness. Radiant health is the birthright of all who are re-born in the spirit world.

There are many "dead" children who awaken on the Other Side quite naturally, and do not need any period of recovery or convalescence. Much depends on the child's age, character, knowledge and the nature of the earthly illness endured.

A sitter was told by Rupert, the control of Edith Clements, that many children awaken quite normally as though from an ordinary sleep. "With perhaps just a little sigh," said Rupert, "they open their eyes and look around them. Spirit nurses and mothers are by their side, waiting to give them a loving smile of welcome and to answer the numerous questions that are asked by alert and active minded children. As it is the nature of a child to wonder and inquire, so do they, on awakening to life on this side, ask whatever questions come to their minds. 'Who are you? Where am I? Where is my mother? Where is my dollie?' All these and many other questions are wisely and tactfully answered. When toys are necessary for a child's happiness they are provided."

This control told the sitter, "Never fear that your dear children are entrusted only to strangers, or to those for whom you never cared in this world. Only those who love, and are fitted for the task, have the right to take charge of a child. Fear, anger or harsh words are unknown in the realm of the children in spirit life."

Children precipitated into the next world as a result of enemy action are the recipients of specialised care and attention.

In all cases, whatever the cause of their passing, the young are tended with love and understanding. Usually they adjust themselves with ease to their new surroundings. They suffer only when they discover they are mourned as lost by their loved ones. Happy are those children who pass over with the knowledge that their parents realise they have survived bodily death, that they are in loving and wise hands, and that they will be able to return to them at the appropriate time.

Spiritualists have accumulated a vast amount of knowledge of life on the Other Side. Through different forms of mediumship, in séance rooms all over the world, accounts of the world they inhabit have been given by those most competent of all to describe their own environment – the "dead" themselves.

Mediums who visit the spirit spheres during sleep or trance state have given lucid descriptions of their experiences. Details of the etheric world have been supplied by astral travellers and psychics who have not, necessarily, accepted the Spiritualist case, and who have credited their "out-of-the-body" experiences to inexplicable circumstances beyond their comprehension.

From whatever source of information accounts of life beyond the veil are received, the principal facts supplied are confirmatory in character. There are no contradictions upon any important points. The moral implications that must be inferred from the accumulated evidence do not differ.

There are many spheres of existence in the spirit world, as, indeed, there are in this world. It is often said that "one half of the world does not know how the other half lives." Were a millionaire and a poor man to describe their own physical world to a hypothetical visitor from Mars, the stranger might be pardoned if he refused to believe they both lived on the same earth. Yet these two human beings would have presented honest accounts of one world, from their own personal points of view. A lama of Tibet exists on an entirely different plane from a materialist living in the Western hemisphere. Yet they both inhabit the same physical world. A coal miner's impression of life differs considerably from that of an airman. The daily existence of a villager has little in common with that of an individual dwelling in an industrial town.

Even in a city like London, there are many spheres of life. The inhabitants of literary Bloomsbury, smart Mayfair, commercial Cheapside, well-bred Kensington, and plebeian Poplar live, cheek by jowl, within one cosmopolitan city. Each stratum of society makes its own contribution to the communal life of which it is an integral part. In any one town, an idle dilletante may rub shoulders with a learned professor. These two individuals inhabit separate states, though they may live next door to each other in the same row of houses.

The varied spheres in the Beyond are not territories in the geographical sense. They may be described as differing degrees of environment, attracting the individual whose evolution is most adapted to the particular sphere of existence.

Arthur Findlay, the author of Spiritualism's best-seller, *On The Edge of the Etheric*, tells in this book how he questioned a "dead" man about life on the Other Side. The writer describes the spirit communicator as one who had a command of language far beyond the normal capacity of the medium, John G. Sloan. "Believe me," said the spirit, speaking at a direct-voice séance, "there are other worlds of substance, finer than physical matter, in which life exists and of which you on earth can form no conception... Encircling your world are planes of different density, and these move in rotation with the rotation of the earth."

The author asked the "dead" man whether the spirit world was real and tangible. "Yes," answered his informant, "it is very real to us, but the conditions in which we find ourselves depend on the condition of our mind. If we wish it we can be surrounded by beautiful country. Our mind plays a large part in our life here. Just as we live in surroundings suitable to our mental development, so we also attract to ourselves minds of the same type as our own. Like attracts like in this world. So also, like attracts like, so far as your world and our world is concerned... We can, at will, take on earth conditions by lowering our vibrations. Our bodies become heavier and more perceptible to the human eye, which accounts for our being seen at times by those who have the faculty on earth of sensing our vibrations... Our world is not material, but it is real for all that, it is tangible, composed of substance in a much higher state of vibration than the matter which makes up your world. Our minds can, therefore, play upon it in a different way than yours can on the material of your world. As our mind is, so is our state. To the good their surroundings are beautiful, to the bad the reverse."

Arthur Findlay wanted to know more. "Do you mean," he asked, "that you live in a dream world where everything appears real but is not?" The spirit communicator repudiated this suggestion. He explained that the spirit world is real, though the atoms of which it is composed differ from those of the physical world. He affirmed that the minds of the "dead" act on this tangible substance in a way that minds in the material world are incapable of doing, because the physical world is one of slower vibrations.

"Do each of you, therefore, live in a world of your own?" asked the inquirer. "Everyone does," said the spirit. "You do and so do I, but if you mean, 'Can each of us see and feel the same thing?' I answer 'Yes.' All in the same plane can sense the same things. We have the same world as you have, but in a finer state...

"I have a body which is a duplicate of what I had on earth, the same hands, legs and feet, and they move the same as yours do... This etheric body is just as substantial to us now as the physical body was to us when we lived on earth. We have the same sensations. When we touch an object we can feel it; when we look at something we can see it. Though our bodies are not material, as you understand the word, yet they have form and feature and expression. We move from place to place as you do, but much more quickly than you can.

The author was told that there were many planes or states of existence in the next world, but only those on the same plane experienced the same sensations. There were houses on these planes. When asked what these houses were like, the spirit replied, "Our houses are just as we care to make them. Your earth houses first were conceived in your mind and then physical matter was put together to make them as your mind first saw them. Here we have the power to mould etheric matter as we think. So our houses are also the products of our minds. We think and we construct. It is a question of thought vibration, and so long as we retain these vibrations we can hold the object."

"What languages do you speak?" asked Arthur Findlay. He was told that various earthly languages were used in the spirit world, but they were conveyed from mind to mind. "Communication takes place mentally from one to another," was the reply, "not only by the spoken word as on earth. This is just as if I were to say that the mind of the spirit gets into telepathic touch with the mind with which he is communicating."

Arthur Findlay learned that great activity prevails in the etheric world. He writes, "Everyone has his or her own work to do. Service to others and love are the ethical standards which prevail there to a higher degree than here." He goes on to say, "There is no night as we understand it, and the light they get does not come from our sun. If they want rest they can get subdued light, but not darkness as we experience it... They enjoy much more freedom of movement, as they get from place to place at a speed we cannot comprehend."

We learn from various sources that only those occupations that are congenial to an individual are continued in the spirit world, where material considerations do not count any longer. The "dead" find no necessity to continue an occupation or profession for which they were unfitted on earth. Scientists, poets, artists, composers and musicians all continue to follow their vocations, if they so desire, but with added and greater opportunities for perfecting their earthly ideas. Teachers, philosophers and writers continue their occupations. Only constructive work is, however, encouraged on the Other Side. When the spiritual vision has been opened, many whose earthly work was destructive turn aside with dismay from the memory of their former callings.

The Rev. C. Drayton Thomas describes in *Beyond Life's Sunset* how his "dead" father told him, "Everything which trains the mind is useful, although purely technical and detailed knowledge gained on earth may be lost or left behind; for it is the effect of the training and education which accompanies you here." The clergyman's spirit sister said of her life, "I continue my painting. On earth I was dissatisfied with it; there was something which eluded me. But now I can put much more into it, and do it more as I wish; it is an expression of oneself and it also gives pleasure to others." Her brother was curious to know what happened to the completed pictures. She told him, "I give them away to those who have no pictures or creative power themselves."

In the Beyond, highly evolved individuals constantly visit those dwelling on a lower plane of existence. The help, encouragement and teaching of these advanced spirits assist the undeveloped to progress from lower to loftier states of consciousness. None of us is so depraved a soul that we may not journey, if we so desire, towards perfection.

Chapter 18

A FEW MINUTES IN ETERNITY

COMMANDER A. B. CAMPBELL, the popular member of the B.B.C. "Brains Trust," was, during an illness, given up for dead by his doctor. While the death certificate was being prepared the patient recovered and described how he had left his physical body and visited the spirit world. He has since recorded his astral experiences in *Bring Yourself To Anchor*.

He became desperately ill when returning home after a journey in the black-out. The doctor was hurriedly summoned by Mrs. Campbell. For the next few days, the patient lay in a dazed condition. He registered vague impressions of having his pulse felt and his temperature taken, but that was all. Then, unexpectedly he became aware that he was standing by his bed looking down on his own physical body. "How pinched and grey I was," Comander Campbell writes, "and the stubble on my chin was about a four days' growth. I felt an urge to get out of the house. It did not astonish me to find that I passed through the closed door of the bedroom with ease. Downstairs, I went through the front door with the same lack of effort. I just wondered why it was not necessary for me to open the doors, that's all."

The moment he stepped out of the familiar garden gate he found himself in an unknown country. Before him, a wide moor stretched as far as his eyes could see. He walked until he reached a narrow, well-worn track. Experiencing a great sense of loneliness, he followed the track until he came to a road. It was thronged with people of all ages; children mingled with old men and women. He joined the pedestrians and discovered they were of varied nationalities. He recognised many of the races of people he had known in his seafaring days. When the trail rose to the brow of a hill, he addressed the man nearest to him. "What road is this and where does it lead?" he asked. The man replied, "You'll know all about it when you get to the top." A few moments later they reached the brow of the hill and looked over the summit. "Never shall I forget that gorgeous picture of ethereal beauty," writes Commander Campbell. "Golden browns, reds and orange chased each other across the scene. As the colours intermingled they seemed to diffuse warmth and love round us all. The comfort of it was wonderful."

The effect of the scene upon the travellers was remarkable. They were overwhelmed with joy and uttered exclamations of delight. Commander Campbell was himself dumbfounded at the sheer beauty of the sight. But the immensity of it all began to dismay him. Feeling rather fearful he asked his companion, "Where does it lead?" The man replied, "Why, this is Death. Isn't it lovely? If only the people on earth would realise it. They are really the dead. We are just going to live." His words came as a shock to the commander. He thought of his wife and asked if he could go back to earth. The man looked at him searchingly, but with tenderness in his eyes, as he answered, "Comrade, you will regret it if you do."

"But my dear wife," said Commander Campbell, "I can't leave her so suddenly." His companion looked at him in a pitying manner before he pressed on with the rest of the throng.

The commander turned to retrace his footsteps. He had to elbow his way through the seemingly endless mass of people. Soon he came upon the narrow trail that had led him towards the road. Within a few minutes he reached his own garden. It did not appear strange to him that he walked straight through the front door and the door of his bedroom. He went to the bed. "There I was," he writes, "lying snugly between the sheets. I seemed a lot better. Gone was the drawn look on my face and I could hear myself breathing quietly and evenly."

Then he opened his eyes to find he really was in bed. He took a deep breath and certainly felt considerably better. He heard his wife weeping softly. He raised himself on his elbow. "What is the matter, darling?" he asked. She gave a sharp, frightened cry which so disconcerted her husband that he relapsed into unconsciousness. When next he awakened the blinds were drawn back, and a thin winter sun streamed into the room. His wife came across to the bed and asked him how he was feeling. When he told her, "Very much better, dear," happy tears poured down her cheeks.

That same morning, the doctor, coming to the house to sign Commander Campbell's death certificate, was greeted by a smiling woman. "Take those papers away, Doctor," she said, "they're not needed." The doctor afterwards told the commander, "For a moment, I thought that grief had turned her mind, but she smiled and led me upstairs to the bed on which you lay. When I saw you I knew that a miracle had happened."

So rapidly did the patient recover that, two days after his return from the grave, he was out motoring.

Commander Campbell's astral experiences of life beyond the veil have been shared by many people who, with no religious "axe to grind," have testified to their supernormal adventures in the next world.

Three days before his passing, the well-known author, John Oxenham, completed one of the most interesting accounts that has been written concerning life in the Beyond. *Out Of The Body*, recently published, is an important work because the author takes pains to explain, in his preface, that he and his daughter, who helped him write the book, have "no connection whatever with supernaturalism, spiritualism or psychic research." John Oxenham had orthodox religious views and his preface suggests that he possessed no personal knowledge of séance-room phenomena. Yet his astral experiences confirm the case for Survival. They agree in every important detail with all the descriptions of the spirit world which, apparently unknown to him, have poured through the channels of mediumship for nearly a century.

John Oxenham calls his astral experiences "a dream," yet he refers to his book as the completion of his work on earth. Indeed, he battled with death itself in order that he might finish *Out Of The Body*.

His psychic adventures began when he was lying seriously ill. A near miss from a bomb rocked the foundations of the house. The shock of the impact had a remarkable effect on the sick man. For the next 15 minutes his etheric body was detached from his weakened physical frame. Freed from physical limitations he underwent experiences in another dimensions from the earthly one. His adventures lasted for a long time in the etheric world. Yet, during the whole course of his remarkable adventures, his watch registered but 15 minutes!

The night the bomb fell, the sick man had lain in bed courting sleep. Wearily, he counted the hours that must pass before the blackout shutters could be removed and the morning light welcomed again. He noted that the hands of the watch on his bedside table pointed to 3 a.m. "And then..." he writes, "without a moment's warning there came a screaming roar outside and a cataclysmic crash... And I knew that the end had come and that I had passed in a moment, as I had always hoped to do, from the little hampered life of Earth to the large free life which only begins when this one ends."

His next realisation was that he was alone in a wide and lofty place. For the moment he felt dazed and could only stand and stare.

"I seemed to be on the very crown of the world," he writes, "and I could see – I whose sight had never been very good – I could see as I had never seen before." His gaze absorbed the lovely aspect. Above his head floated a white cloud in an azure sky. "All round and below me," he states, "I looked over endless distances – forests, rivers, lakes and range upon range of hills and mountains, to what seemed the very ends of the world. And I could hear, as I had never heard in my life before. I could hear the soft whisper of winds in the trees below me. I could hear the ripple and tinkle of many running waters. I could hear the distant shouts of children at play."

He heard the singing of many birds in the trees below him. And his deaf ears had not been able to listen to the song of a bird for many years! With the realisation of his regained sense organs came still further surprises. Three men, deep in conversation, walked towards him. One of them had the appearance of a prophet of old; the second was apparently a native of China. He had a thoughtful inscrutable face, and a very kindly appearance. The third individual looked like a native of Africa. He was of noble proportions. From these men, the author learned the secret of communication between the so-called dead for, although they apparently addressed him in their own tongues, the words reached him as though they were spoken in English. They welcomed him, and explained how it was possible for him to understand their different languages and how they, too, could interpret his own tongue just as successfully.

They informed him that he only had to will himself to be with a certain individual and he would find his desire gratified. But they also said it would be as well to concentrate on one person at a time as his friends might well be scattered anywhere in the universe. "Even here," he was told, "you cannot well be in more than one place at a time." Bidding his new acquaintances farewell, he sped through space to the person whose presence he desired, his wife, who had passed on many years previously. She came towards him with outstretched hands and a face showing happiness and welcome. Soon she led him to other "dead" members of his family, who greeted him joyfully. He re-met his "dead" son; he visited other old friends who had passed over. Everything was tangible, real and solid.

In his new environment in the spheres, this astral visitor saw many places of great interest. In an art centre, he examined masterpieces painted in the earthly world but presented in this "Garden of Art" to the absolute realisation of their creators' highest hopes and ideals. There were present artists of all kinds who were seeking to accomplish the perfect fulfilment of their earthly dreams.

Now that he had found vigorous health, John Oxenham spent happy hours bathing and boating. He discovered also that, when he wished, he could retire to rest. He could eat if he felt he needed sustenance. He found, however, that in the wonderful atmosphere of that sphere of existence, every breath taken restored vitality and supplied all needs.

Later, John Oxenham discovered a "Garden of Music" where one could sit hour after hour listening to great masters playing their immortal pieces on instruments compared with which those of earth were but "tin whistles." "Handel and Bach and Beethoven and scores of others were there," he writes, "and often collected round the player with appreciation and sometimes with kindly suggestion."

In another part of that garden he heard some of the greatest singers the earth has known. These "dead" artists continued, in their new existence, to give joy and happiness to those who wished to listen to their glorious notes. Amongst these singers were Patti, Melba, Caruso, Christine Nilsson and Jenny Lind.

In vast libraries, the author found replicas of every book published on earth. In addition there were records of the thoughts, words and deeds registered by every human being since the beginning of time.

In this new world, John Oxenham met again many of the friends he had known on earth. He found, too, that there were spirit spheres beyond the one on which he was temporarily functioning. In those higher realms there were individuals whose state of evolution had earned them the right to lead a more advanced life. Those on the higher realm could, and did, spend time with the inhabitants of the less advanced planes in order to help them gain progress.

He was told that individuals who wished to do so could still visit friends on earth, watch over them and help those who needed strength from the spirit world. Another discovery made by this "dreaming" author was that all who so desired found congenial occupation in the spheres. Laziness and idleness barred the way to spiritual advancement.

He found that those who, in their earthly lives, had been thwarted of their desire for children were, after "death," given charge of children who needed their love and care. Many such little ones had been suddenly precipitated into the next world through enemy action. During his astral sojourn, he met two people named Mary and Joseph Garth whom he had known on earth. John had been a market gardener. Writing of their physical existence, the author says, "The very greatest sorrow of their two simple gracious lives was the fact that they had no children, though no finer a father and mother could the whole world have produced... Children and their welfare, bodily, mental, spiritual, became the supreme passion of their lives. To help them, no toil or self-denial was too much. They adopted derelict orphans from the slums and turned them out on the world wholesome and gallant men and women."

In the etheric world, John Oxenham discovered that Mary Garth had attained supreme happiness. In her care were some children who had been bombed on earth. The author accompanied Mary's husband to the simple home which they shared with the children. As they neared the house, they were greeted with the sound of joyous laughter. "I see you're as busy as ever," John Oxenham told Mary. She agreed and said how happy she was in being able to take charge of these little ones, who had been air-raid casualties on earth. "They are all so bewildered when they get here," she explained, "that one just has to do everything one can for them."

When John Oxenham said that the little ones could not have anyone better than Mary to care for them, she answered simply, "I love them so, you see," and led the way to a large room where half-a-dozen children were enjoying a meal. The author was informed that they were as yet too unaccustomed to the new existence to realise they could live without food. "But they come to doing without it by degrees," said Mary, "and then it saves a lot of trouble." She showed the visitor over the rest of the house and he saw that each little child had her or his own sleeping room, simply furnished. When the author spoke to her of the work she was doing she replied, "I love it. I need nothing more to make me quite happy."

Mary had indeed found "heaven."

John Oxenham writes, "My little house on the hill-top reeled slightly on its foundations, and then settled down again on an even keel.

"Another bomb had just missed its mark.

"It was exactly 3.15 by my watch.

"For fifteen blessed minutes I had been elsewhere."

His "dream," as he calls it, made such an impression on the sick man that his daughter states in an epilogue to the volume, "J.O.'s greatest wish was that this book should help some in these troubled days – help them to look forward as eagerly as he was doing, to the new life ahead, and perhaps take from them some of the dread and fear that many feel at thought of Death.

"Death for him had always meant New Life and a New Beginning. It was fitting that his last message should be such as this, and he and I both had the feeling that he was being given strength just to finish it."

Three days after the final revision was completed, John Oxenham passed on. His earthly work was done.

Whilst separated from her physical body, Lilian Bailey has seen some of the wonders of the spirit world. It may be due to her intense love of children that she found herself amongst some of the little ones the world calls dead. I asked her to write an account of her astral experiences. Here it is:

"Much has been said and written about astral travelling and astral projection, but I have never been drawn to the study of it, nor had the least desire to experience the condition. I have always been quite convinced of the fact that we do a lot of travelling while the physical body is asleep, and that we meet again and again those who have passed over. The brain is usually unable to give any clarity to such mental and spiritual events. We are so immersed in material cares, anxieties and worries that the experience is distorted, becoming just a vivid dream. I mention this because I do not wish anyone to believe that my astral adventure was the outcome of desire or wishful thinking. No doubt some people will condemn this experience or even laugh it to scorn. I shall not mind that in the least. In fact I shall understand perfectly, for I think that is what I would have done if I had read such an account when I was entirely ignorant of the subject. I only know it happened."

Lilian Bailey describes how, one night after she had gone to bed and lay lost in thought, she became aware of a pool of light hovering above her. It did not take form, but revolved quickly, rather like a glowing wheel. It came lower and seemed to attach itself to the medium. "My heart beat heavily," she writes, "and my breath seemed very rapid, but not through fear. I was far too interested and indeed delighted with the phenomenon to feel anything at all except wonder. Suddenly I seemed to rise. I looked down on the bed and saw my body lying there quite peacefully. I was not at all surprised. It seemed quite natural, but I felt sorry for that inert physical body. It looked rather pathetic and tired, whilst I experienced a sense of lightness and exhilaration. It was rather as one would feel after escaping from a stuffy, airless room. Nothing that was happening seemed strange. I feel certain I have done this same thing on other occasions but have not retained the memory. Now it seemed all too familiar. I was conscious that someone was present but could not record at the time or since the name of the individual. The only memory I retain of transporting myself is that the process was effortless and swift. I did not walk, the effect seemed automatic.

"Soon I found myself in a verdant valley, more beautiful than any written word could convey. I walked then – the luscious-looking grass was deeply, wonderfully green. My tread did not flatten it; each blade of grass seemed to spring back to its previous perfection. Somehow, too, it seemed to radiate a force of strength that gave me energy and invigoration. I loved that grass and, strange as it may seem, I knew that the grass reciprocated that love and was giving me something of its own life essence. Words fail me when I try to express the beauty of the trees in that valley of my adventure. Some were tall and slender, others were gigantic mighty specimens. The foliage was more glossy, more 'living' than any I have seen on earth. A light breeze stirred the leaves into musical notes, like the tinkle of hanging glass on Chinese lanterns, but here there were music and harmony in the sound. I leaned against one of the trees and gazed on the wonderful beauty before me. Again, I felt energy and force coming from the tree. My unseen companion was still with me, probably giving me strength or power to continue.

"There were masses of flowers everywhere. In size and colour I have never seen their like on earth. There were also varieties I had never before seen. Some grew to a great height, their stems were as tall as I am. Physically, I lack the sense of smell. On earth I do not know the meaning of this missing sense. But there, in that valley, I know I could and did smell the wonderful perfume of those flowers."

The medium saw many birds, some covered in remarkably coloured plumage. One bird, dove-like in appearance, alighted on her shoulder. As this happened, she was addressed, for the first time, by her unseen companion, who said in a male voice, "These are the children's birds." Immediately, Lilian Bailey wondered where these unseen children could be. Even as the question crossed her mind, she found she had passed into a large grassy plot, reminiscent of meadow-land, but not quite the same. "There, in that lovely grass-land," she writes, "were 50 or more happy, laughing children, dressed in all colours of clothing. They looked like many-hued petals blown indiscriminately from a mass of beautiful flowers. The little ones were of all nationalities and some were dark-skinned. As I drew nearer they seemed to become aware of my presence. One lovely little girl rushed towards me and flung her arms around me, greeting me as though she knew me well. This did not seem at all strange to me, for I had evidently met this little one before. Later, I heard that through my mediumship this child had been helped to communicate with her dearly loved parents. Hence the great welcome I received from her."

Many of the other children greeted the earthly visitor. Although she did not hear their voices physically, she knew they were saying to her, "We have come here to meet you." Lilian Bailey writes, "I experienced a great wave of love for these children. Just to be with them, in that place of beauty, was a greater joy than I can find words to describe. I have always had a tremendous love for children, but here, on earth, one is not able to tell them quite how one feels. In that meadow on the Other Side they knew it. In the same way I knew that they reciprocated my love. I can only assume that, once out of the physical body and its limitations, we are able to converse without language. Probably, through the radiation of the soul or aura, thoughts are transferred into words.

"These children's ages appeared to range from two to nine years. Never have I witnessed such happiness as they manifested. They were not ethereal looking. They glowed with healthful vitality. With every appearance of gladness, the older ones seemed to watch over their younger companions.

"This, my first visit, seemed to terminate abruptly. I remember returning swiftly. In my own room, I saw my physical body lying on the bed, but it seemed to be moving restlessly. I again thought, 'Poor thing!' for somehow it evoked a great pity within me. The next thing I knew was that I was wide awake, sitting up in bed, and immensely thrilled with my vivid recollections of what had taken place."

Not long afterwards, Lilian Bailey again paid an astral visit to the place she calls "My Valley." On this second journey to the spheres she saw the same scenery as previously, but did not linger until she again reached the meadow where the children were gathered. This time, however, a woman was with them. "She looked very young," writes Lilian Bailey, "yet I was conscious that she was much older than I. Having looked into her beautiful, serene countenance, I now know the true meaning of radiance." This woman told her that the children had come part of the way to meet her because it was not possible for her to visit their actual habitation in the spheres. "You think this is beautiful," said the spirit, "but it is only a fragment of their true environment. Would that those who love little children could know how they are loved and cherished in the spirit spheres. It would bring happiness to your people on earth if they could but see all that is done for the little ones here."

The medium declares, "I watched the children happily playing. I heard their laughter echoing through that valley. The memory of the scene dispels all depression. It is good to know that those who pass through the gate of death go to a life of greater beauty than the one they have left. I wish that every parent in the universe could visit my lovely green valley so that the fear of death would be swept away."

The spirit told the medium, "I am so happy because you have come here. We so much want you to help the little ones."

"How can I do anything for them?" asked the medium in some surprise. "It is all so beautiful here. What could I do for them that is not already done?"

The spirit explained that not all "dead" children were happy and content. "When first they come to this side," she said, "the thought of their parents' grief often causes suffering amongst the little ones. They are so conscious of what is taking place in their earthly homes. They dread to return to witness the grief of their dear ones. They try so hard to tell their parents they are not dead. Their efforts are frequently heartrending. If only you could witness the joy of a child who has been able to convey a word of understanding to those left behind, you would do more – and still more – to help them. Every new experience a child has here is treasured with the hope of relating it to a mother and father. You can help to transform many of these children's suffering into happiness. To those of you on earth who will help these precious children banish their parents' grief and despair, we will bring every aid within our influence."

Then and there, the medium vowed she would do everything in her power to aid the "dead" children. I can vouch for her sincerity when she writes, "I pray that if any sad or sorrowing parents read this, they will believe me when I tell them that their children who have passed on still need their love. Above all, the little ones desire your happiness. If, in their new life, they see you grieve, they cannot enjoy the beauty and wonder of their spirit environment. The boundless opportunities that are presented to them in the Beyond mean little to their loving hearts if they hear you constantly cry out in despair. They are alive. They can hear when you call. If you give them the opportunities for so doing, they will speak with you again.

Chapter 19

"OF SUCH IS THE KINGDOM"

ALL those people whose earthly lives were devoted to their fellow-men continue, in the spirit world, to serve humanity. They may, in their physical existence, have called themselves atheists. Alternatively, they may have lived within the limits of orthodoxy. Whatever their labels, or lack of classified religious doctrine, they followed the call of service and self-abnegation. They may have won renown for their good works; on the other hand they perhaps lived in comparative obscurity, unknown except to a few.

There are individuals whose physical lives were dedicated to spreading scientific knowledge. Others raised the fallen, and comforted the dispirited. With tenderness, sympathy and understanding, noble women have dedicated their lives to the alleviation of suffering and to nursing the sick. Others have devoted themselves to the care and upbringing of unwanted, neglected waifs. Psychologists have specialised in problems of difficult, temperamental and backward children. Others have interested themselves in the important work of training and enriching the minds of the young. Adults, with no special qualifications, beyond a deeply sincere affection for children, have given full measure of their love to all those who came within the orbit of their influence. The work of all who serve humanity is motivated by spiritual qualities which survive "death." It is perfectly normal that, after passing, they should continue to pursue their chosen vocations.

Neither material considerations nor worldly standards of conventional conduct prevail on the Other Side. Those women who, for one reason or another, were obliged to sublimate their strong maternal feelings on earth, find their vocation after "death." They are given the charge of children who never experienced mother love during their short earthly existence. Children who were cruelly treated, unwanted or neglected are compensated after passing by the love of a spirit mother.

Not all women, whether they had earthly children or not, are qualified for such important vocations in the spirit world. But if the maternal urge had, of necessity, to be subdued in physical life, it may be expressed in the Beyond to the mutual benefit of all concerned. There are tiny infants whose spirit bodies have to be nursed. The prematurely born, and still-born, need care and attention until the etheric bodies have attained normal development. Spirit nurses cooperate with doctors and other specialists in this work.

When Rupert, Edith Clements' guide, was questioned about the reception of prematurely-born infants in the spirit world, he replied, "Would that you could see some of the lovely homes to which these tiny mites are taken and reared. In these homes, similar to nursing institutions, although brighter, and often open to fresh air, are nurses and spirit helpers. Some of them watch and care for these little souls, tending them as precious flowers. It is a wonderful experience to visit their quarters and to see the various stages of progression. You can see the minute forms of the 'prematures' lying quite free, but safe. Little movement is noticeable, since they are too small to move their limbs."

Although, as has been stated, the etheric spheres are not territories in the earthly sense, yet "dead" children naturally gravitate to their own appropriate condition of spirit life, which is concentrated in one particular sphere or condition. In the children's own environment is all that can be desired to promote their welfare, happiness and development. They can visit those they love both in earthly and etheric conditions. But their own plane is the centre of their activities. The adults who dwell in this sphere are those whose vocations keep them in that environment. Many of these individuals are evolved spirits who have chosen to remain in the children's sphere rather than claim their rightful heritage in higher planes of existence.

There are no unloved or neglected children on the Other Side. Those little ones with no suitable "dead" relatives to care for them are put in the charge of spirit mothers who lavish love upon them. They do all in their power to help children, newly arrived, to become accustomed to their changed state. In homes, specially planned for their well-being, the spirit mothers gather their charges around them. They tell them the familiar stories to which they never tired of listening on earth. They relate new and wondrous tales of the world they now inhabit. The spirit mothers do their utmost to comfort the hearts of children who are unhappy because their earthly parents mourn their loss and do not realise how often they return to their homes. "Dead" children neither wish, nor are encouraged, to forget their own parents. Whenever it is desirable, they are always helped to return to their home surroundings and see for themselves the ones they love. Given the right conditions they will, whenever possible, make their presence known in the séance room, the home circle and elsewhere.

You may wonder whether the return of "dead" children to their beloved ones retards their progress on the Other Side. Why should it? Would you never have earthly children come home from school? Would you never have them leave their play for a few moments to tell you of the fun they are having? Would you never have them run to you, full of excitement, to relate the experiences you were unable to share? Indeed, would you not have them come to you for the good-night hug and kiss before their bedtime? The desire of spirit children to come back to their parents is perfectly normal. It neither retards their spiritual progress nor unsettles their minds. Only when they find themselves mourned as lost do they become sad and perplexed. Then, and only then, are the endeavours of their spirit guardians to comfort troubled hearts made truly difficult.

When adults pass over, they take to the spirit world the characters they moulded on earth. Their new environment is conditioned by the lives they have led on earth. We adults cannot expect to escape the consequences of worldly behaviour and actions on passing to the next world, although we can make retribution. Our spiritual progress is determined by the restitution we make for past misdeeds. The Creator has bestowed on us the dignity of personal responsibility. There is no divine mediator between ourselves and God. But, in the spirit world, we also receive compensation for the suffering we have experienced through no fault of our own.

When a child "dies" the position is different. The young pass to the spirit world comparatively unpolluted by worldly error. They have not been subjected to the stress and strain of adult cares, responsibilities and temptations. They do not have to make retribution for misdeeds they never committed. They claim, immediately, their rightful heritage of brightness in the spirit world. Yet, the scales of justice are perfectly balanced. Because children have escaped worldly snares, they are also the poorer in human experience. Their untried souls have never reached the lofty heights of human endeavour, or known the joys of conquest over difficulties. They know little of the attainment of noble ideals in the service of humanity. They have not experienced the sense of satisfaction that follows success after long struggle and effort. Their mentalities are immature. Their characters have still to be tested. They have lessons to learn in the spirit world that adults have already mastered in the school of earthly life. Those who pass over at a tender age must acquire knowledge and gain experience so that their progress and evolution may not be retarded.

In that classic, *Spirit Teachings*, received through the automatic-writing mediumship of the Rev. W. Stainton Moses, a highly evolved communicator deals with some of the questions that arise from the "death" of children. This wise spirit teacher states, "The absence of contamination ensures a rapid passage through the spheres of purification, but the absence of experiences and knowledge requires to be remedied by training and education, by spirits whose special care it is to train these tender souls, and supply to them that which they have missed. It is not a gain to be removed from earth life, save in one way – that misuse of opportunities might have entailed greater loss and have more retarded progress... Many a child-spirit leaves the earth-life pure and unsullied who would have been exposed to temptation and grievous trial; and so it gains in purity what it has lost in knowledge."

The spirit communicator points out, "Love and knowledge help on the soul. The child may have the one qualification, it cannot have the other save by education."

The playgrounds in the spheres, the woods and the glades, the hills and the valleys, the lakes and the meadows resound to the voices of happy, carefree children. Under ideal conditions, they play many kinds of organised games. It is just as necessary for spirit children to have healthy and varied exercise as it is for the young on earth. Their recreations promote the development of grace and rhythm in their growing etheric bodies. But organised games are co-operative rather than competitive. They are devised to eradicate selfish accomplishment and pride of prowess. To win a game need not necessarily mean personal achievement, but co-operation and good will. In the children's spheres are no sports or pastimes that exploit the strong at the expense of the weak.

A number of necessary lessons are taught to the children through the medium of games, postures and exercises. They learn enthusiastically when lessons are presented in an interesting and novel manner.

Sometimes, the wonders of the universe are presented to spirit children in pageant or dance form. They see the story of the heavens depicted as an impressive spectacle of motion and rhythm acted for their benefit by spirit individuals whose names, when on earth, may have been famous for their artistic accomplishments. The children themselves are encouraged to take part in different artistic presentations that are designed to develop in their natures an appreciation of all forms of true beauty.

As in the case of adults, on first passing over, the young gravitate to the same etheric "locality" as others of their race and nationality. A Chinese girl or boy might feel out of place and miserable in a spirit home planned on a Western scheme of habitation. Children are usually greeted by members of their own race or nationality. But ingrained prejudices of race and colour, creed and caste are soon overcome in the children's sphere, for these are false barriers of the material world. Providing their temperaments and stages of evolution are suitable, dark-skinned and fair-skinned children mingle happily in the Beyond in work and play. Qualities of the soul are the only standards of spiritual superiority.

Pamela Nash's coloured child control, Topsy, who passed on with a bitter resentment against the white people in her heart, was gently led by her spirit mother's influence until the little girl conquered her antagonism. She told Norman Swaine, at one of his sittings with Pamela Nash, that when she had been in the spirit world for a while, she was unable to resist the attraction of the other "dead" children with whom she mingled. As this author records in his *Autobiography Of Two Worlds*, Topsy told him the children were so lovable that they broke down the barriers of reserve she had unconsciously built around her soul. "I learned to love them," she said, "and to share my thoughts with them almost as freely as they shared theirs with me. I learned something of the joy and happiness which came with the knowledge of someone to love and someone who loved in return, and gradually my resentment lessened as my understanding grew."

This is what Topsy told the author about her experiences on the Other Side: "Many children of about my own age came to our home where they were cared for by the spirit mothers. We were a happy crowd of children, learning of the beauties of the flowers and the trees and the wonder of spirit-life and soul-growth, taught by our gentle spirit mothers whose one diploma was that of childlove. We learned so much, too, from our daily conversations together

– children of all colours and nations, here united into one happy family. We would talk upon all subjects concerning ourselves, for there was no reserve or shyness as upon the earth-plane, and many happy hours we spent in the gardens, exchanging experiences and stories."

In the same way as earthly children go to school, so also do the little ones in the spirit world. When they have reached a certain stage of mental development they begin to attend classes conducted by specially qualified adults.

A "dead" teacher told Mr. Guy P. J. L'Estrange at one séance that she specialised in the instruction of spirit children between the ages of 11 and 13. He published a record of this sitting in the *Yarmouth Independent*.

"Can you tell me something about your school?" he asked the spirit teacher. "It is not a building, but a garden," she replied. "All the necessary tuition is given in the open air, amongst the trees, the flowers and the birds. The children like that so much better than being enclosed by four walls."

The sitter asked whether the outdoor conditions were likely to distract the pupils' attention from their lessons. Telling him that this was not the case, the spirit declared, "It is the first duty of every teacher to hold her or his pupils' interest. When one can do this, there is no need to fear lack of proper attention."

"You, as a teacher, love your work," said Mr. L'Estrange. "Are your pupils equally as enthusiastic over their studies?"

"Of course they are," she replied. "Children would not come to classes if they did not thoroughly enjoy their lessons. School attendance is not compulsory in the spirit world."

She explained that, although some of the school instruction of earth life was not considered necessary in the Beyond, there were many lessons that helped the spiritual and mental development of the children. "They must be taught," she explained, "about the wonderful universe of which they are a part. They have to gain an understanding of the great natural laws which prevail. They are shown how, if they fail to act in accordance with these laws, their neglect brings about its own punishment."

"Is there more than one class at your school?" was the next question. "No," replied the spirit teacher, "older and younger children go elsewhere. I have tried to specialise in the instruction of pupils at a particular stage of mental development. Even when, with the help of friends, I was planning my garden, I carefully schemed to produce a result which should have the happiest psychological effect upon my future scholars." The sitter exclaimed, "I marvel at the thoroughness with which everything is achieved in the spirit world."

"In our spheres," said the teacher, "people take up only the work which they love with all their hearts, so naturally everything is done very thoroughly."

Her garden class-room was constructed to encourage the children to appreciate many of the beautiful things they had overlooked on earth, merely because they held no material value. The "dead" woman instanced the fact that earthly children often disregard wild flowers because their parents attached no value to them. "This habit," she said, "persists in later life and becomes extended to other things, with the result that false ideals are slowly formed in the mind, and the sweet, simple things in creation, which can give so much pleasure, are forgotten." The spirit teacher said that, in her garden on the Other Side, she had given as prominent a place to the daisy and the hedgerose as to the prized lily, the orchid and other cultivated choice blooms.

"Children note these things," she stated, "and after they have got over their first astonishment, they begin to analyse their emotions. 'What a funny thing!' they say. 'We never before noticed that these flowers were so beautiful.' And because they are pleased with the discovery that loveliness may lurk in unsuspected places, they keep their eyes open for it elsewhere. They soon begin to appreciate all sorts of things at their true worth, untrammelled by conventional ideas."

Sometimes the teacher told her pupils the life story of great individuals who now lived in the spirit world. Occasionally they received visits from some of the great personages about whom she had lectured. "When such a visit occurs," she told the sitter, "the children are especially delighted. From their point of view, it is like a story-book hero coming to life."

Asked at what age children ceased from attending school, the teacher replied, "There is no age limit. I can assure you there are some very elderly pupils in certain schools, for there is always much to learn in our spheres."

In the material world, the young are often prevented from pursuing a certain course of study merely because of their parents' lack of means. This is never the case in the spirit world, where monetary considerations do not prevail. Providing the chosen vocation is a constructive, and not a destructive one, the student will find specialists in that particular field of interest willing and anxious to impart knowledge and instruction on the subject required to be mastered.

In the spirit world, travelling from one place to another is not conditioned or restricted by physical boundaries. "Dead" children can pursue their studies in a far more interesting manner than earthly students. Naturalists and botanists can take their pupils to any part of the etheric or the earthly world they desire. If a specimen of animate or inanimate life is required to be examined at first hand, the pupils and their teachers can travel immediately to the desired place. There are laboratories, equipped with all kinds of scientific instruments, where pupils may experiment under expert tuition and guidance. Beautiful and useful crafts may be learned from masters of these accomplishments. There are workshops humming with activity where the students, applying their own skill, can put their creative ideas into practical operation.

Many of the artists, composers, musicians and, designers who follow their vocations in the spirit world are generally willing to give promising students the benefit of their own knowledge.

"In our world," said Silver Birch at a séance, "we have teachers who take one look at their pupils and see if they are musical or artistic. At once they begin to teach the young soul how to express the natural talent it possesses. No attempt is made to force the growth that is unsuited to the soul. They do not try to make the musician paint or the artist compose. We have in our world a much greater range than you have to interpret all the variety of forms and colour shown to the children by the creation of their own thoughts.

"If we want to describe anything, all we have to do is to think of it. We make it grow by our thought. Now, having obtained it, we have to concentrate on a certain shape and then our colour. If it is to be a lesson in painting, the teachers will think of the colours and shapes of the models the children wish to paint and draw for themselves. All our models are natural and are drawn from the most plastic substance – thought."

At another séance Silver Birch described the halls of music where all who wished could hear any desired work of a composer. "These compositions," he said, "are played for us by any of the great masters who have ever dwelt in your world. Every piece is recorded. We can have several masters playing the same piece for us, one after another, so that we can have different interpretations of beauty and artistry."

He explained that evolved individuals could also produce music of their own creation. Because of the great facilities that are available on the Other Side, the "dead" can experiment with musical ideas in a manner quite impossible in the material world.

Life for many of us in the spirit world would be incomplete without the companionship of animals. As in the case of humans, when the tie of love still binds, our "dead" pets await us in the Beyond. Many children are overjoyed to be greeted by a wellloved animal whose "death" preceded their own. The young, as a rule, have an intense love for animals. Those who, in their earthly lives, were never able to lavish affection on a domestic pet, are given an opportunity in the Beyond of having this longed-for companionship. There is a great camaraderie between young animals and children. Have you ever watched a child and a puppy playing? I think it is a charming and rather touching sight. They seem to embody the natural affinity which should exist between all young creatures, regardless of species. In Great Britain, and many other countries, children are usually encouraged to love their domestic pets. They are taught to appreciate the fact that such animals are dependent on humans for their well-being, and require consideration and sympathetic treatment. Children observe that their animals respond in an unqualified measure to the affection bestowed upon, them.

Unfortunately, there are some earthly children who are allowed by their elders to indulge in cruelty to certain helpless creatures. They are taught to treat the household pets with love and respect, but may be permitted to kill creatures of other species. Children who were brought up to hunt the fox find, on passing over, that a different standard of "sporting" ethics prevails. They learn that all helpless creatures have equal rights to considerate treatment. They learn that other animals, besides domestic pets, have reactions to pain and discomfort that are similar to those experienced by humans, for our common heritage holds us together. Children are usually reasonable individuals. When glaring inconsistencies in the treatment of animals are pointed out to them, they find little difficulty in readjusting themselves to other standards of conduct.

Conventional earthly behaviour is not necessarily good behaviour in the spirit world. Some earthly parents think that the conduct of the young should, on all occasions, be modelled upon the standard of convention set by their elders. Any deviation by the children from a set code is frowned upon by their parents. The young ones are not encouraged to think or act for themselves, or allowed to depart from the rigid line of what is "done" and what is "not done." It is not surprising that some children grow up cramped in outlook – standardised products of a material or social code of behaviour. Individuality is stifled, and self-expression is deplored.

In the spirit world, originality of thought and outlook is always encouraged amongst the children. They learn to express themselves without self-consciousness. Their impressionable minds are guided, but never forced, by their teachers and guardians.

There are earthly parents who yield to every whim and caprice of an adored darling. A sweet and lovely disposition can be ruined by over-indulgent relatives, and a potentially fine character be distorted into one of selfishness and inconsideration for others. A spoiled, ill-tempered or selfish child does not, by the act of "death," suddenly become transformed into a sweet, angelic cherub. But, by a process of wise and specialised re-education, the little one is gently, but firmly, guided towards a new standard of conduct. Spirit mothers, guardians and teachers help and encourage difficult children to unfold the innate good qualities which were not given a fair chance to develop on earth.

Pampered, over-indulged children are seldom happy ones. Neither their physical bodies, nor their minds, are completely healthy. Often, too, they are misunderstood and unpopular with their contemporaries in age. On the Other Side, they find there are many young people who are well-disposed towards them and willing to share with them their games and pastimes. They discover that a system of fraternity and harmony prevails in the children's spheres. They learn that friendly co-operation in work and play means, for them, the end of misunderstanding, boredom and loneliness, and that thoughtful conduct towards others brings hitherto undreamed – of happiness into their previously discontented lives.

The great American seer, Andrew Jackson Davis, inherited his mediumship from his mother. He was the forerunner of Modern Spiritualism. In 1847, he wrote in his *Principles of Nature*, these words, "It is a truth that spirits commune with one another while one is in the body and the other in the higher spheres, and this too when the person in the body is unconscious of the influx and hence cannot be convinced of the fact."

The following year, the Fox sisters in their Hydesville home, established communication with the "dead." On the same day, far away from Hydesville, Andrew Jackson Davis recorded in his notes that he heard the voice of a spirit visitor say, "Brother, the good work has begun – behold, a living demonstration is born." He was left wondering what the message meant. But modern Spiritualism began on that day!

Andrew Jackson Davis, in visionary states of clarity which he described as "the superior condition," visited the children's spheres a number of times. He retained a clear memory of all he saw. The seer was profoundly impressed with the system of education, which embraced moral, mental and spiritual instruction. He witnessed the methods of exercise devised to promote grace and beauty in the growing etheric bodies. He observed how the appreciation of music and art was encouraged and developed.

Because he realised that "the child is the repository of infinite possibility," Andrew Jackson Davis devised a similar scheme of mental, spiritual and physical training for earthly children based on what he had witnessed in the Beyond.

In his day, the system of education he advocated was a revolutionary one, breaking down many conventional ideas of the manner in which girls and boys should be taught. But although nearly a century has elapsed since this great psychic's detailed plans were put into operation on earth, the movement he founded is still in being. These Lyceums, as they are called, are Spiritualism's equivalent to the orthodox Sunday schools, but there is little similarity between the two methods of training. The students are divided into groups according to their age and mental development, but there is no age limit for Lyceum membership.

As Mr. A. T. Connor points out in his admirable pamphlet on Lyceum education, the work of the teacher is to make the lessons interesting, and to ensure that education does not deteriorate into mere instruction. He quotes Lord Avebury, who said, "It is far more important to cultivate the mind than to store the memory. Instruction is only a part of education... studies are a means not an end."

Children in the Lyceum movement grow up without fear of death. They are taught that personal survival is the natural law of the universe. They learn that it is perfectly normal for those who have passed on to return to their loved ones on earth. Whilst no attempt is made to force the psychic faculties of the young, the children quite naturally accept the facts of mediumship.

The purpose of Lyceum training is not merely to teach the truths of Spiritualism, but rather to provide students with a training that will enable them to find for themselves tenets that appeal to their own reason and intellect. Theological or sectarian dictums of any kind are not permitted in a Lyceum. The teaching is designed on a broad and harmonious plan.

Based on Andrew Jackson Davis's observations of spirit children's education, the earthly system is an attempt to stimulate the students' own mental powers. Self-confidence is promoted by encouraging the individual efforts of the children. Songs, dances, recitations, instrumental performances are given by the students at Lyceum demonstrations. To quote again from Mr. Connor's pamphlet, "The point of outstanding importance is not what has been done or how it has been done, but that the attempt has been made. A child, three or four years old, who has stood up before the Lyceum and muttered the simple rhyme of 'Jack and Jill,' gets as hearty applause as is given to the recitation of a masterpiece. In such an atmosphere the latent ability of every child is encouraged to expand, and by degrees our boys and girls get into the habit of feeling confident of their ability to do whatever they have undertaken."

Self-reliance is encouraged in the pupils. They learn that the most worth-while rewards are those earned by personal effort. The children are always urged to express their own individualities and not to become mere copyists of other people.

The young who possess calm self-confidence, self-reliance, and who have the gift of self-expression may go through life with a serene outlook. They develop the habit of reasoning for themselves. They possess confidence in their own ability to execute their plans, solve their problems, and pursue their ideals without fear.

Chapter 20

CITIZENS OF TOMORROW

EARTHLY women and men, of high character and integrity, devote their lives to the teaching of the young. Their knowledge of child psychology is considerable. They labour unceasingly to inspire the children with a sense of their responsibilities as future citizens of the world. But the knowledge they are able to place at the disposal of the young can be measured in terms of the earthly experience these teachers and guardians have accumulated – a few score years at most.

In the spirit world are evolved individuals who, having acquired considerable knowledge in their earthly lives, have not ceased, since their passing, to absorb still further wisdom and spiritual discernment. This wealth of knowledge is available to those still on earth.

People who are unfamiliar with the Spiritualistic case sometimes affirm that only trivial or commonplace messages come from the Other Side. A short examination of the literature of Spiritualism easily confounds such statements. The "dead" have made, and continue to make, valuable contributions to science, invention, learning, literature, music and other arts. Here are just a few examples. Through Mrs. J. H. Curran, an American medium of average education, there came, in automatic writing, scripts in Chaucerian prose. The spirit communicator, Patience Worth, said she lived in the 14th century. Mrs. Curran recorded thousands of words which, though meaningless to her, were pronounced by literary experts to be 14th century English. Some of the poems received through her mediumship were awarded prizes for their merit. The judges were not told of their spirit origin.

Oscar Wilde has proved his survival by writing messages in his inimitable manner. Typical Wilde epigrams besprinkled the pages of the automatic writing that came through Hester Dowden's mediumship. Here again, experts have given their testimony, as they did with the characteristic Jack London messages through another medium.

Dr. W. Osterley, Examining Chaplain to the Bishop of London, and one of the greatest authorities on the Bible, has described as "veridical evidential" the script, purporting to be a continuation of the Acts of the Apostles, received through the mediumship of Geraldine Cummins. Some of this automatic writing, obtained in the study of a former Bishop of Kensington, attained a speed of 1,714 words an hour!

A remarkable contribution to Egyptology has been made by "Rosemary," a Blackpool medium. A spirit communicator, who passed on 3,000 years ago, has told, for the first time, how ancient Egyptian was spoken. The pronunciation of this dead language was almost unknown, only its written form being made available since the discovery of the Rosetta stone. Incidentally, this same spirit communicator has given valuable information about the life and customs of Ancient Egypt.

The psychic powers of two women – one of them is the famous violinist, Jelly D'Aranyi – enabled the hiding place of a lost concerto by Schumann to be discovered, a fact that the B.B.C. acknowledged when Jelly D'Aranyi played the composition the first time it was broadcast.

Sir Oliver Lodge, the "Grand Old Man of Science," has paid tribute to the spirit help he received in his researches. "I know that I am helped continually by those on the Other Side," he once said. "I am grateful to those higher powers who have led me thus to become convinced of the reality of a spirit world."

The renowned philosophers, sages and teachers of the past, whose physical lives were examples to all humanity, still return to earth. They offer the fruits of their accumulated wisdom to those who would absorb the knowledge. As I have previously stated, some of the great teachers return wearing a cloak of anonymity. They come in unassuming guise, but so eloquent are the words, so profound the truths, so wise the counsel they give us that we can but wonder at their wealth of understanding.

The wise teacher of simple truths, Silver Birch, tells us, "We care not for creed, doctrine or dogma unless they enable a soul to live a better life. We are not concerned with aught but action, for it is the living of your daily lives that is of fundamental importance. No creed, no dogma, and no ritual can alter by one hair's breadth the sequence of this law of cause and effect; neither can they detract one iota from, nor add a particle to, your spiritual state, which is determined only by your daily lives. Our allegiance is not to a creed, not to a book, not to a church, but to the Great Spirit of life and to His eternal natural laws."

Children brought up in the atmosphere of a Spiritualist home are able, on suitable occasions, to talk with the wise spirit guides who have gained the love and respect of the family circle. These children can tap a higher source of knowledge and wisdom than is available in ordinary earthly circumstances. From these evolved guides, the young learn of their own inherent spiritual natures and the implications and responsibilities that this awareness brings.

The Nazarene did not turn aside from the company of little children. On the contrary he loved to talk to them. "Forbid them not," he rebuked those who would have removed them from his presence, "for of such is the kingdom of heaven." No less than this man of compassion do the highly evolved spirit teachers reject the friendship of little children.

The direct unbiased outlook of the young makes them, as a rule, excellent sitters. I do not advocate that they should indiscriminately attend public séances. But, in the atmosphere of the home circle, or at a sitting with a medium whose guide is loved and trusted by the parents, children may find joy and interest in listening to words of wisdom from those who dwell in the spheres.

As I write, I bear in mind a friendship between two children I know and Silver Birch. Ruth and Paul have always been taught by their parents to accept, quite naturally, the facts of personal survival. For several years past, they have counted Silver Birch as their "guide, philosopher and friend." On occasions, they have a special trance sitting with his medium in their own home. These two children have a deep love for Silver Birch, who they know watches over them at all times with a parent's care. Despite the great respect they have for the spirit guide, they have no reticence or fear in his presence. Silver Birch on his part is, I know, touched by the children's devotion.

Their special privilege is to talk with Silver Birch every Christmas time. Although the "grown-ups" in the family are present it is none the less the children's own séance. Ruth and Paul are no exception to the majority of children. Their thirst for knowledge and information seems well-nigh unquenchable. What tortuous, complicated questions the young expect to be answered! How many adults have racked their brains in an attempt to provide their children with reasonably simple replies to questions that have engaged the minds of human beings for centuries!

The very simplicity of a child's question sometimes makes the adult's response difficult to frame. It is hard to return the direct gaze of a child who asks such questions as, "Why do men kill each other? Why are there poor people when some are so rich? Why do some people have to starve when others get plenty to eat?" It is not easy to reply to such unconscious indictments of "civilisation" without a blush of shame that these innocently plied questions should be necessary in the world of abundance God had provided for us all.

Before their sitting with Silver Birch's medium, Ruth and Paul usually prepare a list of questions to ask the guide. He is used to answering questions. Members of different religious denominations, men of letters, well-known people from all parts of the world have, at times, visited our home circle and presented Silver Birch with involved questions on all kinds of subjects. I have never known him at a loss to reply immediately, in direct language, to the most complicated inquiry.

The first time Ruth and Paul spoke to Silver Birch was when the girl was eight and the boy six years of age. They were told beforehand by their parents that the medium would "go to sleep" and the guide take possession of the body. With great interest they watched the control take place. There is always a marked difference in the medium's countenance when Silver Birch manifests.

The children's father, Paul Miller, a journalist and author, recorded the séance at which I was also present. I am indebted to him for the following account.

Silver Birch began. with an invocation in his inevitable custom.

"Oh Great White Spirit, may we be able to approach Thee with the simplicity of the child's heart and mind and learn those great truths that are revealed only to those who have the perfect trust of children in a loving and an all-wise Parent. May we learn to approach Thee without fear, knowing that Thou art perfect wisdom, love and kindness."

When the children were seated one on each side of the medium, Silver Birch said, "We will not talk to the big children tonight, we will pretend they are not here. You know I often come to play with you."

"You have such a beautiful voice, and I can hear you so easily," declared Ruth.

"This is my voice and not the voice of my medium," answered the guide. "I make it specially."

This raised the question in the little girl's mind, "How do you talk in spirit land?"

"We don't speak," explained Silver Birch. "We send our thoughts out to each other on little wings and, carried by the stars, they fly quickly through space. And then we receive other thoughts in reply; we do not have to find words. When we have a beautiful picture in our minds we can send it at once. We have so many beautiful things here, many more than you have – trees and flowers and birds and streams. Whenever we want a beautiful picture we can make it immediately for ourselves. We can make everything we need."

"How long is it since you were born?" asked one of the children. Silver Birch said he had been in the spirit world nearly 3,000 years. "And I am still very young," he added.

"I don't call that very young," said Ruth. "When we die will we become spirits?"

"You are little spirits now, growing up to become big spirits," said Silver Birch.

"But we are not the same as you," Paul declared.

"We are all children of the Great Spirit you call God," the guide replied, "and as all the little parts of the Great Spirit are linked we are one family of the spirit."

The boy pondered. "God must be very big," he said.

"He is as big as the whole wide world," answered Silver Birch. "And there is much that you cannot see."

"But did God make the Great Spirit?" was his next question. "He did not make it, for God is the Great Spirit Who is always there."

"Does He ever come to earth?" Ruth wanted to know.

"Yes," answered the guide. "He comes every time a baby is born, for then He puts a part of Himself into it."

The children said that they were glad that they knew about the spirit world. "You are fortunate," Silver Birch told them, "because you know you are surrounded by the light and love from those who have passed from your world to mine. They are protecting you always."

"Is your world bigger than ours?" asked Ruth.

"It is much, much bigger," replied the, guide, "and it contains many more beautiful things than you have in your world, such beautiful colours, such wonderful music, such big trees – and flowers and birds and animals."

Paul wanted to know more about the animals and Silver Birch assured him that no animals were killed in the spirit world.

"I wonder why men kill animals," said Paul a little later. "Because they have not yet learned it is wrong," he was told. "Some men feed animals just to kill them," remarked Ruth. "You try to live without eating animals," said Silver Birch.

(Ruth and Paul are vegetarians.)

"Do you get hungry in the spirit world?" asked the little boy.

"Never," replied the guide, "because we are surrounded always by life, and when we get a little tired we just breathe in more life. When you go to your bed at night, you stand and breathe in air, and when you do that you also breathe in life."

"When shall I see with my spirit eyes?" asked Ruth.

"You have spirit eyes and ears, hands and fingers, and legs with spirit toes, for you have another body – that is, the body of the spirit. You can see with your spirit eyes now, but you do not remember what you see while you are in the little physical body you have now. But gradually, you will be able to catch what you have seen and hold it."

"Will my spirit eyes be ever so big?" asked Ruth with feminine curiosity.

"It does not matter, for the eyes of the spirit can see ever so far."

"Can they see right over the world?" Paul wanted to know.

"They are like a telescope which can bring distant things into the range of your vision."

"When can I see you properly?" the little girl asked.

"You will have to wait a little. You see us very often, but you do not remember. When you go to sleep I take you by the spirit hands. Both of you leave your earthly bodies asleep on your beds and we travel to my world and have such wonderful adventures. But when you get back to your bodies you forget them. You just say, 'What a funny dream I have had?'"

Ruth seemed still to be fascinated by the guide's voice, for she repeated, "You really have a beautiful voice," and Paul added, "I think it is rather unusual."

The children thought it was a good thing that people had different voices. "If we were all the same," declared Paul, "it would be very dull."

The guide told them that although we were all different, we were also all very similar, because we belonged to the Great Spirit. "Some people," he told the children, "have big spirits in little bodies, and some have big bodies with little spirit."

After Ruth had inquired whether all spirit guides were the

same, Silver Birch asked them to watch while he transfigured his instrument's features so that they could see the difference between the medium's face and his guide.

The children thought that the guide had a longer face and a sharper chin than that of the medium. Ruth also declared that, while the change was taking place, she saw a light shining from the medium's face.

The little boy, usually very reticent about declaring his affections, then said to Silver Birch, "I love you."

"The Great Spirit is full of such love," answered the guide, "such love as there is between us."

Silver Birch spoke to the children of a festival in the spheres to which he was going. Ruth and Paul wanted to know more about it. "The guides meet," he told them, "having left their mediums behind. We take counsel and learn of the things we have done and tried to do. We get a new outlook, and perhaps new wisdom, perhaps even more love, faith and power to take to your world when we continue our work."

"What is wisdom?" asked Paul.

"It is what you know," came the reply.

"Where is heaven?" Ruth asked.

"Heaven is in your hearts when you are happy," was the simple answer.

"It is not in your heart when you are unhappy?" declared the girl.

"You need never be unhappy," she was told. "You can always be in heaven when you want to be. I am always with you and I try to help you. If you ever forget and cry, I will come and wipe away your tears and bring back the laughter to your eyes that you may grow in happiness."

Paul Miller thus describes the end of his children's first séance with the beloved guide: "Placing a hand on each little head, the guide, whose words had struck wonder into the grown-ups and made them silent listeners of the free, frank and loving talk between a great soul and two children, left them with this blessing, 'I bless you in the name of the Great White Spirit Who is love and wisdom and beauty and truth. I pray that you will retain through the whole of your earthly life that simplicity which enables you to be in the kingdom of heaven now. I pray that you will respond to the influence that is round and about you and that you will become instruments of the Great Power we seek to serve.'"

Writing later in *Psychic News* of a similar séance, the journalist said of the spirit teacher's influence on his growing children: "Here is the unseen guiding hand directing their spiritual education, not to the conning of catechisms prepared by men ignorant of the truths of the spirit. Here is a guide advising young people to develop their own innate spiritual powers that they may themselves behold the intelligences who stand guardian to all humanity. Here in the sanctity of the home, the power of the spirit makes contact with the growing minds of two children, setting them the high example of tireless service, leading them without threat or fear to the vision of a nobler life."

Silver Birch told the children, towards the end of this sitting: "I cannot offer you the things of your world. I cannot bring you money, jewels, clothes. I cannot tell you where to look for gold or silver or diamonds. But I can show you where to find the gold of wisdom, the silver of understanding, the diamond of knowledge. I can show you the riches of the spirit which have a lustre that is for ever undimmed, that will be brilliant long after all the gold in your world has not the importance it has for so many today. These, then, are the riches I can offer you; riches which will endure, which you cannot lose so long as there is no desire to lose them."

Paul once asked the guide, "Do my prayers help you?" Many of us have pondered on this question of prayer. Silver Birch's reply is as appropriate to the adult query as to the one asked by the child. "All prayers help," he said, "whenever there is sincere desire. Prayer creates its own wings and projects itself into the stillness until it finds its objective. Sincerity give it accuracy and enables it quickly to get home. So, whenever you pray and mean it, it always helps, because all those who, like myself, come down to your world, have to work with prayer, with love, with all the things which are unseen but which are beautiful and real.

"You go on with your prayers and know that if you do not get the answers as quickly as you would like, each one is heard, each one is weighed and each receives its reply at the right time."

At a recent sitting, Paul Miller's two children asked Silver Birch, "What happens to children who are killed in wartime?"

"Many, many things happen to them," answered the guide. "First they are put into a hospital, a hospital where outside in the gardens there are thousands and thousands of beautiful flowers, wonderful trees, and lakes with shimmering fish, and in the trees there are birds with gay plumage. When the little babies are weak they are looked after by nurses, and when they are properly awake mothers are found for them, for they often leave their own mothers behind on earth.

"And all the women who come to our world without having had children on earth, though they desired them, look after the babies until their real mothers come for them. And they grow and grow and grow, just as they would have done in your world. But they do not get older. They grow like fruit; they get ripe.

"And they have schools and games – everything that you have – and teachers who encourage any gifts the children possess. If, for example, it is seen that a child has a talent for music, then all the great music teachers come and give lessons. If it has a gift for painting, then all the great artists come and help the child to paint. And as they have more colours in our world than you have in your world, they can paint more wonderful pictures. We have more music in our world because we are not limited to the same range of sound that you are.

"Where parents of the children know about what happens after what you call death, then the children are brought back to them again and again and again. But where fathers and mothers do not know, the children are kept away, because it is not good for them to be in an atmosphere of sorrow. They are spared unhappiness."

"Do you know what kind of world there will be in the future?" asked Ruth.

The guide said it depended on many things. "But," he said, "I do know the kind of world you will have, though it may take a long time to get it. It will be a world in which there are no dictators. It will be a world in which there are no more rich having too much and the poor not having enough; it will be a world where there will be opportunities for the spirit of man – the spirit of God within man – to find full expression. It will be a world not dominated by the tyrant, be he political or religious; it will be a world where all the great bounty lavishly bestowed by the Great Spirit will be freely distributed to all His children.

"It will be a world where boundaries will have vanished, where the colour of a man's skin does not matter, where there will be no divisions because one is white, another yellow, another brown or black, because they will have realised that they are all part of God. It will be a world of beauty, where ugliness will have receded; it will be a world where the kingdom of heaven will be established, for men will have found God because they will have found themselves. That is the world that is coming, the new world, the world which has been seen for centuries, by poets and artists, by seers and prophets – by all those who possessed the eye of the spirit and who caught glimpses of that new world which must be."

In these words, Silver Birch visualised the new order towards which we all hopefully turn our eyes. Its realisation can be hastened or retarded by our own efforts. But, to a great extent, it will be shaped by the children of today – the potential citizens of the world of tomorrow.

Meanwhile, there is no doubt that the holocaust of destruction brought about by the war has raised a crop of problems in regard to the education and the upbringing of this generation of children. Most of us realise that there is much to be done to help eradicate from the minds of the young the evil consequences of war conditions. Thousands of children have witnessed scenes of horror and destruction. They have seen their homes wrecked by bombs, and their relatives and friends killed or injured in air raids. A war mentality has, almost unavoidably, taken the place of the peaceful ideals many of us tried to instil in their impressionable minds. Children, whilst playing with their toy tanks, guns and aeroplanes, have heard their parents and other adults declaiming against the enemy who has wrought so much havoc. Children have spent night after night in air-raid shelters where they have seen fear manifested by adults unable to control their emotions. These young have heard uttered clamorous demands for air-raid reprisals to avenge those who have suffered, and seen others suffer, at the hands of the enemy.

In a *Psychic News* article, Mr. A. T. Connor faces the problems that lie before those adults who have the welfare of children at heart. He asks, "Spiritualist parents, what have we done, and what are we doing to save our children from the results of their war memories, and prepare them for the anti-war, peace-loving world they will have to construct? Let us consider, dispassionately, how dependent on us are our children for their ideas and ideals of life and human relationships and whether we are making of them fit builders or worthy citizens of a world of lasting peace and sincere good will between individuals and nations."

Mr. Connor points out that, from the time the young begin to speak, until they learn to read, every word they use is one they have heard others use. When they are faced with a problem, they base their own solution on the knowledge they have gained from their personal experiences – what they have learned, what they have seen, heard or read. As with adults, the mental complexes brought about by their war memories and experiences do not help children to overlook the crimes of the enemy, or to admit them, or their descendents, to equality in any new dispensation.

"It seems unlikely," writes Mr. Connor, "that they will be broadminded, pacific or impartial in their treatment of their parents' former enemies – or even that they will have many non-military ideals about a new world system."

He considers that the position would be rather hopeless were it not for the fact that the memories of the young can be dimmed, and their complexes sublimated, by proper teaching. Nevertheless, he visualises that a League of Collective Security and its purpose will be a serious handicap to the ideals of equality and fellowship. He writes, "Children will question why they are being asked to accept Germans and Italians as equals and friends while all the world remains in arms against them. But all this could be truthfully explained as a temporary precaution against any nation resorting to aggression whilst all nations are developing the habit of not appealing to armed force as an international argument; and that the sooner all nations become friendly and peaceful, the sooner will world disarmament become possible."

He goes on to say, "It could be pointed out that friendship and good example may, and possibly will, give 'enemy' children – who are not to blame for the crimes of their elders – an incentive to adopt our habits of life and thought; whereas contemptuous 'maddog' treatment would be certain to embitter them and make them look forward to a war of revenge – as their parents did after the 1919 'peace.'" He suggests that an appeal be made to our children by telling them that "enemy" children, like themselves, have undergone bombing, wrecked homes and the loss of parents and friends. In addition, hunger and privation, such as we were largely spared, were experienced by them.

Mr. Connor thinks that, compassion thus aroused, could be cultivated into a kinship of fellow-suffering which later would develop into true friendship and comradeship.

Chapter 21

THE BIG ADVENTURE

"TO die will be an awfully big adventure!" J. M. Barrie, the celebrated author and playwright, put these words in the mouth of the most famous character conceived by his genius – "Peter Pan, The Boy Who Would Not Grow Up." Within recent years, Barrie has himself embarked on the "big adventure," but he has returned many times from the world of spirit. Not only has he proved his survival through mediumship, but he has demonstrated that the flame of his imaginative inspiration still burns. Ruby Miller, the well-known actress, psychically received the plot of a story dictated to her by the "dead" author. The story was published. It is impregnated with Barrie's own inimitable style.

In Barrie's play, which is beloved by most children and "grown-ups" alike, the words used by Peter Pan reveal the author's profound understanding of the mentality of children. Important new events that occur to them are regarded as "adventures." The experience of death is a fresh and wonderful adventure, and the first thing children want to do, after such an experience, is to return to their mothers and fathers to tell them all about it. Peter, if you remember, left his parents and went to live in the Never Land. But he flew back to his home so that he could tell them about his wonderful new experiences. Alas, when he tried to enter the house, he found he was locked out; the windows were closed and barred, because his mother could not believe that her little boy would ever return. Sadly and disconsolately, Peter turned away from the home from which he was shut out and went back to the Never Land.

Parents, do not close the windows of your hearts to your children who have gone to the land beyond the veil. As soon as they recover from the transient effects of their passing, they are helped to return to their earthly homes. To inform their beloved ones that all is well is their first desire. Retain your faith in your children's continued existence until knowledge opens the psychic door through which they can return and prove their survival. Do not make it difficult for them to reach you. Your uncontrolled grief will be an obstacle.

Their simple, immature minds cannot be expected to comprehend why you continue to grieve when actually they are still with you.

They may not understand, at first, why you are not aware of their presence, since they can see you. Do not cause distress, therefore, by what would appear to them to be indifference to their presence. Your thoughts are real and tangible to your "dead" children. It is on your mental attitude that their happiness depends. Once they realise you know they still live, they will be content.

Even though you may have little psychic ability, if you relax your minds you will sometimes be conscious of their closeness. The little ones will be with you often, particularly at the time of the day they were accustomed to spend in your company. At a mother's knee as evening approaches, at a father's side when day is done, there are the "dead" children.

Evidence of Survival is available to all who seek the truth with a sincere, unbiased attitude of investigation. It is always advisable to wait for a few months before you start on your quest. This interval will not only permit your children to become accustomed to their new conditions, but will allow sufficient time to elapse for your own state of mind to gain calm and poise. A tense, pent-up condition at a séance may easily disturb the psychic vibrations and prevent a successful manifestation.

Because mediums are sensitive instruments, a sitter's over-wrought emotions can affect the psychic power and even distort the spirit communication. Do not, before or during the séance, volunteer any information which will detract from the value of the evidence. Reputable mediums are strongly averse to being told anything about your reasons for desiring a sitting. They, as well as you, want the séance to be successful. Do not, however, attend a sitting in an unbending, unyielding frame of mind. You can, by your well-disposed, receptive attitude be helpful and encouraging without giving away any evidence.

Before you set out to prove Survival, it is advisable to gain a little knowledge of the subject by reading some literature or books on Spiritualism. Read them with an unprejudiced mind, unhampered by previously-held religious convictions, superstitions or hidebound dogma. I would suggest that, before sitting privately with a medium, you attend one or two public Spiritualist services. Meetings sponsored by reputable societies are usually advertised in the weekly psychic press. If you live in a place where these meetings are not advertised, it is generally advisable to attend a service organised by one of the many reliable Spiritualist societies.

Because of ancient statutes that are still unrepealed, Spiritualists cannot prevent any "fortune-tellers" from calling themselves "Spiritualists," or stop a totally incompetent person from setting up a "Spiritualist church." Practically all worth-while mediums belong to recognised associations which exist for your help and protection.

The time to arrange a private sitting with a medium is when you feel that you possess the knowledge that ensures success at séances. There are a number of Spiritualist organisations who will make all necessary arrangements. Their addresses appear in the psychic press.

I do not think you will be disappointed with the result of your inquiry. During my long experience of Spiritualism, I have never known a sincere mourner who left a séance room uncomforted.

There is no reason why you should be an exception.